THE LOWELL
EXPERIMENT

THE LOWELL
EXPERIMENT
Public History in a Postindustrial City

CATHY STANTON

UNIVERSITY OF MASSACHUSETTS PRESS   *Amherst and Boston*

Copyright © 2006 by University of Massachusetts Press
All rights reserved
Printed in the United States of America

LC 2006003180
ISBN 1-55849-546-0 (library cloth ed.); 547-9 (paper)

Designed by Sally Nichols
Set in Janson Text
Printed and bound by The Maple-Vail Book Manufacturing Group Inc.

Library of Congress Cataloging-in-Publication Data

Stanton, Cathy.
    The Lowell experiment : public history in a postindustrial city / Cathy Stanton.
        p. cm.
    Includes bibliographical references and index.
    ISBN 1-55849-547-9 (pbk. : alk. paper) — ISBN 1-55849-546-0 (library cloth :
alk. paper)
    1. Urban renewal—Massachusetts—Lowell. 2. Lowell National Historical Park
(Lowell, Mass.) 3. Urban anthropology—Massachusetts—Lowell. 4. Lowell
(Mass.)—History. 5. Deindustrialization—Massachusetts—Lowell—History. I.
Title.
    HT177.L73S83 2006
    307.3'416097444—dc22

                                                                    2006003180

British Library Cataloguing in Publication data are available.

CONTENTS

ILLUSTRATIONS

PROLOGUE
The Map in the Museum

In the summer of 2002, while I was completing my fieldwork in Lowell, nine coal miners became trapped in a flooded mine in Somerset, Pennsylvania. The underground landscape in that region is riddled with abandoned mines, which are supposed to be mapped definitively whenever a company stops working a particular deposit. For a variety of reasons, this final mapping does not always happen, and mining companies are sometimes left guessing about exactly what they are digging into when they follow a vein close to an older shaft. In this case, the miners discovered—too late, when they broke through a rock wall into an old, flooded mine—that they had been working with an inaccurate map. Over three hot July days, rescue workers struggled to locate and reach the nine trapped men. Media coverage was intense, and in Lowell, as in the rest of the United States, it was impossible to be unaware of the accident, the rescue efforts, the eventual exhilaration as all nine were brought to the surface alive. There was praise for the miners' solidarity and courage during their three-day ordeal and for the ingenuity and determination of the rescuers. It was an uplifting story, the kind that reinforced images of the nation's blue-collar workingmen as unsung heroes, putting themselves on the line in countless ordinary but self-sacrificing ways. Obliquely referring to Lowell's own dogged fight to overcome adversity and economic decline, the Lowell *Sun* editorialized, "Hanging on when there is little hope is one of the harshest of human experiences.

That it paid off early Sunday morning in Somerset, Pa., seems miraculous. But some miracles are rooted in human persistence. The lesson in Pennsylvania is to never give up hope" (Lowell *Sun* 2002b).

As it turned out, however, an accurate map of the old mine did exist. Just a month before, it had been donated to the Winber Coal Heritage Center, where it was rediscovered only after the accident (P. Boyer 2002:65). This small museum, less than twenty miles from Somerset, is part of an extensive industrial heritage effort in southwestern Pennsylvania designed to attract tourism and new white-collar development to the area. No one, apparently, thought to look in the museum for the information that could have averted the Somerset accident.

My husband and I visited the Winber Coal Heritage Center almost exactly at that time. We were in Pennsylvania because I wanted to compare its culture-led redevelopment efforts with those in Lowell, which has been in many ways a model for other deindustrialized places in the United States and beyond. In Winber, I talked to the museum director, an energetic and entrepreneurial young man who was cheerfully frank about the role the museum was expected to play in turning Winber around. His words echoed rhetoric I had already heard from many people in Lowell: the goal was to become a desirable address again, to keep the best and the brightest from leaving the area, to clean up the old buildings and try to fill them with start-up businesses on the cutting edge of new technologies, such as biogenetics and telecommunications. The museum was one way of adding to the general quality of life in Winber, contributing to the kind of cultural milieu that upscale workers and residents would expect.

The museum was clearly not intended to function as an aspect of the diminished coal industry still existing in the region. Like all industrial history museums, it came to praise *and* to bury—to extol the workers whose labor created these places and frame that labor as something essentially finished. These places, in fact, are instrumental in creating the past. Often this sense of "pastness" is created at the expense of people still living in the present—not the energetic curator in Winber or the new-economy workers he hoped to attract to the town, but people who have not been able to prosper in the changing U.S. economy, or those associated with older patterns of living and working: miners, factory workers, farmers, people from groups associated in some way with "tradition." In an extreme case, as with the map that would have allowed miners to avoid the Somerset calamity, history museums and culture-based revitalization projects may literally sever a still-active link between past and present. In the more ordinary course of things, they prod along processes already well under way, reframing people and places to conform to a changing economic and social order. This is what Barbara Kirshenblatt-Gimblett has called "the reciprocity of disappearance and exhibition" (1998:56)—the process by which museums, monuments, historic sites, and similar types of display not only reflect and memorialize change, but actually help to create it. She adds, "Display not only shows and speaks, it also *does*" (1998:6). What it does—specifically, what it is doing in the former textile city of Lowell, Massachusetts—is the subject of this book.

The book is organized in three sections. Part I situates Lowell in relation to the contemporary public history movement, and analyzes that movement as a form of cultural performance, an approach well suited to capturing the dynamic, contested character of all processes of history-making. Chapter 1 chronicles the emergence of public history in the United States since the 1970s, a development very much interwoven with the creation of Lowell National Historical Park and Lowell's reinvention as a postindustrial place. Chapter 2 uses a discussion of my methodology as a springboard for assessing some of the complexities of conducting ethnographic research among peers and colleagues.

Part II looks at the city's history and its cultural and geographic landscapes through the lens of a particularly performative medium: the guided tour. In selecting these three tours, I drew on the national park's mission statement, which spells out the tripartite role the park was asked to play in the city when it was created in 1978:

> Lowell National Historical Park preserves and interprets the nationally significant historic and cultural sites, structures and districts in Lowell, Massachusetts that represent the most significant planned industrial city in the United States and symbolize, in physical form, the Industrial Revolution. The Park tells the human story of the Industrial Revolution and the changing role of technology in a 19th and 20th century setting [Tour 1].The cultural heritage of many of the ethnic groups that immigrated to the United States during the 19th and 20th century, and which continues today, is still preserved in Lowell's neighborhoods [Tour 2]. The park provides a vehicle for economic progress in the community, encouraging creative and cooperative preservation and interpretive programs [Tour 3].

The first tour is one of the standard "mill and canal" tours given routinely by national park rangers. The second, a walking tour of Lowell's poorest neighborhood, is presented occasionally as part of an effort to acquaint visitors with aspects of the city outside its public historical space. The third tour was a special offering focusing on historic preservation efforts within the city's economic redevelopment project.

I am asking these three tours to do triple duty. First, these chapters are a way to provide considerable background information of the kind that will help the reader form a larger picture of how the city has evolved over time. They also serve as an introduction to the national park—its physical components, some of the key factors that have contributed to its creation, and its basic themes and interpretive approaches. Finally, I offer counterreadings of the park's interpretations, using these tours to begin advancing my own analysis of how history-making processes and professional public historians have functioned within Lowell's cultural experiment. By doing so, I do not mean to imply that my own reading of Lowell's past is necessarily more authoritative than the park's. Any interpretation, including mine, involves choices and omissions. My decision to begin with these three tours is, in part, designed to foreground the fact that all historical knowledge comes through particular sources at particular times and places, and to underscore the performative, contingent nature of all historical interpretation. I do argue, however, that there is a clear pattern to the choices and omissions reflected in park interpretation, and that this pattern is ultimately shaped by the park's role within the city's broader revitalization effort, which works in many ways to support the celebratory multiculturalism and narrative of economic rebirth on which the city's reinvented identity is based.

The first two chapters suggest that the public history movement is rooted in part in a politically progressive, socially democratic impulse to link scholarly historical inquiry with broad public participation and a critical questioning of the status quo. The "Three Tours" section suggests that, at least in Lowell, the impulse has been unable to sustain truly critical linkages between past and present or the kinds of social relationships and encounters that would make those linkages operative in the contemporary life of the city. Part III inquires more closely into the reasons these disconnections have occurred. Chapter 6 begins with a demographic analysis of Lowell's public historians and visitors and proposes a close link between recent socioeconomic mobility and the appeal of Lowell NHP both as a workplace and as a tourist destination. Following Victor Turner's model of social drama, I suggest that park visitors and public historians alike use this site in ritual ways, coming to terms with their separation from ethnic and working class forebears while simultaneously seeking a means of locating themselves more securely within a changing postindustrial economy. The final chapter examines the creation and operation of two distinct poles of discourse within Lowell's new experiment, one organized around localness and the other around outsiderhood. Using as a case study the Mogan Cultural Center, which was designed as a point of intersection between the park and the people of the city, I show how the carefully balanced authorities of local cultural activists and professional public historians ensure local participation in the new Lowell experiment, but do so in ways that further limit critical discourse about the meanings of Lowell's past and present history.

Of course, this book itself is part of precisely such a critical discourse, and I want to acknowledge some of the many sources of information and support on which I have drawn in producing it. Two individuals deserve my most particular thanks. David Guss recognized what I was doing long before I knew it myself and has been an exceptional teacher, mentor, and friend throughout my graduate study. It has been a joy to share this intellectual journey with him. And Fred Holmgren has been both ruthless and loving in anchoring my feet to the ground even when (or particularly when) my head was in the clouds. His unconventional wisdom has been invaluable in helping me keep these scholarly pursuits in perspective.

This study would not have been possible without the generosity of numerous people at Lowell National Historical Park, including former Superintendent Pat McCrary and former Chief of Interpretation Jim Corless, who opened the door for me to conduct my fieldwork there. Among the many other park staff members who participated in interviews, accommodated my presence at meetings and on tours, and shared their insights and experiences with me, I wish especially to mention Mehmed Ali, Audrey Ambrosino, Peter Aucella, Gray Fitzsimons, and Carolyn Goldstein. Former staff members Larry Gall and Bob Weible were most open-handed with their time and ideas, as was Marty Blatt, who has inspired and encouraged countless people, including me, to think more deeply about public history as a field of endeavor. Many other people in and around Lowell assisted me during this project, including Jane Becker, Mary Blewett, Jeffrey Gerson, Larry Gross, Samkhann Khoeun, Paul Marion, Martha Mayo, Chath pierSath, Janice Pokorski, Jean Pyle, Sak Seang, and Cheryl West. The exceptional southern hospitality of Caryn and Dennis Bell enabled me to spend far more time living in Lowell than would otherwise have been possible.

Finally, I am most appreciative of the support of the Interdisciplinary Doctorate Program at Tufts University's Graduate School of Arts and Sciences, and of the many colleagues and students at Tufts and elsewhere who helped me to bring this study gradually into clearer focus. John Brooke, Richard Handler, and Andrew McClellan deserve particular thanks, as do David Glassberg and Ed Linenthal, both of whom have been valuable interlocutors as well as models for those of us striving to blend scholarship with participation in public projects. Other advisors and colleagues who have offered a great deal to this inquiry include Mark Auslander, Myrna Breitbart, Kelly Britt, Rebecca Conard, Sally Duncan, Paula Hamilton, Pat Larson, Pat Reeve, Margo Shea, and Rosalind Shaw. I have been honored and stimulated by my exchanges with these and many other fine scholars and teachers. Carol Betsch and Paul Wright at the University of Massachusetts Press and Mary Capouya, my copy editor, have been a delight to work with, and I am also indebted to the Center for Lowell History, Bill Hayward, Jack Herlihy, Jim Higgins, and Joan Ross for their help in providing images.

I follow convention here by acknowledging that many of the insights in this book are owed to the people named above, while any errors or omissions are entirely my own. Beyond the conventional truth of this statement, however, I want to underscore the many ways in which my study of Lowell is part of a collective endeavor rather than a stand-alone statement by an individual researcher. Ethnographers in recent decades have become highly aware of how our texts are always produced in collaboration—sometimes unwitting or unwilling—with the people we study. In a project like this one, however, where neither cultural nor spatial difference separates me from my informants, the collaborative nature of ethnographic research becomes much more inescapable. For me, it has also been highly desirable—an opportunity to participate in the discussions taking place both inside and outside the academy about the roles that museums, historic sites, cultural performances, and intellectual inquiry might play in shaping a more just and open society. At a time when that vision of social justice is being eroded on many sides, such questions become more urgently important. Thus I offer my critical views of Lowell and public history in the hope that they can contribute something to the wider conversation and offer some new insight into what happens in the public history realm and why.

PART I
HISTORY, PERFORMANCE, ETHNOGRAPHY

CHAPTER I

Lowell and the Public History Movement

The flagship project of Lowell's culture-led redevelopment is Lowell National Historical Park (NHP), created in 1978. Unlike traditional national parks, it is not a neatly bounded piece of real estate owned outright by the National Park Service, but a series of buildings and open spaces within the downtown area and along the canal system that once powered the textile mills (see map, pp. 42–43). This kind of decentralized park and its successor, the "heritage area," have now become more common in the Park Service, but when Lowell NHP was being developed, it was an entirely new concept. Visitors—and even local residents—are often still confused about where the park actually *is*. And so most park rangers begin their guided tours by addressing that point. After posing the question "Why Lowell?"—that is, "Why is there a national park here?"—they talk about the steep drop in the Merrimack River that provided the initial waterpower for the mills, and the planned industrial city that was quickly built once the waterpower was harnessed. Then they try to convey to visitors that what is being interpreted at the national park is not just isolated mills or canals or corporation boardinghouses, but an entire city, whose life today is in many senses an outgrowth of its industrial past—in the words of the park's first historian, "an artifact of the industrialization process" (Weible 1991:xi). To get this idea across, the rangers sometimes use a phrase that was heard often during the park's early years: "The park is the city and the city is the park."

Similarly, I want to begin by setting out the reasons I focused on Lowell, and specifically on the public historians at Lowell NHP. Lowell offers an exceptional opportunity to investigate the processes of redevelopment and representation currently occurring in many places around the globe and to consider the role of historians and other public intellectuals within those processes. The city has always been on the leading edge of the cycle of capitalist production, beginning with its creation as a planned industrial community in the 1820s. The "Lowell experiment," as some called it, was an attempt to create a manufacturing center that would combine efficiency in production with democratic moral values and social structures—to nurture what seemed best about industrial capitalism while avoiding its worst dangers and excesses. As such, the Lowell model was widely studied and emulated in America and abroad. One of the earliest American places to become industrialized, Lowell was also among the first to experience the shock of deindustrialization. By the 1960s, it had gained a reputation as one of the most down-and-out of New England's depressed mill towns. When it turned to a culture-based revitalization approach in the 1970s, it was riding the edge of another wave. Faced with the need to restructure their economies as manufacturing activity moved elsewhere in the second half of the twentieth century, towns, cities, and regions throughout the industrialized world increasingly began turning to culture—in the form of heritage trails, museums, arts districts and public art projects, sports facilities, waterfront recreation areas, outdoor festivals and other performing-arts events—in an attempt to repair some of the social and infrastructural damage done by the loss of industries, and to draw new kinds of people and businesses into decayed and abandoned downtowns and industrial areas. This repertoire of strategies and the perception of cultural vibrancy they promote have become a familiar characteristic of contemporary cities worldwide (for useful discussions of this, see Dicks 2003: 67–92, and Ward 1998: 188–208).

Lowell was not the first city to adopt this culture-based approach to revitalization, any more than it was the single birthplace of the Industrial Revolution. But the city has been an exceptionally important nodal point for both industrial and cultural production, giving this small city a symbolic weight out of proportion to its size. In both endeavors, people associated with Lowell took existing ideas and innovations and combined them in new, more rationalized and purposeful forms. Lowell's nineteenth-century creators gained a competitive edge because they were able to remove many of the variables of everyday life from the manufacturing process and to control every aspect of textile production from generating power to housing and feeding their workers. A century and a half later, the originators of Lowell's postindustrial experiment took a similarly integrative approach to reinventing the city. They intentionally began to blur the lines between museums, classrooms, tourism, art, festivals and other local celebrations, recreation, economic development, and the cityscape itself, and found new ways to yoke public and private investment together in aid of turning the city's fortunes around. At the time, this was largely uncharted territory. In subsequent decades, this paradigm—the new "Lowell experiment" that gives this book its title—has been adopted and adapted not only in deindustrialized places throughout the world, but in many kinds of communities seeking to strengthen their economies and make themselves more visible and "visitable."[1] New terminology has developed to describe the cluster of strategies pioneered in places like Lowell thirty years ago. More and more towns, cities, and regions worldwide are seeking to promote their "creative economies" or "cultural industries," broadly defined as the whole range of commercial and nonprofit cultural and artistic activities from museums and farmers' markets to sports, advertising, and new expressive technologies like digital media.[2] A term now widely used in Britain, "culture-led regeneration," perhaps comes closest to capturing the essence of this overall approach, particularly the notion that cultural activities may be useful in establishing a kind of beachhead from which other kinds of economic and social growth can take hold. So ubiquitous is this tactic, particularly in former industrial communities, that one pair of observers has written recently about "the rise and rise of culture-led urban regeneration" (Miles and Paddison 2005).

Within such efforts, the specific histories and landscapes of particular places are seen as invaluable assets that can be mobilized to help "brand" (or in depressed areas, to re-brand) places so that they are immediately associated in people's minds with memorable images, stories, and impressions. As in Lowell, many of these projects emphasize obsolete industries or ways of life, endowing them, in Barbara Kirshenblatt-Gimblett's words, with a "second life" as heritage (1997:7). Heritage areas, historic canal corridors, cultural routes, regional parks, and similar developments are proliferating in the United States and internationally. Along with countless nonfederal projects, there are currently twenty-three federally designated heritage areas in the United States, with more waiting in the wings. Like Lowell, many of these places seek to capture the prize of supralocal designations of significance—that is, official declaration that their unique local characteristics are somehow significant on a national or even global level. The United States National Park Service has generally taken a subsidiary role in these projects (in Lowell, for example, it is a central but by no means the dominant player in the city's preservation and interpretation efforts), but its presence has been tremendously important in legitimating the overall enterprise. In Asia, where tourism is one of many rapidly expanding economic sectors, many development projects are linked with designation by UNESCO as World Heritage sites. Many of these ventures are, like Lowell's, essentially local efforts, but increasingly they also occur on much larger scales, echoing the way Lowell's industrial experiment was not only copied but expanded in other places. The Tennessee Civil War National Heritage Area, authorized in 1996, encompasses the entire state, while some heritage areas span state and even international borders. The National Park Service's National Underground Railroad Network to Freedom initiative seeks to make thematic connections among sites in many parts of the United States, and a number of projects at U.S. borders with Canada and Mexico promote "two-nation vacations" and use cultural partnerships and conceptual connections to further trade or security agendas. Some of the Asian heritage-area projects, such as China's Tea Route and Southern Silk Road, have adopted a regional partnership structure explicitly modeled after heritage areas in the United States.[3] The future of heritage- and culture-based development projects, then, appears to be the Lowell model writ large.

Because it adopted this repertoire of culture-led development strategies earlier than most places, Lowell is an obvious place to ask how those strategies are playing out a generation after they first came into use. None of these strategies is unproblematic, and many questions have been raised about whether their benefits are distributed evenly and whether they will be any more durable and accountable to a wide range of local needs—more "sustainable," in the current rhetoric—than older economic patterns proved to be. In Lowell, as in many urban communities, these questions are sharpened by changing demographic realities that have brought large influxes of new immigrants from Asia, South and Central America, and elsewhere in recent decades. As the city busily woos new residents and visitors at the high end of the new economy, it also continues to draw many at the lower end of the socioeconomic scale, who are seeking refuge from hardship elsewhere or a toehold in the American economy. Many of these newcomers struggle in Lowell's new economy, often working in the remaining manufacturing jobs in the area or in the least lucrative parts of the growing service sector. Not only does Lowell's changing population mirror general demographic trends in early-twenty-first-century Western places, but it reveals the widening split between rich and poor that is characteristic of postindustrial economies. The presence of these newer migrant groups both plays into Lowell's celebration of history and ethnicity and unsettles it.

The city thus offers a site to explore many of the questions raised by the adoption of strategies of cultural display as a vehicle to benefit any community. How can places be made attractive as tourist sites without trivializing or erasing difficult and complex histories? Can prosperity generated with the help of these strategies be spread far enough to benefit poorer neighborhoods and residents? And what of the longer-term prospects for the "new economy"? Just as imitation and competition within the early textile industry decreased profitability for all, will the cultural market eventually become saturated with ethnic festivals, sports stadiums, and history museums, undermining the ability of all but the most iconic places to stand out among the crowd? There are already signs of a "race to the bottom" in various new-economy sectors. The delivery of many kinds of information and services, seen as cutting-edge products in the United States only a decade ago, are already being "outsourced" to places with cheaper labor (Madhavan 2005). Successful competition means being able to deliver ever more complex and innovative combinations of knowledge and experience, and the exponents of such concepts as the "creative class," "creative city," "experience economy," "placemaking," and "branding"— the contemporary heirs of Lowell's nineteenth-century innovators—are greatly in demand by places and organizations seeking a foothold in this intensely competitive global marketplace.[4] Meanwhile, cycles of boom and bust are shorter and shorter throughout the global economy, to the extent that deindustrialization—the loss of manufacturing jobs due to the de-skilling of workers and the mechanization of production—is now occurring even in countries still in the process of industrializing. How can places and workers in the United States and abroad contend with the volatility and mobility of these new kinds of production? What happens when the cultural institutions that might be positioned best to raise critical questions about these processes—for example, universities and museums—are intimately involved in efforts to promote economic redevelopment in places like Lowell? What are the social costs, in terms of our ability to understand and respond to the changing economic circumstances of our lives, of linking the production of knowledge so closely with the quest for economic growth?

There is an additional reason Lowell is such a useful site for posing these questions. The mix of voices speaking about history and heritage in Lowell has included a concentration of professional public historians—workers in a field that has been emerging over the same period of time in which the city has been reinventing itself. The presence of these people—trained to think critically and analytically about the causes and consequences of historical change—means that there have been voices raising precisely these kinds of questions throughout Lowell's ongoing redevelopment efforts. This adds an element to Lowell's focus on its industrial past that makes it much more useful for investigating not only a wide range of history-making processes but also the role of critical scholars in the contemporary American public sphere.

The Public History Movement in the United States

"Public history" is not the same as "history in public." Many kinds of people and institutions—schools, museums, tour companies, historical societies, government agencies, filmmakers, and individual researchers and enthusiasts—are involved in history-related activities in public, and many of these activities have longer lineages than the historical profession that developed in the late nineteenth century. But within the larger arenas of public history-making and professional history, a specific movement emerged in the United States in the 1970s whose adherents termed themselves "public historians." In essence, the movement represents an attempt by academically trained historians to re-establish a place for themselves in the public history making sphere after almost a century of retreat from it, and to assert within it that their methods and insights are of value to the society outside academy walls. Because the work of public historians in Lowell is the primary focus of this book, it will be useful at the outset to look at the development of the field.

History as a scholarly discipline emerged in European universities in the late nineteenth century and took root in the United States via young American scholars pursuing graduate study in Germany. The professionalizing of the American field—the establishment of credentials, standards, and review processes—is often considered to have begun in 1884 with the creation of the American Historical Association (see Novick 1988 for a detailed account of these processes). The AHA was one of many Gilded Age and Progressive Era organizations that reflected a broad interest in the past, an interest often linked with a parallel concern about the sweeping changes of the industrialism, immigration, and rapid social and technological shifts of the present.[5] Although the AHA originally encompassed many amateur historians and subgroups, a gradual parting of the ways between professionals and amateurs occurred during the first half of the twentieth century. Eventually, the AHA and the professional field as a whole came to be dominated by academic historians, most of whom talked only to one another. Between 1890 and 1910, only one-quarter of the AHA's members were college teachers, and local historical societies and self-trained historians and writers were well represented; after 1927, almost all of the presidents of the organization held a Ph.D. (Novick 1988:49). Over the first half of the twentieth century, many of the amateur affiliates slipped away as they found the AHA less and less congenial to their interests. The Conference of Archivists left the AHA after twenty seven years to become the Society of American Archivists in 1936, and the Conference of State and Local Historical Societies became the independent American Association of State and Local History in 1940, after a thirty six-year affiliation (Conard 2002:148). As Peter Novick points out, many historians in the new profession expected that they would dominate the production of historical knowledge at all levels of public history-making, including collegiate and precollegiate education and popular publishing. Over time, however, they managed to retain full control only of college teaching. The scholarly emphasis on scientific method and personal objectivity very often produced works that did not appeal to general audiences, while various levels of government and the professionalizing field of pre-collegiate education took the lead in determining what kind of history was taught in public schools (Novick 1988:185).

Although the overall arc of the historical profession moved away from the public realm over the course of the twentieth century, there were some small crossovers and areas of overlap between academically trained historians and the practice of history in public. Rebecca Conard has traced some of these overlapping areas, showing that many elements of the public history field were in place long before the field began to try to define itself in the 1970s (Conard 2002:148–164). Two World Wars and the Great Depression turned the attention of many in the federal government to history as a tool for documenting and promoting their own war and recovery efforts and for stimulating community and national identity—and employment—during the 1930s. Federally sponsored history projects in this period include the well-known oral history collections and local guidebooks produced under the auspices of the Works Progress Administration (WPA) and the development of new historic sites and professional positions for historians within the National Park Service (NPS), which had been created in 1916.[6] At the same time, private corporations discovered the public relations value of establishing their own museums and collections, a development that led to the creation of many corporate archives and archivist positions. More indirect corporate-sponsored history could be found in the creation of sites such as John D. Rockefeller's Colonial Williamsburg and Henry Ford's Greenfield Village, both projects of the 1920s and 1930s. Yet historians working in all of these areas remained largely isolated from one another and from academic historians, whose professional dialogue usually remained within the college gates.

There was no collective attempt to bridge the public–academic gap until the 1970s, when two developments converged to produce a new field that its exponents dubbed "public history." First, young historians leaving American graduate schools were encountering a rapidly shrinking academic job market. Almost fifty new doctoral programs in history had been created shortly after World War II (Novick 1988:406); by the 1970s the field was glutted, and few new Ph D.'s could look forward to a secure collegiate teaching position. In response, some academic historians who already had experience as planning and policy consultants or expert court witnesses began to consider what other kinds of gainful employment their graduate students might pursue. A handful of programs focusing on historical archives, management, or preservation already existed in the United States; the first academic training program for public historians per se was started at the University of California at

Santa Barbara in 1976, with the ambitious goal of helping to bring about a gradual change in American public life "so that the historical method of analysis becomes an integral element in all decision-making" (quoted in Conard 2002:164–65). By the end of the decade, there were almost fifty degree programs that fit the definition of public history, although not all claimed the title. This was a period of increased public investment in educational and cultural ventures, and many graduates of public history programs found jobs directly or indirectly funded by institutions that had benefited from this expansionist moment—for example, the state historic preservation offices created by the National Historic Preservation Act of 1966, new national parks and heritage areas, and countless Bicentennial-era heritage projects.

Not everyone saw this as a positive development for the historical discipline. Some historians, for example Peter Novick, lamented the intrusion of "particularist" agendas into a scholarly mode of inquiry built on the ideal of looking impartially at the past (1988:510–21). For Novick, the whole notion of a "public history" challenged the foundations that the profession was built on. He argued that much of what passed for public history was actually *private* history, assembled to order for corporate clients or government agencies, while historians who worked in museums and similar settings were involved in *popular* history that was answerable to its audiences' interests but not necessarily to the norms of solid historical research as upheld in the academy. For many historians who went to work in the public sector, though, these realities were not distractions from their work, but welcome opportunities for a radical rethinking of how and why historians did what they did. In other words, there were philosophical as well as practical reasons to work outside the academy. Much of this philosophy was linked with the impact of various leftist causes—feminism, civil rights movements, environmentalism, anticolonial struggles—of the 1960s and 1970s. This fluorescence of radicalism was felt throughout the academy, prompting the development of new disciplines and directions in some places and a defensive circling of the wagons in others. Within the historical field, this social climate was influential in sparking a "new social history" focused on "ordinary" and often nonprivileged subjects—workers, women, immigrants, ethnic and racial minorities—rather than on the traditional "great men" and momentous events.[7] But the changes went beyond the content of historical writing, shaking up what had been in many ways a conservative discipline and prompting many historians to join in the general scholarly soul-searching about what their own social role should be in the world beyond the academy.

Many historians believed that active civic participation was not incompatible with doing methodologically sound history, and that historians' perspectives had the potential to inform public debate and corporate and government policy in positive ways. The more radical of these historians argued that it behooved scholars, in Michael Frisch's words, "to redefine and redistribute intellectual authority, so that this might be shared more broadly in historical research and communication rather than continuing to serve as an instrument of power and hierarchy" (1990:xx). For Frisch and many other progressive historians who became involved with the fledgling public history movement, a crucial element of this task was to make their work meaningful outside the academy and to try to forge the kinds of connections with lay audiences that most professional historians had long since ceased to strive for—in the words of labor historian James Green, "to break down the walls that separate people from their past and that divide those who study the past from those who have lived it" (2000:1). Overall, these historians aimed at raising public consciousness of the countless ways that individual lives and choices intersect with larger political and economic forces, with a larger goal of fostering social and economic justice—in short, in the words of Thomas Dublin, whose research on Lowell's "mill girls" laid the foundation for much of Lowell NHP's interpretation, "to combine serious historical scholarship with a commitment to social and political change in the present"(1993:xvii). Dublin's own influential 1979 book *Women at Work*, he freely admitted, was "a product of the women's movement of the 1970s" (1993:xix), an example of the convergence of historical and political discourse in the period. Thus progressive public historians argued—to return to the metaphor which gives the prologue its title—that the maps in our museums contain a great deal of useable information for the present day, which we neglect at our peril and which historians should be working to share more widely with many audiences. The merger of this leftist strand with the job crisis in the U.S. historical profession has underpinned the new field of public history in many ways and creates some of its enduring tensions, as this book will show. For some historians, the new field offered an avenue for finding a job; for others, it was a way of broadening the constituencies for historical knowledge or contributing to the kind of society they hoped to see; and, perhaps for most, including many who have been involved with the national park in Lowell, it has been both.

Defining public history and finding common ground for public historians—and thus for those who would study them—has always been a challenge. The University of California at Santa Barbara continued to be a leader in the early phases of this professionalizing endeavor, founding *The Public Historian* as a quarterly journal in 1978 and hosting the first national public history conference the following year. Out of that conference emerged the National Council on Public History (NCPH), still an active organization and perhaps the closest thing the field has to a collective body. Rebecca Conard, a public history graduate student during the period of these early organizing activities, has said that, in 1979, the public history movement was "brash, brim-full with optimism, and headed in several directions at once" (2002:168). This variety has meant that although many people practice what may technically be defined as public history, not all of them choose to identify themselves as public historians. Some—archivists, museum curators and interpreters, government historians, those in local historical societies—work in fields that have long since created their own professional organizations, publications, and credentials. Although some find enough interests in common with the public history movement that it is worthwhile for them to belong to the NCPH as well as to societies of museum or archive professionals, many do not. Others may identify themselves primarily in terms of their institutional affiliation (for example, as National Park Service employees) or their specific occupational niches (for example, exhibit designers or self-employed researchers and consultants). Technological, cultural, and economic changes since the 1970s—the Internet, cable and reality television, changes in funding patterns and political climates, to name just a few—have opened some new territories for public history and curbed others, further complicating the task of defining and positioning the field. To some extent, the movement has also become international, with some early adherents in Canada, Australia, England, and more recent ones in other parts of the world as well. In each of these settings, the theory and practice of public history is shaped by differing kinds of relationships with state agencies and policies, the private sector, and various academic disciplines.[8]

Public history, then, remains an open-ended concept even among its own practitioners, a fact that complicates the task of analyzing the work of public historians. One progressive historian who worked at Lowell NHP during the 1980s told me that "the first time that I saw a group of people coming together as professional public historians in a self-conscious way" was at an NCPH conference in the early 1980s. Attending a session presented by historians working in the military, he remembered being "somewhat taken aback and thinking that I have nothing in common with them. A big part of me still feels that way." He and many others choose to identify themselves as public historians because it gives them a professional platform from which to assert the value of their historical training in the public sphere. But not all the workers in the interpretive division of Lowell NHP would necessarily choose the label of public historian, a subject I discuss in Chapter 6 in the section "Lowell's Public Historians within the Public History Movement."

Is it realistic, then, for me to treat the park's interpretive workers as members of a single professional field, as I do in this book? I believe a case can be made for doing so. First, the very lack of precision in defining the field means that, to some extent, public history is always in the eye of the beholder. Paradoxically, the fact that some interpretive workers at Lowell NHP identify themselves as public historians and others do not is highly characteristic of public history sites. And second, Lowell NHP is undeniably an important public history site with many long-standing links to the professional field as it has developed in the United States. Lowell NHP was founded concurrently with the contemporary public history movement, and the two drew on many of the same raw materials. The focus on labor and immigrant history that developed during the planning stages for the park in Lowell resonated deeply with the interests of new public and social historians. One of the first historians on the park staff recalled: "One point very early, certainly within the first year, those of us who were working on this just after work one day we were just standing around and we all realized, 'Oh, my God, there's no road map here. We're doing something that people will look back on some day.' I mean, it was very conscious, that we were doing something that was different and was going to set new rules. And we were aware of that." Lowell NHP, then, was in many ways a flagship development for both the new social history and the emerging public history field. It retains that status for many in the field; as the current curator, a somewhat younger Ph.D. historian, told me, "In my universe, both national and international, of industrial history and public history of technology, Lowell looms very large on the horizon. . . . [E]verybody I studied in graduate school or studied *with*, had a hand in this place."

My research centered around the effect that leftist, even radical public historians have had in the public interpretation of Lowell's history. This element—what I will refer to as "progressive public history"—has never wholly dominated the field in the United States, and it has tended to be concentrated in the areas of the profession that overlap most closely with the academy. Nonetheless, it has been a significant ingredient since the movement's beginning, providing much of its energy and certainly inflecting its general politics. The connection between progressive public history and Lowell National Historical Park is particularly clear and important. In many places, progressive historians find themselves struggling with the legacies of existing exhibits, collections, or institutional structures—a struggle that Richard Handler and Eric Gable term "the new history in an old museum" at Colonial Williamsburg (1997). But when Lowell NHP was created, everything—even the very concept of an urban or industrial history park—was new, opening myriad possibilities for the small but influential group of young public historians who were among the first planners, historians, and interpreters at the park. "Most of us young people on the staff," one member of this group told me, "thought of ourselves as a little subversive." Many of my informants at the park, especially the more academically oriented staff historians and consultants, spoke of their belief in the potential of historical inquiry to provoke public reflection and social change. "I'm not really an activist," one told me. "But I am an activist in the sense that I really see my role as a professional and as a historian to help people reflect upon current conditions." Another, in response to my question about the value of including critical perspectives in museum exhibits, stated plainly that it could help to produce "*A better world*. In the end, you know, of course, it won't reach, in terms of how many people in the world you reach, it reaches a minute number of people, but you just hope that if you get people to think critically about the past and how the present has come to be, they can think somewhat critically about these issues in their own lives. And that can only be towards a better world."

It is this activist, progressive strain within public history, and specifically within the national park in Lowell, that I analyze in this book. These are the people trying most explicitly to link critical scholarship with public participation, an endeavor that is of concern to those of us in many academic fields who envision an active social role for our work. Although I believe my characterization of public history as generally left-leaning is accurate, my focus in this book is also clearly a reflection of my own concerns and questions, a bias I readily acknowledge at the outset. I turn now to a discussion of the theoretical frameworks that I used to explore those questions.

Public History as Cultural Performance

During my graduate coursework at Tufts University, I set out to write an essay about historical knowledge in Deerfield, a preserved village in western Massachusetts. I was interested in how various kinds of historical interpreters—traditional academic historians, ethnohistorians, tour guides, public historians, indigenous cultural leaders, and costumed performers—dealt with gaps in the historical record about the famous "Deerfield Massacre," an attack on the village by French and Indian raiders in 1704. I conducted a number of interviews, attended several public tours, performances, and lectures, familiarized myself with recent academic work on Deerfield and the 1704 raid, and then sat down to write.

Years later, the essay is still not finished, and it probably never will be. After several unsuccessful drafts, I finally identified the central problem. Without realizing it, I had collected two quite different kinds of data from the people I talked with. In my interviews with the professional academic and public historians, I asked questions only about their professional training and experience—how they approached the study and writing of history, where they had gone to school, how they located themselves within various intellectual debates about historical authority and interpretation. It would have felt jarring to include more personal questions about their socioeconomic or ethnic backgrounds, or to note down information about their clothes, mannerisms, and other aspects of their personal presentation—so jarring, in fact, that it never occurred to me to do it. But with my other informants—the part-time docents, the Mohawk cultural leaders, a costumed interpreter who was part Abenaki—it was perfectly clear to me that I needed to know the answers to some of those personal questions before I could begin to understand how these interpreters were presenting the story of the 1704 attack. I felt free to ask about things that would have felt inappropriate and intrusive had I raised them in my interviews with the historians. And I drew on the kinds of observations about demeanor, dress, and setting—the docents' expensive tailored clothing, the costumed interpreter's theatrical techniques—that I had simply not registered when I was sitting in the historians' offices and meeting rooms.

In retrospect, I saw that I had run up against a powerful taboo of the academic and professional tribes. Anthropology took a well-known "reflexive turn" in the 1980s and 1990s, during which the discipline became much more self-aware about the roles its members play in constructing accounts of human cultures. Despite this, however, we still use our intellectual and analytical tools primarily on "others," not on people like ourselves. Because the historians at Deerfield were people very much like myself, encountered in familiar and authoritative settings, my anthropological antennae were not operating as they should have been. With my other informants, I had been a much more competent anthropologist: attuned to many kinds of detail, trying to take nothing for granted, working to reach as broad an understanding as I could of my informants' views of the world. With the informants who were essentially my colleagues, I had been essentially just that—a colleague. And when it came time to write my essay, I realized that I was trying to compare apples and oranges. I was talking about one set of informants as inhabitants of complex social settings, while discussing the historians' words and ideas without reference to any social context at all.

It was reassuring in some ways—though troubling in others—to recognize that I was not the only researcher to have fallen into this trap. In recent years, scholars from many fields have focused a good deal of attention on the processes of memory and commemoration. At the same time, a very large academic literature on tourism has been developing. As a result, we now have a considerable number of historical, ethnographic, and other kinds of studies of historic sites, memorialization, cultural and heritage tourism, and history-making in general. Yet within this sizeable and growing body of work, I could find no models for investigating the people most like ourselves in the same way that anthropologists have investigated our ethnographic "others." To date, most historiography (that is, studies of the work of the historical profession), and virtually all of it that pertains to public history as a field, has been written by historians themselves (for examples of the literature on public history per se, see Benson et al. 1986, Blatti 1987, Conard 2002, Frisch 1990, Glassberg 1996, Grele 1981, Howe and Kemp 1988, Leffler and Brent 1990, Leon and Rosenzweig 1989, Wallace 1996). These writers have had neither the theoretical nor the personal inclination to look searchingly at historians as social beings operating within particular social contexts. Historian and historiographer Peter Novick notes how this taboo operates in the historical profession when it comes to writing about peers and colleagues: "Out of understandable but misplaced tact and courtesy we apply a different standard when writing historically about historians—particularly, of course, living historians. Occasionally, when historians write of dead historians, they 'sociologize' or 'psychologize' their views, but here, too, there is a double standard at work: these. . . . explanations are almost always applied to the views of those with whom we disagree (1988:12)."

The ethnographic literature on professionals in the historical field offers no examples to counter this taboo. In his detailed study of state-sponsored historic preservation in a Cretan community, for example, Michael Herzfeld draws a definite line between the "social time" of local residents and the "monumental time" of the state's historic preservation program, whose efforts are both resisted and used in paradoxical ways by local property owners (1991). Although the locals appear in Herzfeld's book as active participants in a multifaceted social world, the day-to-day lives of the state bureaucrats are virtually invisible, even though many of them appear to be local people themselves. In their groundbreaking study of professional historians at Colonial Williamsburg, Eric Gable and Richard Handler acknowledged precisely the same critical lapse that I experienced in Deerfield: "Like anthropologists drinking gin and tonics on the colonial officer's veranda, when we went to dinner with the historians, we had conversations with them rather than interviews. . . . We rarely subjected them to quite the same anthropological technology that we turned, microphone in hand, on both the front-line workforce and the business-side managers (Gable and Handler 1993:27-28)." Erve Chambers notes how anthropology's traditional focus on the exotic and the powerless has similarly limited the scope of ethnographic studies of tourism: "Anthropologists have tended to view tourism as a manifestation of international and mainly unequal relationships between tourists and their 'hosts.' They have given much less attention to domestic tourism or to touristic exchanges among social and economic peers" (2000:ix).

In many ways, then, existing scholarly and ethnographic patterns and preoccupations have kept us from producing studies of professional history-making that place professionals like ourselves within the kind of broad and holistic frameworks that anthropologists have traditionally aimed for. Where fieldworkers *have* focused on professional historians working in public settings, their attention—like mine at Historic Deerfield—has been confined solely to their informants' professional or working lives. Stephen Snow presents a detailed analysis of the work of costumed interpreters at Plimoth Plantation, but he is interested only in what they do as performers; just four paragraphs of the book are devoted to the question of who these people are outside their jobs (1993:121–22). Similarly, in the most substantial and important ethnographic study to date of historians at an American historic site, Handler and Gable's study of Colonial Williamsburg, the new social historians whose work is the main focus of the book appear in its pages already fully formed. The authors state quite plainly that they were "by and large not concerned to relate people's arguments to their personal lives and backgrounds" (1997:26)—an approach that limits our understanding of the larger social contexts in which these sites operate. Historian David Glassberg has at least nudged open the door toward a fuller contextualization of professional history-making in his survey of the borderlands between professional and popular understandings of history. Noting that "over the past century, the historical profession has not only chronicled [the] changes in American life but also experienced them" (2001:209), he raises the question of how the uncertain job market for historians has affected the kinds of histories they write and the kinds of understandings they are able to develop of particular places. But this is not the central focus of Glassberg's book, nor has anyone else explored these issues more thoroughly.

Ethnographers and historians must constantly make choices about what to include and what to leave out, of course, and there are many good individual reasons for the scholars mentioned above to have made their choices in the ways that they did. But the consistency with which these lines are drawn between the personal and the professional, the dominant and the marginal, the official and the vernacular (to use John Bodnar's [1992] terminology) suggests that other considerations are at work here as well. For better or worse—that is, out of an attempt at balanced, dispassionate observation or a reluctance to probe too deeply into the implications of our own motivations and social positions—we almost never use the same kinds of intellectual and methodological tools on people like ourselves that we use on others. One result for the new literature on historic sites and history-making is that we have no empirically grounded studies of professional historians operating as social actors within a context that goes beyond their work lives. As David Glassberg notes, "Only a few case studies have examined the complex relationships between public history and political culture, popular culture, and the culture of place-making in a particular time and place. And we are a long way from a synthesis of public historical practices over time, in the same way that we can isolate a historiography of the historical profession" (1996:21). And anthropologist Richard Maddox has argued that this kind of imbalance "inevitably skews our understanding of the contemporary world because it makes it difficult, if not impossible, to trace and analyze the linkages between what is going on in places near the top and centers of the global pecking order and what is happening in sites near the bottom and on the margins" (1997:289).

In other words, our reluctance to probe into our own roles and those of our social peers has left us with an astigmatic view of what is actually happening at historic sites, and this keeps us from gaining a fuller sense of how these sites function in our culture. It is this astigmatism that I am working to overcome in my study of professional public historians at work in Lowell—in my attempt to be, in Bernard Cohn's phrase, "an anthropologist among the historians." Not all of the information offered by my research will be startling or new—for example, no one familiar with the museum, cultural tourism, and public history worlds is likely to be shocked to hear that these are heavily populated by well-educated, middle-class people of European descent. But a closer consideration of the social and professional positioning of specific people in those places may yield some insights about *why* these sites seem to continue to reflect dominant or mainstream culture despite scholars' critiques and practitioners' many efforts in recent decades to connect with more varied constituencies (see, for example, Drake-Wilson 2000, Floyd 1999 and 2001, Goldsmith 1994, Karp and Lavine 1991, Karp et al. 1992). And in a larger sense, this kind of study may create a clearer map of the terrain on which public historians—and, by extension, other cultural workers in the public sector—currently find themselves maneuvering. Such a mapping exercise may help to clarify some of the internal and external factors that shape our ability to voice our critical analyses and to contribute to the social changes we would like to see in our world.

Performance, like memory and tourism, has been a popular interdisciplinary subject in recent years, and some researchers have begun to bring the resources of performance studies to bear on the question of how people approach and use the past (see Desmond 1999, Edensor 1998, Pollock 1998, and Snow 1993 for examples). At first glance, thinking of history as a performance may seem counterintuitive, but the field of performance studies offers unique advantages for the task of analyzing what happens at historic sites. Below, I briefly outline how scholars understand cultural performance, set out the rationale for applying this body of theory to the work of professional public historians, and show how this approach is particularly suited to the kind of postindustrial setting found in Lowell.

As scholars have come to see human societies more and more as something in process, being constantly constructed and contested, the idea of performance has come to seem more apt as a way of thinking about how culture works. In an important early work in the field, Erving Goffman famously argued that everyday human life is itself intensely performative: "Ordinary social intercourse is itself put together as a scene is put together, by the exchange of dramatically inflated actions, counteractions, and terminating replies... [L]ife itself is a dramatically enacted thing. All the world is not, of course, a stage, but the crucial ways in which it isn't are not easy to specify" (1959:72). All social life, in this view, is performed to some extent.[9] But some things are performed to a greater extent, creating sites where cultural meanings and questions are condensed, collected, and made visible. Milton Singer (1972) coined the term "cultural performance" to describe such intensified performative events, which share several central characteristics. They are somehow set apart from everyday reality, in space, in time, or both. They offer participants and audiences an opportunity to reflect on culturally significant materials and symbols. And they may also present openings to argue or negotiate about the meaning of these materials, often in ways that have social or political consequences beyond the actual experience of performance (see Guss 2000:8–12 for a more detailed discussion of these characteristics).

It is this last quality—the porous boundary between cultural performances and everyday social life—that has appealed to scholars interested in exploring how social meanings are produced in particular times and places and specific, embodied ways. Victor Turner, whose work constitutes one of the cornerstones of cultural performance studies, spoke of the "exemplary, model-displaying character" of all rituals, and commented that "in a sense, they might be said to 'create' society" (1969:117). Similarly, David Guss points out that "what is important is that cultural performances be recognized as sites of social action where identities and relations are continually being reconfigured" (2000:12). And Dean MacCannell, writing of what he terms "cultural productions," notes that these "are not merely repositories of models for social life; they organize the attitudes we have toward the models and life" (1999:27). Focusing on sites of cultural performance is one way that scholars have been able to look at context as well as text—that is, at the politics of cultural production as well as its poetics. And the concept of cultural performance itself provides a useful way to bring many different kinds of expressive behavior within the same analytical framework, including, in the instance of a place like Lowell, not only vernacular, "traditional," and commercial uses of history, but professional and scholarly ones as well.

There are two central reasons I found this theoretical approach congenial to my study of Lowell. First, history itself—our inquiries into the past and the various forms of display based on those inquiries—has a strongly performative character. A museum exhibit or an archive does not appear to be performing anything—it simply sits there while visitors look at it. But following the definition of cultural performance above, it constitutes a place and an experience outside visitors' everyday routines, where participants can reflect on expressive materials with cultural and symbolic significance for them and for others. And its production and presentation are interwoven with social networks of relationship that both shape its content and may in turn be affected by whatever is collected, interpreted, and displayed. Della Pollock has written that performance is "action enfolded in the resources of representation," while representation is "itself a form of action" (1998:27). Kirshenblatt-Gimblett concurs: "Exhibitions are fundamentally theatrical, for they are how museums perform the knowledge they create" (1998:3). In an important sense, according to this perspective, the entire enterprise of historical inquiry is performative.

Historians themselves have often struggled with this quality of their work. On the one hand, Western conceptions of history depend largely on the notion of a "past" that is finished, knowable, and separate from the present (Certeau 1988, Fabian 1983, Wolf 1983). Historians have built their disciplinary authority on their ability to speak more knowledgeably about that past than nonhistorians. But there is more than ample evidence from the hundred-plus years of the historical profession that interpretations of the past change constantly; that these changes are shaped in important ways by the conditions and concerns of the present; and that multiple interpretations, each valid in its own way, can often coexist. Peter Novick (1988) has devoted a weighty book to examining how this paradox has played out in the American historical profession. Novick frames it as a tension between the quest for objective fact and the recognition of historical relativism, and shows how during various periods—for example, during the social turmoil of the 1930s and the deconstructive self-questioning of the 1970s and 1980s—American historians have wrestled more openly with this question, while times of greater national coherence or uneasiness have frequently prompted a general return to the notion of a more stable, knowable past.[10] Over time, however, we can trace two broad and parallel arcs: historians have come to acknowledge that their authority to speak about the past is not, after all, absolute, and they have retreated gradually from the public sphere in ways that I described in the previous section. If historians' interpretations could be challenged—if it could be successfully argued that history *was* a matter for interpretations rather than a set of unassailable facts—then it seemed safer to limit professional historical discourse to people who were playing by the same rules. As Michel de Certeau phrases it, "A place [i.e., the historical discipline] was marked 'off limits' just when the fragility of what was being produced therein was revealed" (1988:59). No matter how individual historians might feel about it, then, historical inquiry is a dynamic and social endeavor—a form of cultural performance. As performance theorist Richard Schechner has put it, "History is always in flux; that is what makes it so like a performance" (1993:259).

Framed purely as a question of determinacy versus indeterminacy, the issue has proven ultimately unresolvable. Even those historians willing to acknowledge the indeterminacy of what they can know about the past are often reluctant to cede the authority that comes with being experts on that past. Cultural critic Tony Bennett, however, offers one way around the problem. He has argued that, although it is important to acknowledge a certain amount of indeterminacy in what historians are able to know about the past, a much more interesting and productive question is the degree to which scholarly debates about historical subjects resonate with various historical publics. In other words, the important issue for scholars is whether they are able to find ways to link their professional discourse with broader discussions about the past. Public acceptance of historians' authority, Bennett writes, "depends on the relations which obtain between the practice of history and the other institutional contexts and discursive regimes within which representations of the past are produced and circulated." When distorted histories—for example, fascist myths or Holocaust denials—gain public currency, in Bennett's view, it is because of "the failure of the specific form of reasoning embodied in the procedures of history to establish their pertinence or carry much weight in the general political arena" (1990:57). Taking such an approach, as I do in this study, allows us to work toward what anthropologist Charles Briggs (1996) has termed a "metadiscursive" analysis—that is, an understanding of the social and political relationships among the many different kinds of voices speaking about the past.

Much more than their academic colleagues, the practitioners of public history cannot avoid—and often actively seek out—engagement with other forms of historymaking, including the kinds of celebratory projects that are often connected with the realm of "heritage." Indeed, it is probably fair to say that of the professional historians who practice their craft outside the academy, it is those who welcome broad public engagement who are most likely to identify themselves as public historians, while those who prefer to remain in enclaves with more limited public participation—for example, in government or corporate archives— are more likely to affiliate themselves primarily with other professional labels and associations. Politically progressive public historians, in particular, embrace the openness that their work entails and often promote a constructivist view of history—one that acknowledges its incomplete, ongoing nature—as a way of helping to make public historical inquiry more participatory, and hence more democratic.[11] The more progressive of public historians in Lowell and elsewhere have willingly extended this openness to include the economic redevelopment project that their work was a part of. As one of the first public historians at Lowell NHP told me,

> We were activists. . . . and we felt that the purpose of public interpretation
> is to give people a sense that you make your own history, and if making

your own history means using your history to make money, then that's a good thing.

Because it's active?

Yeah. Right. But the issue was, then, you know, who owns the history? Which is always up for grabs.

Public historians spend much of their time negotiating within the areas that are "up for grabs." Framing their activities as performative—as part of the play of ideas, symbols, and strategies that makes up any cultural performance—can be a useful way to see more clearly what is happening in those areas.

A second reason to take a performance-oriented approach to public history is that space and culture themselves—the larger contexts in which public historians work—are becoming increasingly performative. As Richard Schechner has put it, "Performance studies assumes that we are living in a postcolonial, performatized world where cultures are colliding, influencing and interfering with each other, and hybridizing at a very fast rate" (2002:160). The culture-based strategies being pursued by places and people throughout that world in effect make spaces into settings for the staging of cultural experiences. These strategies, in the words of sociologist Bella Dicks, transform places into "exhibitions of themselves" (2003:1). They are designed to create a sense of meaning, identity, and what Dicks terms "visitability." This "visitable" quality is not created for outside visitors only; it is a part of the larger effort to rejuvenate and "brand" places by mobilizing their unique histories, cultures, and landscapes in ways that can create a desirable quality of life and attract and retain talent and capital. James Abrams, a public folklorist working in deindustrialized southwest Pennsylvania, has written (1994) of the "documentary landscapes" now being created in such places, while Dennis Frenchman, a designer and planner who helped draft some of Lowell's key redevelopment proposals, notes that, "There are increasing demands that public spaces be not only convivial but *communicative*" (2001:258). Frenchman and his students in the MIT Department of Urban Studies and Planning have pioneered such concepts as "narrative design" and "experience architecture," essentially the storyboarding and enhancing of existing landscapes so that they more clearly communicate a particular set of images and stories. As Abrams notes, "Space becomes playful" in such ventures (1994:27). Cultural materials—symbols, stories, landscapes—

are put into play in ways that make them available for audiences and participants to reflect on and negotiate about their multiple meanings. In short, they become performative.

The work of public historians is more and more interwoven with these kinds of developments. Public historical interpretation in Lowell is part of an interlocking set of cultural productions within the overall project of rejuvenating an old industrial place. Such larger projects often come under the rubric of "heritage" (heritage tourism, heritage areas, World Heritage sites), an apparently simple term that actually requires some discussion here. In the view of critical commentators, heritage is not simply an unproblematic legacy from the past, but rather a complex mode of present-day cultural production in which local places and memories are displayed—often with the aid of professional interpreters—for a range of purposes that usually includes stimulating local pride and economic growth through tourism and other means. These components are perpetually in tension with one another, with the result that heritage production tends to be a highly contentious business.[12] Many observers have argued that the parochial and celebratory character of heritage overwhelms its potential to act as a critical commentator on historical processes. "Heritage is not the same as history," one such detractor has written. "Heritage is history processed through mythology, ideology, nationalism, local pride, romantic ideas or just plain marketing, into a commodity" (Schouten 1995:21).

The perceived tension between history and heritage is in some ways the entire basis for this book, which explores how critical historical viewpoints have fared within a large-scale heritage-oriented project. In another way, though, this study works to *erase* the idea that we can make any clean distinction between history and heritage. Indeed, a central characteristic of contemporary culture is the erasing of boundaries between what were previously more discrete cultural genres and social sectors—a phenomenon, as we have already seen, that took hold in Lowell earlier than in most other places. In a piece on the future of ritual, Richard Schechner has argued that what were once more circumscribed spheres of performance—for example, education and entertainment— are now "in play with each other. . . . What used to be a tightly bounded, limited field has expanded exponentially" (1993:20). Similarly, the lines have continued to blur among festivals, museums, shopping, advertising, sports, journalism, politics, memorialization, websites, television dramas, travel, and so on. Turner (1982:41–44) noted the development of what he called "liminoid" rituals in postmodern societies. These are optional and innovative rather than obligatory, often individual rather than collective, but they nevertheless fulfill many of the same functions as more conventionally defined sacred rituals: negotiating change and conflict, establishing group and individual identities, creating opportunities for participants and spectators to reflect on culturally important symbols and ideas. Among such liminoid rituals, tourism and tourist sites have attracted a great deal of attention from theorists (for example, Dorst 1989, Graburn 1976, MacCannell 1999[1976], and Urry 1990), who have argued that tourism typifies much about contemporary culture, including the blurring of surface and substance and—a key point—the pervasive *marketing* of culture as a commodity and an experience. Noting that "the current structural development of society is marked by the appearance everywhere of touristic space" (1999:100), MacCannell argues that tourism is a contemporary ritual whereby people try to bridge many perceived discontinuities and disconnections that industrial and postindustrial societies themselves have created: among generations and different kinds of people, between past and present, modernity and tradition, work and leisure. These cultural developments have created public spaces and activities that are not only performative but multilayered and complex.

It is within these layered settings that public historians ply their trade, making it more difficult to analyze public history per se but also—because these visitable, documentary, narrative places are becoming such a salient feature of our world—more important to do so, particularly for those of us who believe that the critical tools of the historical discipline are crucially important for democratic citizenship. This book, then, poses questions about how public history has fared in postindustrial Lowell. It approaches public history as a form of cultural performance because of the performative nature of history itself and of the world in which we are living. Like Handler and Gable's (1997) work on Colonial Williamsburg, it examines cultural workers in an elite historical institution, but instead of focusing on "the new history in an old museum," as Handler and Gable do, I examine the new history (now a considerably older history) in a new economy. That is, I work to historicize the political, cultural, and economic currents within which Lowell's public historians have been maneuvering for the past twenty-five years. During this period, the postindustrial economy in the United States and beyond has been much more elaborated and become entrenched, producing significant changes in the social settings in which public history first emerged as a self-conscious field. As Tony Bennett (1995:161) has pointed out, "The search for the tourist dollar has become the primary driving force of museums and heritage policy," a shift from the more reformist or community-oriented, government-funded projects of the 1960s and 1970s. These recent developments raise new and sharp questions about public history and about public scholarship in general. Nationally and globally, we are seeing an increasing neoliberal emphasis on marketbased solutions to social problems and the continued rapid growth of cultural and heritage tourism as an industry. Within the U.S., public funds for cultural projects have dwindled, and the historic preservation movement, as Mike Wallace notes, has shifted "toward its real estate right and away from its populist left" (1996:205) in response to Reagan-era legislative changes that have made it expedient and necessary to forge allegiances with development interests. Within such a setting, how much room is there for the progressive component of the public history movement? To what extent are public historians able to comment critically on the workings of capitalism when their own work has become to some extent a product within an advanced capitalist economy? Where do progressive public historians fit within the postindustrial Lowell that their own work has done so much to help bring about? These are the central questions I explore in this study. I will now turn to a discussion of how I approached those questions.

CHAPTER 2

An Ethnographer in Public Historical Space

My goal in Lowell was to try to understand professional public historians as social actors within a postindustrial city undergoing considerable socioeconomic and demographic change. I wanted to investigate how public historians were responding to the kinds of social and economic forces that were shaping the city, and how the historians in turn affected the changes taking place in Lowell. Identifying specific fieldwork sites within this larger context proved challenging. I found it helpful at the outset to locate what I thought of as "public historical space"—the areas and activities created and controlled by public historians. Although Lowell's public historians are involved in many aspects of the city's culture-led redevelopment, not all of their activities take place within public historical space. For example, the national park is one of the primary sponsors of the annual Lowell Folk Festival, and park staff members put in countless hours on festival-related work each year. But I do not consider the festival to be a public history event per se, because it is not based on the specific modes of historical inquiry and display used by historians. Rather, it is one production within the overall Lowell experiment to which public historians contribute substantially. Museum exhibits, ranger tours, and wayside plaques, on the other hand, do create public historical spaces. Some of these are physically contained within places controlled by public historical institutions, while others—canal or walking tours, for instance—stretch deep into other areas of the city. In some parts of Lowell, public historical space overlaps with other kinds of space. Lucy Larcom Park, which lines a block-long section of one of the downtown canals, contains interpretive plaques placed there by public historians at Lowell NHP, as well as public art works and landscape restoration accomplished as part of the overall redevelopment project. The park is also a public walkway that functions in many ways as a schoolyard for the city high school, whose buildings line both sides of the canal. This overlap of lived and representational space is becoming, more and more, a feature of our shared landscapes, and public historical space often appears within the mix.

Identifying its presence, however, did not solve the dilemma of how to study it. "Public history in Lowell" still presented far more institutions, events, bodies of knowledge, and overlapping social and professional realms than a single fieldworker could hope to understand in any real depth. The national park itself, my primary focus, is a large institution which had at that time more than one hundred employees and some two dozen "cooperative agreements," or active partnerships, with other cultural institutions in the city and beyond. To answer my central questions, I had to identify the various realms public historians operated within and to become at least somewhat familiar with enough of them to be able to understand public historians' roles there. The scope of my central inquiry meant that from the outset, I had to sacrifice some of the depth that ethnographers typically aim for while realizing that my two-year span of fieldwork would not be nearly long enough to provide a compensating breadth. That is, I knew I would only begin to grasp the workings of the interlocking ethnic, economic, political, familial, and professional worlds that make up a city of more than one hundred thousand people. Like most ethnographic projects, then, this one was a series of compromises, estimates, and omissions as much as it was a consciously designed strategy for answering specific questions.

My principal fieldwork was conducted between July 2000 and August 2002. My central focus throughout was on the interpretive division of the national park—the rangers, historians, curators, tour guides, and administrators who are Lowell's most visible public historians. I took many park tours, spent a good deal of time in the park's exhibit spaces, attended public forums and special park events, and observed many internal park meetings and workshops, including festival- and exhibit-planning meetings. I also interviewed 29 park staff members.

Most were from the interpretive division, including some key former staff members; 4 were administrators at the park. Overall during this project, I taped and transcribed interviews with 54 informants, with interviews of from a half hour to four hours in length. To become somewhat acquainted with two of the park's principal partnerships, I observed a small number of workshops and other programs at the Tsongas Industrial History Center and was a participant–observer at the Lowell Folk Festival for three consecutive years, including acting as a volunteer during the 2002 festival. Throughout, I looked particularly for moments when the park's public historians were working at the boundaries between past and present, or when they were talking about the relationship between the actual city and the park's representations of the city, on the assumption that these would be the places where the performative quality of history-making would be most evident. I found many of these moments in meetings of the Mogan Cultural Center Community Committee, which was charged with creating programming for the park's most community-oriented space. The park was also planning exhibit renovations for its Visitor Center (which serves as an introduction to the city and its history) and the concluding section of the Boott Cotton Mills Museum exhibit (which brings the story of Lowell into the present). Both of these processes proved particularly useful in understanding past–present, city–park, reality–representation relationships and the processes of negotiating those representations in public historical spaces.

I identified four groups of "supporting players" whose interactions with park public historians were of particular interest to me. First, I quickly saw that public historians' activities in Lowell had been shaped and circumscribed in important ways by their relationships with local people who had a vested interest—personal, professional, or both—in the overall history- and heritage-related project. I interviewed 15 people who fell into this category, whom I have labeled "local cultural activists" (this term, and the people associated with it, are discussed in detail in Chapter 7). Park visitors formed a second supporting group in my study. During the summers of 2001 and 2002, I conducted 162 short interviews (from 5 to 20 minutes in length) with randomly selected groups of visitors, as well as 74 "spot" interviews with audience members at the Lowell Folk Festival.[1] A third, smaller, but crucial set of informants was composed of scholars who have been among the park's consultants on exhibits and other projects. I interviewed 3 historians, 2 folklorists, a language scholar, and 2 designers who had been involved with the park in these ways; I also read published works by the many scholars who have contributed to the park's interpretation of Lowell's history since the 1970s.

Finally, I became somewhat acquainted with a number of civic and cultural leaders and organizations in Lowell's large Cambodian community.[2] I tried to observe as many Cambodian events as possible that seemed to abut, parallel, or overlap with the city's existing heritage productions, especially those involving the national park. I looked most closely at the annual Southeast Asian Water Festival, attending it (and planning meetings for it) during three consecutive summers and participating as a volunteer in 2002. I attended Khmer language classes in two different settings and gained a working acquaintance with some of the programs and projects associated with the Cambodian Mutual Assistance Association, at that time the city's largest and most influential Cambodian organization. I also organized two focus groups of monolingual Khmer-speakers to tour the national park with me and a translator in the summer of 2002. I initially expected to focus considerable attention on the intersections between the national park and Cambodians in Lowell, but this aspect of my project assumed much less importance when I realized that there were, in fact, very few points of intersection between them. This fieldwork was nonetheless helpful in enabling me to understand something of the overall relationship of newer immigrant groups in the city to the established heritage realm and the construction of localness, which I discuss in Chapter 5.

In general, I do not quote people by name in the body of this study. In this, I am following two basic conventions of cultural anthropology and ethnography. First, researchers in these fields are usually more interested in thinking about social patterns than individual motivations (although the two are, of course, linked). Thus I have usually chosen quotations that reflected the underlying patterns I saw operating in Lowell's public history world, rather than stand-alone opinions of single individuals. And second, like most social scientific researchers, I have tried to err on the side of protecting the confidentiality of the people I was studying, even when there was no pressing reason for anonymity. Two classes of people are referred to by name in the chapters that follow: those who have produced published work about Lowell's postindustrial experiment and those (like the assistant superintendent of the national park) who can be considered public figures and who customarily make public statements about Lowell's redevelopment project. A third class—those who hold unique jobs or who belong to very small categories (like the handful of park rangers who lead walking tours of the Acre neighborhood)—are not named but will be identifiable to those familiar with the setting. All of the people quoted here were aware of my presence and my project; they understood that they were speaking "on the record" and that I might wish to quote from their interviews, tours, and statements in meetings and other gatherings.

Although I live only an hour away from Lowell, in a much smaller Massachusetts mill town, and was able to undertake fieldwork on a part-time basis beginning in the summer of 2000, I wanted to be more than a commuting anthropologist during at least part of my fieldwork. For a total of ten months during 2001 and 2002, I lived in Lowell, subletting accommodations from two University of Massachusetts Lowell professors. The first was an apartment in a renovated textile mill, one of the more "upmarket" examples of adaptive reuse in Lowell. The second was a unit in one of the few remaining blocks of corporation boardinghouses—the brick row-housing built by Lowell's early textile corporations to house their workforce of young, single women. Most of these boardinghouses were torn down before or during the urban renewal efforts of the 1960s; indeed, in this period, the block in which I lived had been truncated to make room for a four-lane road. Across the street I could look out at the Suffolk/Wannalancit Mill complex, which had been in operation until 1980 and which now houses a number of small high-tech companies, state agencies, university programs, and the national park's waterpower exhibit. On the other side of the boarding-house block was the neighborhood known as the Acre, long a point of entry for new immigrants and symbolically important in terms of the city's pride in its ethnic heritage and its anxiety about present-day crime and poverty. In both places, I was in the midst of the palimpsest that is Lowell—the layers of structures, uses, and meanings that have been built and erased, rediscovered, and transformed over the past 180 years. The time I spent living in Lowell gave me an opportunity to experience something of the everyday life of the city, to get to know the downtown area—the focus of Lowell's culture-led redevelopment efforts—quite well, and to get a sense of some of the other clearly defined neighborhoods that make up the city. I often felt immersed in the worlds of history, preservation, and redevelopment, as I went from my apartment in one former textile mill to the national park spaces in three other mills or the Cambodian Mutual Assistance Association in yet another. Because my research focus was on public historians' work lives—something that I did not, in the context of this fieldwork, actually participate in—living in Lowell added the kind of participatory element to this study that ethnographers typically seek as they try to comprehend a place or a group of people as holistically as possible.

Of course, in some important ways, I *was* a participant in the social and professional worlds of many of my informants, and I will conclude by considering what that meant for this project. The more I talked to public historians in Lowell, the more I realized that the boundaries between me and my principal informants were very porous, indeed. This is not surprising in a study of people much like myself, in a general cultural setting with which I was already very familiar.[3] However, it was not just that we were all English-speaking white people of European descent, college-educated, middle-class, with an interest in history. In much more specific ways, our socioeconomic backgrounds and personal values were highly similar. So were the kinds of dilemmas we had faced and continued to face in finding a compatible niche in contemporary America. Most of us, I discovered, were from families that had only attained middle-class stability or status quite recently, usually in our parents' generation. The memory of the first family member to go to college or the first to take a professional-class job was still fresh. In my case, it was my father who made the move away from his family's rural farm and summer vacation-lodge business, attending university so that he could become a history teacher. Although I grew up in comfortable circumstances—in a roomy suburban house and at a cottage on a lake during the summers—I always had a sense that my parents did not take this prosperity for granted. They knew it had been achieved, not given, and they always lived with an uneasy sense that it could be lost again.

During the time when I was growing up—the 1960s and 1970s—many of the post–World War II socioeconomic gains made by middle-class people in the United States and Canada *were* lost to a large extent (Ehrenreich 1989, Newman 1999). In the expanding industrial economy of the late-nineteenth to the mid-twentieth century, a large base of working-class jobs, a rapidly growing white-collar sector, and enormous state support for personal credit (including home ownership) had provided the means for upward mobility for very large numbers of people. There was widespread expectation that each generation would do better than the one before it, and that new immigrants would continue to be able to live out the "American dream" of those who had arrived in the earlier part of the century. My husband's father, for instance, came to the United States as the youngest of a large family of Swedes, most of whom ended up employed in metal-working and munitions factories. The only one in his generation to go to college, my father-in-law earned his doctorate in chemistry and went on to work in the growing pharmaceutical industry. Chemists, like engineers, were at that time becoming more professionalized and more central to the increasingly important knowledge sector of the U.S. economy; David Noble has traced how these fields helped to transform the old industrial model pioneered at Lowell into an increasingly rationalized and scientific mode of production (Noble 1977:5–6,12–13). My husband, like me, grew up in the kind of comfortable suburban home that could, at that time, be afforded on a single professional salary. Like me, like many of the people we knew, like many of the public historians I was meeting in Lowell, he was part of a three-generation progression from the working class to middle-class professionalism to whatever came next.

"Whatever came next" has been the sticking point for many of us in the "baby-boom" and subsequent generations. As one observer has put it, "The thing that comes after growth is elusive" (McKibben 1999:68). The kind of prosperity that our parents' generation achieved proved to be the product not only of their own and their parents' efforts but also of a particular set of economic forces that have now changed drastically. In the postindustrial American economy, it has become more difficult to gain and keep a comparable level of prosperity. Entry-level middle class jobs face pressures from both directions—to become ever more skilled, credentialed, and professionalized (as continues in education and engineering) or to accept working conditions more like those of the lower-paid, lower-status jobs in the service sector, where there is little career security or worker control over jobs (as is happening in many parts of the health care field). And beyond the increasing difficulty of following in our parents' footsteps economically, many of us have been ambivalent about taking that route to begin with. Those of us who lean leftward politically are part of a segment of the population that has questioned "mainstream" middle-class values and goals since the 1960s and 1970s, too often finding both the high and low ends of contemporary corporate life soulless and unsatisfying, and searching for work that is more compatible with our social consciences while still providing something that at least approximates the comfortable middle-class standard of living we are used to.

In my own case, I spent many years working in odd corners of the arts, education, and service sectors until I hit a series of occupational dead ends during the recession of the early 1990s. I had always been perversely proud of having only a high school diploma in a world that assumed a college degree was necessary for any kind of success, but I finally had to admit that my lack of credentials was leaving me with precious few options for making a living. Somewhat reluctantly, I entered college for the first time in my mid-thirties, intending to get a degree that would equip me to do something that would be immediately useful and productive. Instead, I fell in love with intellectual inquiry and ended up pursuing graduate study in anthropology, with a focus on a question that had always deeply engaged me: how we use our knowledge of the past in our present-day lives. And so I found myself, ten years later, in the midst of an ethnographic study of people in Lowell whose backgrounds and career trajectories were in many ways strikingly similar to my own. My informants and I very often seemed to be seeking the same things and also trying to avoid the same things. Their dilemmas were similar to mine: how to make a living in an economic system that all too often felt hostile to our most cherished values and too seldom rewarded the things we found most worthwhile. And in the case of Lowell's public historians, especially those in the more radical left wing of the field, there was the added paradox of wanting to make some kind of comfortable living within an economic system that they were personally, professionally, and intellectually critical of, or at best ambivalent about. In critiquing how well public historians in Lowell have achieved this balancing act, as I do in this book, I have been forced to consider how well I am doing at it myself, and to think about how a critical observer might assess my own professional choices and ethnographic work. At times, I felt as though I were doing fieldwork in a hall of mirrors, confronted with my own questions and choices at every turn. Through previous ethnographic study I had learned to "bracket" my own beliefs so that I could study those of my informants with some degree of detachment, but it was almost impossible to do so in this case. My informants' beliefs were substantially the same as mine, and because we held those beliefs, our lives had played out in some extremely similar ways. These similarities suggested avenues of inquiry that I have found very fruitful in this study, but they have also challenged me in ways that were much more personal than I expected them to be.

This kind of project also points to some areas that still need further attention from anthropologists undertaking studies in museums and other privileged institutions, especially within our own cultures. Handler and Gable (1997:13) note that such studies typically ask about the ideological meanings produced in such institutions, how those ideologies relate to the interests and intentions of those who produce them, and how they are reproduced or resisted by those who receive them. Handler and Gable correctly argue that this triangular model—producers, product, consumers—is too simple to capture the complicated web of overlapping relationships and interests that combine to produce and use the social knowledge that museums and similar institutions help to create. Their own study of historical meaning-making breaks new ground by treating a historical site as "a complete social world" (1997:10), whose structure, norms, and practices are susceptible to ethnographic investigation. It also provides a model—one of comparatively few, despite calls for anthropologists to spend more time "studying up"—for studying informants who are peers and even colleagues, people who have been trained in the same intellectual and professional traditions and are likely to read what we say about them and respond in the same forums that we use to disseminate our own findings.[4] By using conventional ethnographic methods to study an elite and characteristically Western institution, and by opening the door to an ongoing and even-handed discussion with their informants, Handler and Gable have made an important contribution to an anthropology that is less fraught with the kinds of unequal power relationships and social distances attacked so vigorously by scholars since the 1960s.

But if *The New History in an Old Museum* is an important model for the kind of study I undertook in Lowell, it also falls short in ways that are both revealing and troubling. In traditional anthropological fashion, Handler and Gable *do* attempt to separate their own beliefs and values from those of the people they studied at Colonial Williamsburg, with the result that they leave themselves out of the web of meaning-making that they are examining. The separation is a very artificial one in this case. As with my study of Lowell, there are many areas where their own social, intellectual, professional, and economic worlds closely overlap with those of their informants. Handler and Gable are severely critical of the apparent failure of progressive social historians to mobilize their political and intellectual convictions in their work at Colonial Williamsburg. They point to an "abdication of responsibility that is characteristic of the intelligentsia at Colonial Williamsburg and elsewhere in American society" (1997:231) and go so far as to suggest that scholars, as well as public historians, have evaded their responsibility to be more critical and active in American society. But they draw the line at asking what this means for their own work and the choices they have themselves made. Tellingly, they relegate their criticism of the academy to a footnote, which reads:

> University professors are "free" to promulgate in the classroom stinging critiques of class inequalities in American life even as they ignore, for example, the relationship between the institutional resources devoted to their own salaries and those devoted to the wages of the largely invisible (to them) custodial and maintenance workers who clean up after them. Or it could be argued that they are free to be critical as long as they continue to credential the sons and daughters of the middle classes, thereby fitting them for work in a corporate world where the critical lessons they may have learned in college will not be of much use to them. (1997:231)

This point is vitally important in considering the kinds of institutional, economic, and social pressures that affect progressive movements and ideals in contemporary America. But the authors do not permit it to inform their overall discussion of the public historians' failures at Colonial Williamsburg. It is also noteworthy that Handler and Gable refer here to university professors in the third person, further veiling any personal connection between themselves and the conditions they criticize so articulately.

Likewise, Handler and Gable never really acknowledge the leftist assumptions that undergird their own analyses, although it would be a very obtuse reader who did not see those assumptions in action throughout the book (as Bixel 1998 and Shaffer 1998 comment in their reviews of *The New History in an Old Museum*). Nor, as I have already noted, did they inquire into their informants' lives beyond their work setting.

Colonial Williamsburg is *not* "a complete social world," after all—it is a workplace, and its workers come to it from specific backgrounds that significantly shape their motivations, perceptions, and behaviors. Yet the authors chose not to confront either or both of these issues—their own social and political positions and the broader circumstances of their informants' lives—leaving some important larger questions about historical knowledge and cultural production unasked and unaddressed. In most anthropological studies, maintaining such a distance is still quite easy, even if we now question it to some extent. But in my study of the public history sphere in Lowell, this kind of separation would have been highly contrived, as it was contrived for Handler and Gable at Colonial Williamsburg. This present study, then, attempts to build on the important work of *The New History in an Old Museum* and to extend it by asking questions that originate in—rather than masking—my own role as an interested observer and active participant in the social scene that I am studying. These are the questions that occupy me as I begin to search for ways to integrate scholarship with citizenship, and theory with participation in public culture. And they are the same questions that have occupied a generation of progressive public historians in Lowell and elsewhere. To what extent can museums, tourism, and public history act as critical, counterhegemonic sites—that is, as places to question and perhaps challenge the dominant forces in our lives? And if we, as leftist scholars and practitioners believe that there is potential in these social forms to critique and change what we do not like about the society in which we live, how might our own work help to bring about the changes we hope to see? I could have approached Lowell's cultural experiment from other angles, but I have chosen to frame my inquiry in this way because these are the questions that matter most to me. And there is no better historical site at which to ask these questions, because Lowell's culture-led redevelopment itself is based on a particularly unfinished history that continually raises questions about capitalism and the kinds of opportunities, inequities, and tensions that exist within it, including those that shape and confine all of us today.

PART II

THREE TOURS OF LOWELL

Lowell's Industrial Heritage Sites

1. Visitor Center
2. Railroad Exhibit
3. New England Quilt Museum
4. Old City Hall
5. Moody Street Feeder Gatehouse
6. St. Anne's Church
7. Agents House/Park Headquarters

8. Mogan Cultural Center/ Boarding House Park
9. Boott Cotton Mills Museum
10. Kerouac Commemorative
11. Lower Locks
12. Industrial Canyon
13. Swamp Locks
14. American Textile History Museum
15. Whistler House Museum of Art

16. Tremont Gatehouse and Power House
17. Suffolk Mill Turbine Exhibit
18. Pawtucket Gatehouse
19. Francis Gate/Guard Locks

UNIVERSITY OF MASSACHUSETTS LOWELL NORTH CAMPUS

113

Riverside

Veterans of Foreign Wars Highway

University

Hydroelectric Plant

NORTHER

Mammoth

PAWTUCKET FALLS

NORTHERN CANAL

Fathe

Merrimack

Moody

Varnum

18 PAWTUCKET GATEHOUSE

PAWTUCKET DAM
elevation 101 feet

Pawtucket

Nuestra Señora del Carmen Church (formerly St. Jean Baptiste Church)

Salem

Varnum

Pawtucket

To Lowell Heritage State Park's Vandenberg Esplanade

PAWTUCKET CANAL

NORTH COMMON

Fletcher

St.

FRANCIS GATE PARK

Walker

School

FRANCIS GATE   GUARD LOCKS

19

Broadway

UNIVERSITY OF MASSACHUSETTS LOWELL SOUTH CAMPUS

PAWTUCKET CANAL

Canal levels shown on map

UPPER RIVER	GUARD LOCKS 2-foot drop	
UPPER CANAL	SWAMP LOCKS 13-foot drop	32-foot vertical drop from upper river to lower river
	LOWER CANAL	LOWER LOCKS 17-foot drop
	LOWER RIVER	

NATIONAL PARK SERVICE/LOWELL NATIONAL HISTORICAL PARK

Middl

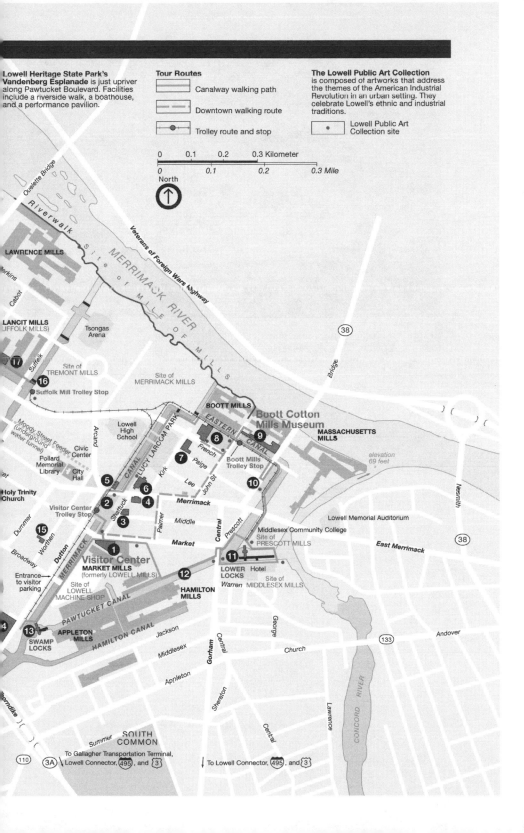

Lowell Heritage State Park's Vandenberg Esplanade is just upriver along Pawtucket Boulevard. Facilities include a riverside walk, a boathouse, and a performance pavilion.

Tour Routes

Canalway walking path

Downtown walking route

Trolley route and stop

The Lowell Public Art Collection is composed of artworks that address the themes of the American Industrial Revolution in an urban setting. They celebrate Lowell's ethnic and industrial traditions.

Lowell Public Art Collection site

0   0.1   0.2   0.3 Kilometer
0   0.1   0.2   0.3 Mile

North

LAWRENCE MILLS

Perkins

Cabot

LANCIT MILLS
(SUFFOLK MILLS)

Suffolk

Tsongas Arena

Site of MILE OF MILLS

Site of TREMONT MILLS

Site of MERRIMACK MILLS

Suffolk Mill Trolley Stop

Ouelette Bridge

Riverwalk

MERRIMACK RIVER

Veterans of Foreign Wars Highway

Bridge

38

BOOTT MILLS

Boott Cotton Mills Museum

MASSACHUSETTS MILLS

elevation 69 feet

Nesmith

Moody Street Feeder (underground water tunnel)

Lowell High School

Civic Center

Pollard Memorial Library

City Hall

Holy Trinity Church

Visitor Center Trolley Stop

Arcand

CANAL

LUCY LARCOM PARK

EASTERN CANAL

French

Paige

Kirk

Lee

John St

Boott Mills Trolley Stop

8

9

7

5

6

2

4

3

Shattuck

Merrimack

Middle

Market

Palmer

Central

Prescott

10

Middlesex Community College

Site of PRESCOTT MILLS

Lowell Memorial Auditorium

East Merrimack

38

15

Worthen

Dummer

Broadway

Dutton

MERRIMACK

1

Visitor Center
MARKET MILLS
(formerly LOWELL MILLS)

Entrance to visitor parking

Site of LOWELL MACHINE SHOP

12

HAMILTON MILLS

11

LOWER LOCKS

Hotel

Warren

Site of MIDDLESEX MILLS

PAWTUCKET CANAL

APPLETON MILLS

HAMILTON CANAL

13

SWAMP LOCKS

4

Jackson

Middlesex

Appleton

Gorham

Central

Sheraton

Church

George

Central

Lawrence

CONCORD RIVER

133

Andover

Thorndike

110

3A

Summer

SOUTH COMMON

To Gallagher Transportation Terminal, Lowell Connector, 495, and 3

To Lowell Connector, 495, and 3

FIGURE 1. Trolleys and canal boats carry visitors along the national park's tour routes in Lowell. CATHY STANTON.

CHAPTER 3

The Run of the Mill

The "Run of the Mill" tour is one of several tour programs regularly presented by Lowell National Historical Park from late spring through early fall. These ranger-led tours are among the park's most popular offerings and are often filled to their twenty-seven-person capacity. Most tour itineraries include a trolley and canal-boat ride, lasting from ninety minutes to just over two hours (fig. 1). The Run of the Mill is one of the longer tours, incorporating not only a ride along one of the canals but also a visit to an exhibit about waterpower in the Suffolk Mill, a location somewhat distant from the park's downtown sites (see map). The purpose of the tour, according to the outline used by the rangers, is to show "how human, natural, and financial resources interacted to impact the operation of the mills." Like most park tours, this one focuses largely on the early period of Lowell's development, from the 1820s to the 1840s, when the city's defining system of canals, textile mills, and downtown streets was first designed and built. This early nineteenth-century infrastructure forms the core of the city's 137-acre Historic Preservation District and the main area that the national park is mandated to interpret. Park staff members sometimes refer to this area as being like an octopus, with its concentrated downtown center and far-flung system of "arms" snaking out into the city in several directions.[1]

I took many "mill and canal" tours during my two years of fieldwork, but this chapter draws on a single Run of the Mill tour that I took in

August 2001, which combined the standard features of most tours with some small but very striking exceptions. The tour was led by a seasonal park ranger who was working for the National Park Service during his summer vacation from his regular job as a teacher.[2] In his brief introductory orientation, he offered an alternative to the octopus metaphor by describing the city as being layered like an onion—a useful notion for understanding early Lowell's distinctive landscape and its founders' unifying vision. The outer layer of the onion consists of the Merrimack River, which makes a right-angled turn at Lowell, and an eighteenth-century transportation canal built to circumvent the rapids at that point (see map). Together, the river and the old Pawtucket Canal form a rough circle, which originally enclosed all of Lowell. By the early nineteenth century, the canal had been supplanted by another canal route that ran directly to Boston. But a group of Boston entrepreneurs saw a new use for the obsolete Pawtucket Canal, and for the waterpower that could be generated by the thirty-two-foot drop in the Merrimack River at what was then the farming community of East Chelmsford.

This group, which has subsequently become known informally as the Boston Associates (see Weil 1998), had already experimented successfully with a textile mill development on the much slower-moving Charles River in Waltham, Massachusetts.[3] These men were innovators on a large scale. One of their members, Francis Cabot Lowell, had memorized the workings of an English power loom while on a tour of Europe, thus illicitly exporting a piece of the closely guarded technology that had made Britain the first industrialized nation in the world. Britain's Industrial Revolution was largely built on the labor of an impoverished underclass of manual laborers displaced by spatial and socioeconomic changes in the eighteenth century. The United States had no such available labor pool, but the Boston Associates solved the problem by recruiting the daughters of New England farmers. At a time when agriculture was no longer expanding in the region and the economy was becoming increasingly cash-based, these young women had few options for making a living and they eagerly embraced the opportunities offered in the new textile mills. Lowell and his fellow investors had all made fortunes earlier in the risky but lucrative long-distance shipping trade, and thus were able to capitalize their Waltham mill at an unprecedented level—ten times the investment in competing textile mills in Rhode Island's Blackstone River Valley (Dublin 1993:17). This wealth gave the Waltham and later the Lowell enterprises an unusual level of stability in the volatile early days of American industrial entrepreneurship and allowed them to create large and efficient organizations that brought together all of the many operations needed to make cloth. The Boston Associates were also among the earliest to grasp how the corporate structure—originally conceived as a way to enlist private capital for the public good—could be used as well to minimize investors' risks without restricting their capacity for profit. After tapping out the limited water resources of the Charles River, the group quietly bought up all the farmland along the more vigorous Merrimack River in East Chelmsford, along with the old Pawtucket Canal, and laid out plans for an integrated industrial operation on a scale not yet seen in the New World. The first Lowell mill began operations in early 1823. By the time Lowell was formally incorporated as a town in 1826, its population was 2,500; by 1850, it had grown to 33,000 people, with ten mills in operation (Malone 1991:149).

The interior layers of Lowell's onion consist of these mills and the canals that powered them. Using the Pawtucket Canal as a starting point, the engineers hired by the Boston Associates constructed a network of power canals that drew the water of the Merrimack River inland and through a series of new brick mill buildings. By 1848, when the last canal was dug, the system was 5.6 miles long and capable of carrying the entire volume of the river's water to the mills, where it turned huge waterwheels (later replaced by more efficient turbines) that powered the looms and other machines on the floors above. This engineering feat has created a strange landscape. The Merrimack River veers abruptly at the Pawtucket Dam; its waters are diverted through the city and then added back to the nearly empty riverbed at various outfalls along what became known as Lowell's "mile of mills." Many of the giant factory buildings were demolished during the urban-renewal efforts of the 1960s, but many remain, creating red-brick canyons at places along the still-existing canal system. The final, inner core of the onion is the downtown area. Most older cities and towns have grown up gradually around a central business district or common area, but Lowell's downtown is at the city's center largely by default. The original planners fit their business district into the only land area not needed for manufacturing space within the main mill and canal system (Ryan 1987:140). The textile mills were paramount in early Lowell; everything else existed to support the production of cloth.

One integral piece of Lowell's original mill-and-canal layer has all but disappeared over time. When the Boston Associates recruited young New England farm women to work in their textile mills, they were not merely being pragmatic in the face of a chronic American labor shortage or seeking to avoid the kind of resistance that they feared they might encounter among male workers with entrenched artisanal traditions and previous experience in the wage economy (Gross 1993:9). Indeed, Lowell's founders were deeply and sincerely disturbed by the poverty and misery that the English Industrial Revolution had brought to British workers and towns. They sought to avoid the most degrading human and social effects of industrialization by hiring republican-spirited young women who would work in the mills for only a few years. Because there was no existing town with residential areas where these workers could live, and because of the belief of the times that young single women needed close moral supervision and chaperonage, the Boston Associates constructed row upon row of corporation-owned brick boardinghouses next to each mill complex.

Lowell's founders might well have approved of the park ranger's onion image. The metaphor echoes their own somewhat utopian vision of Lowell as a coherent, unified manufacturing community where the social and environmental degradation and conflict of the English Industrial Revolution could not occur. Like many Americans, the Boston Associates believed that tremendous economic and technological progress could coexist within the purifying natural landscapes that have supposedly shaped a uniquely democratic set of American values. They constructed their city so as to balance nature and industry. Their "distinctly collegiate" (Dalzell 1987:68) factory campuses originally consisted of several freestanding mill buildings clustered around green courtyards, next to their attendant rows of boardinghouses. Tree-lined, landscaped parks and promenades were an important part of early Lowell's design, and walkways along the canal system were provided for the workers' enjoyment and recreation (Malone and Parrott 1998). Idealized views of Lowell were used throughout its first decades to sell both the textile companies' products and the concept of the ideal manufacturing community itself (Wright 1989) (fig. 2). These images usually showed the city in the distance, as seen from a pastoral foreground, emphasizing the harmonious relationship between what Leo Marx has famously termed the machine and the garden (Marx 1964). Dalzell has argued that this

FIGURE 2. Idealized pastoral images of early Lowell were often used to advertise the city's textile products, as on the cover of this sample folder from the Merrimack Print Works. LOWELL MUSEUM.

spatial harmony was designed to produce social harmony, and to preserve the Boston Associates' superior wealth and social status without fomenting the new kinds of class antagonisms that they saw simmering dangerously in England's industrialized cities. The substantial corporate investment in "respectable" worker housing, the relatively short terms of the mill girls' employment, the greenways and other amenities were all part of a grand social experiment aimed at "controlling the process of change, of channeling its direction so that it did not simply sweep everything before it" (Dalzell 1987:25). And for a very short time, the plan worked. Lowell became a showplace visited by politicians, celebrities, and tourists, a major American industrial center and a world leader in textile production, famous for its workforce of young women. Although the labor was hard, with workdays averaging about twelve hours, Tom Dublin has noted that the workers at least initially considered it a fair bargain, and that, "As long as their expectations were met, women workers did not challenge the power and authority of the corporations" (1993:86). In a changing society and economy, Lowell's mill girls appeared to welcome the opportunities for income and experience that the city presented to them.

Just over a decade after Lowell was founded, however, its founders' utopian hopes were challenged by the realities of industrial capitalist development. Rapid economic growth, prompted in part by the very success of the Lowell experiment, led to competition and the need for the Lowell mills to expand and cut costs in order to stay profitable. Pay cuts and new production demands in the 1830s and 1840s prompted resistance and work stoppages by the mill girls, many of whom turned out to be far less tractable than the paternalistic Boston Associates had anticipated. Ironically, shared life in the close quarters of the paternalistic corporation boardinghouses actually fostered the women's activism and ability to organize (Dublin 1993:103). By the 1840s, impoverished Irish immigrants were arriving in the northeastern United States in great numbers, providing a labor force willing to work for the lower wages being offered by mill owners.

The gradual shift from Yankee women to an Irish workforce was a sign of a new phase of industrialism in America, driven by the demands of competition and growth and fueled in large part by the labor of the enormous numbers of immigrants who came to the United States in the late nineteenth and early twentieth century. As the workforce changed, so did the built environment. Increasingly, workers lived in ethnic enclaves that often resembled the overcrowded, impoverished working-class districts in Britain's industrial cities that had so horrified the Boston Associates (Dalzell 1991:64). Starting around 1840, once-ample textile wages dropped steadily in relation to those for other jobs. Never as thoroughly unionized as those in other industries or even other textile cities (for example, in neighboring Lawrence, site of the famous 1912 "Bread and Roses" strike), workers in Lowell saw a long erosion of their earnings over the next century (Gross 1993:78, Miller 1988:2–4).

As the corporations and their production expanded, the neat, campus-like mill complexes became more like fortresses, the grass courtyards and river views gradually walled in by new and larger brick buildings (figs. 3, 4). The canal system that had been the state of the art in the 1820s was quickly outmoded, despite extensive revisions and new turbine technology introduced in the 1840s. By 1880, steam had become the major source of power for the mills, introducing a pall of coal smoke that added to the growing environmental costs of textile production in Lowell and made the city look much like any other grimy industrial center (Malone 1991:151, Steinberg 1991:245). The shining vision of the Boston Associates had

FIGURE 3. By the late nineteenth century, Lowell was a densely built industrial city, as this 1876 bird's-eye view attests. CENTER FOR LOWELL HISTORY.

FIGURE 4. Textile workers pose for a company photograph in the courtyard of the Boott Cotton Mills, c. 1878. LOWELL MUSEUM.

succumbed to what Dalzell calls "the relentless logic" (1987:226) of industrial capitalist expansion and competition. The original vision, in his view,
"suffered not from an overdose of practicality but from the reverse: from
too strenuous a determination to counteract the economic logic inherent
in the situation" (1987:68)—a logic that continues to work itself out in
present-day Lowell and most other places around the globe.

Making a Communicative Landscape

The recent reinvention of Lowell is part of that same cycle of capitalist
logic. This makes present-day Lowell a deeply ironic place, because its
new "communicative landscape" contains many unusually critical statements about how capitalism has operated in the past, yet in many subtle
ways—for example, in the kind of mill and canal tours I am analyzing
here—the same landscape is used to mask how that system operates in
the present. Before I return to the Run of the Mill tour, I want to give an
overview of how industrialism is interpreted at Lowell NHP.

Early in the life of the park, its interpretive planning staff decided to
focus on five main themes: waterpower, technology, labor, capital, and the
industrial city. Lowell NHP could hardly ignore the role of technology in
the city's early history, but the inclusion of the categories of "labor" and
"capital" in the park's interpretive themes signaled that this would be an
industrial story focused on people as much as on machines or cloth. As
the official Run of the Mill tour outline states, "Water provided the power
to run the machines but the run of the mill ultimately rested with the
people on all levels including corporate investors, engineers and workers."
To a significant extent, this aspect of the park's interpretation was building on earlier work done by the coalition of educators, new social historians, preservationists, architects, planners, and others who had gradually
gathered around the idea of creating a national park in Lowell (this process is described in the following chapter). A key document in early park
planning was a publication known as the Brown Book, published in 1977
as a lobbying and educational tool during the city's pursuit of Congressional approval for its park plans.[4] The Brown Book laid the groundwork
for concentrating the park in the downtown area while linking it to the
more far-flung canals and riverbanks—the tentacles of the octopus. This
decision was by no means universally popular; some saw (and still see) it
as supporting downtown business and real estate interests at the expense

of the city's neighborhoods. But from the standpoints of many historians and planners engaged in the writing of the Brown Book, including some of the most politically leftist people involved in the project, the focus on downtown offered advantages because it enabled a certain kind of story to be told succinctly and powerfully. That story centered on the relationship between capital and labor.

This focus signaled that Lowell NHP would be a significant departure from existing industrial museums—and indeed, it has remained unusual among the many industrial history sites created since the late 1970s. Many history museums, as Mike Wallace notes, were created by industrialists themselves, or by inventors and engineers who have historically tended to lionize technical and entrepreneurial achievement and to see technological development as "a blind and automatic process that moves according to its own inner imperatives" (Wallace 1996:85) rather than a contested and asymmetrical social process. Many industrial history sites created in recent years continue to reify the notion of economic and social change as a natural and inevitable progression, often because these sites were part of economic redevelopment projects conceived during the New Right era that began in the 1980s rather than the more socially and politically progressive period of the 1960s and 1970s, as Lowell NHP was. For instance, one visitor-center exhibit in the Massachusetts/Rhode Island Blackstone River Valley National Heritage Corridor (created in 1986) depicts industrialization and deindustrialization as vast forces moving through human affairs as impersonally as weather fronts:

> During the late 1700s and early 1800s, the Industrial Revolution swept across the ocean from England and straight up the Blackstone River Valley—the first area in North America to be industrialized. . . . Industrialization of the Blackstone River Valley produced prosperity until the turn of the century, when the mills moved south and workers began to leave. The Great Depression speeded the decline until, after the end of World War II, almost all the mills closed. Today, the growth of service industries, together with Congressional recognition of the Blackstone River Valley as a historically significant region, have inspired a new era of revitalization.

Lowell NHP, in contrast, acknowledges agency, contestation, and multiple perspectives in the development and aftermath of industrial capitalism. The park's main exhibit at the Boott Cotton Mills Museum includes a wall display and slide-show treatment of the debate between Thomas Jefferson and Alexander Hamilton, in which Hamilton argued that the United States should follow Britain's course in pursuing greater industrialization while Jefferson maintained that the country's republican values would be better served by its remaining a primarily agricultural society. From the beginnings of Lowell's new experiment, there had been contention over the portrayal of the Boston Associates who founded the city. Should these men be lauded for their accomplishments or vilified as rapacious capitalists who were primarily interested in using the city and its people for profit? The park's first public historians found some middle ground in this debate by portraying the founders as men who sought social good as well as profit, but who became caught in the logic of a system whose consequences they had not been able to foresee.

The park's interpreters took a more partisan stance about the period when those consequences—competition, wage cuts, labor unrest—began to become clearer. The introductory slide show at the Visitor Center and a second slide show, "The Wheels of Change" in the Boott Cotton Mills Museum both state forthrightly that it is in the nature of capitalism to produce social and economic inequalities, and that workers have often fought back against those inequalities. Indeed, the park's overall interpretation is strongly pro-labor. The Yankee mill girls are central to this interpretation for several reasons. As I show in the following chapter, the National Park Service preferred to emphasize Lowell's early development, which it saw as the city's most nationally significant period and hence the era that made Lowell worthy of commemoration in a national park. Focusing on the mill girls was a way for the new public historians to accomplish this goal while moving beyond the more conventional focus on technology and the celebration of industrial achievement. It was—and still is—remarkable to encounter a historic site where women are depicted as industrial workers. In this way, Lowell NHP reflects the new interest of the 1970s in women's history, an interest sparked by the feminist movement and linked with it to other social movements that questioned and challenged the status quo. As we have already seen, historian Tom Dublin, whose work provided much of the basis for the park's interpretation of the mill girls, explicitly connected his research with the influence of the contemporary women's movement (1993:xix). And women were shown not only as workers at the park, but also as labor organizers and activists. In fact, the mill girls were Lowell's most active labor agitators. Their cultural homogeneity, assumption of social equality with their employers, and ability to return home to their farms made them much bolder than their immigrant successors in challenging the decline of working conditions and wages in the textile mills. Even so, they were ultimately unsuccessful, as their eventual withdrawal from the industrial labor market shows, and subsequent textile workers were also generally unable to organize effectively against the closely allied textile companies (Richards 1991, Zaroulis 1976).

One of Lowell's first public historians acknowledged to me that "the whole notion of interpreting organized labor in Lowell's history is not a big story. . . . There was labor activity in Lowell, but it was never a place where labor was wildly successful." But organized labor and class relationships *were* a central interest of the new social historians and public historians, who succeeded in making these subjects an important part of the park's interpretation. Focusing on the mill girls also offered a pragmatic advantage from the perspective of the professional planners who were active in drafting the Brown Book and other important planning documents. Although most of the boardinghouse blocks that originally housed Lowell's workers had been torn down, enough remained so that it was possible to show spatially how the relationship between labor and capital had evolved. The boardinghouses' proximity to the mills, the close quarters shared by the mill girls, the organization of the entire city to support a single economic activity—these physical legacies in Lowell's built environment allowed the planners to map the city's early history and to begin to make it "legible" or "communicative"—to create, in the terminology of one of the planners who drafted the Brown Book, a "narrative place" (Frenchman 2001). There was also one final advantage to focusing on the mill girls. As we will see in Chapters 4 and 7, the subject of Lowell's later immigrant workers was declared largely off-limits to the critical, leftist approach of the public historians by the local cultural activists who had helped shape the revitalization experiment from the outset. These local founders of the new Lowell experiment felt a proprietary interest in the immigrants that they did not feel for the mill girls; the mill girls, then, were more available to the planners and historians—most of whom were not Lowell natives—for their own interpretations.

The park's interpretation of industrial capitalism, then, acknowledges agency and contestation but also shows a clear sympathy with labor, as represented most centrally by Lowell's first labor force of Yankee women. A final important feature of park interpretation is that, to some extent, it uses the living city itself as part of its exhibitry. In fact, in the late 1970s and early 1980s, the city was almost the *only* exhibit the park could offer. The permanent Market Mills Visitor Center was not completed until 1982; before then, ranger tours took visitors to the existing Lowell Museum, created during the planning and lobbying process for the park. But the primary exhibit on display was Lowell itself—the canals, the still-unrenovated mill buildings, the stores, restaurants, and people on its streets. The park began running mill and canal tours immediately after its creation in the summer of 1978, and these have remained among its most popular programs.[5] In search of realism and authenticity like most tourists, visitors appear stimulated by the fact that they are touring a living city rather than a simulation or a museum display. The park's first interpretive planners hoped to capitalize on this porous boundary between audience and exhibit in a way that would further progressive public history's aims. They wanted to encourage people to make connections between their own lives and the material being interpreted and to see industrial capitalism as an ongoing process within which countless individual and collective actions—our own as well as others'—continually shape the world in complex, contingent ways. They also sought to link the twinned phenomena of industrialization and deindustrialization, rather than separating them as was the usual practice in industrial history exhibits.

As the park itself has been more fully developed, with permanent exhibits at the Visitor Center (1982), the Suffolk Mill (1985), a renovated boardinghouse (1989), and the Boott Cotton Mills Museum (1992), this porosity has diminished somewhat. Visitors can now remain more fully within public historical space when they visit Lowell. Because many still choose to take a mill and canal tour while they are at the park, the door is left open for a potentially more direct encounter with the history and consequences of industrialism. However, as the Run of the Mill tour will demonstrate, tentative movements through that open door are carefully circumscribed in ways that work against their considerable potential for breaking through the taken-for-granted acceptance of economic and social conditions in modern industrialized or deindustrialized places. Some incidents from the Run of the Mill tour illustrate the patterns and paradoxes that I found typical of the park's interpretation and that show how the park in some senses invites, and in others inhibits, a fuller consideration of the operation of capitalism in our lives.

Creating Unilinear Time

The basic mill-and-canal tour route at Lowell NHP takes visitors by trolley from the park's centrally located Visitor Center in a former mill building, a short distance to a nexus of the canal system known as Swamp Locks, and then by boat along the original Pawtucket Canal toward the Merrimack River. Much of the rangers' interpretation during this section is devoted to explaining how the original waterpower system worked, often with some attention to the environmental impacts of industry. On the return boat trip, rangers usually point out some of the industries that still operate along the canals, including steam and hydroelectric generating plants, and some factories producing specialty textiles. One of these, operated in 2001 by a company called Collins and Aikman, borders the Pawtucket Canal. On warm days when windows in the unair-conditioned building were open, workers sometimes leaned out to wave at passing tour boats. On the August 2001 tour, our ranger drew the group's attention to several Asian women workers who were waving:

> There's some folks waving to us, they're working here. [To workers:] How you doing? [To tour group:] This factory is a smaller factory. Lowell used to be a one-horse town. It used to be cotton textile mills. And then in the 1950s those mills went down south. [In the]1970s, Wang Computers came to Lowell and everybody was happy. They thought, "Wow, we're going to get jobs from the computer factories." And then Wang Computers left. So now the city of Lowell is much more diversified, a lot more smaller businesses. This is one example, this Collins and Aikman, the people work twelve-hour shifts three days a week, and then they have four-day weekends. And the factory's open twenty four hours a day. So there's a night shift, you might work midnight to noon, or you might work noon to midnight, just three days and then a four-day weekend. That's a lot different than what the mill girls had. They had a twelve hour day, sometimes more, but it could be six days a week. These folks also have a good opportunity for overtime pay.

In the ranger's telling, this company and the kind of work it offered its employees are part of an overall narrative of improvement and progress, in which the city has continually learned from its past mistakes and avoided repeating them. He made no mention of the extent to which these workers in a still largely nonunionized industry were able to control the length of their working day or the conditions under which they worked. Nor did he speak of their continued vulnerability to fluctuations in an ever more globalized textile market. In fact, Michigan-based Collins and Aikman was the new owner of a division of a locally owned textile company, Joan Fabrics, which had just sold its Lowell automotive fabric and yarn-dying operations to the Michigan corporation (Heartland 2001). Not long afterward, Elkin McCallum, the local owner of Joan Fabrics, acquired a textile mill in Mexico, his first outside the United States, with the stated goal of "bring[ing] low-cost production to the United States" via Mexico's cheaper labor pool (Sloan 2002)—a direct admission that textile production is, in McCallum's own words, "an industry that is dying here in the United States" (Murray 2002). A second textile operation frequently pointed out by rangers on park tours, Freudenberg Nonwovens, moved all its remaining manufacturing jobs to North Carolina in the summer of 2002, leaving another 100,000 square feet of empty mill space just a block from the national park's Visitor Center (Tutalo 2002) and continuing a southward movement of textile plants and jobs that has been going on in Lowell for nearly a century.

The global pattern of mergers, plant closings, and the shifting of manufacturing jobs to places with lower labor costs continues to reshape Lowell's economic and social landscape in ways that do not fit neatly into the linear story of progress and improvement as told by the ranger. His description of working conditions at the Collins and Aikman plant carefully avoided placing these companies within the rapidly shifting context of global capitalism—a context that also encompasses the story of Wang Laboratories. When Dr. An Wang, a pioneer in microcomputer technology in the 1970s, located his world headquarters in Lowell in 1978, he was widely heralded as a new incarnation of the innovative merchants and engineers who had created the city 160 years earlier. By the early 1990s, though, Wang Laboratories was bankrupt, a casualty of the fast-paced boom-and-bust cycles of the growing electronics industry, and its tens of thousands of workers in the area—including many of the Cambodian refugees who had moved to Lowell in the 1980s—were left to find other work if they could. (Wang's history is treated in more depth in Chapter 4.) The story of Lowell's few remaining textile mills and their high technology successors, then, could be used as an illustration of the ongoing working out of the "relentless logic" of industrial capitalism and competition. In this cycle, as Mike Wallace has pointed out, rational short-term decisions made in the interests of individual corporations all too often result in the larger social irrationality of places and economies that are less and less sustainable in the long term (1996:90)—a conclusion very different from the happy ending sketched by the ranger above. His was a linear narrative, masking the many repetitions of the cycle of industrial capitalism in Lowell and beyond. Deindustrialization is not ignored in this narrative, but it is placed on a one-directional continuum that supports the story of birth, decline, and rebirth told by the city's overall redevelopment project. As Walter Benjamin noted, "The concept of the historical progress of mankind cannot be sundered from the concept of its progression through a homogeneous, empty time" (1969:261). The ranger's interpretation reinforced the notion of this kind of time, disregarding the layering and overlapping that actually connect seemingly separate historical actors—the tourists in the boat, the workers at the windows—with one another across both space and time.

Despite the sharply critical interpretation of labor strife, class relationships, and capitalist logic reflected in the national park's depictions of industrial Lowell, then, many of its cultural productions deeply undercut critical historical perspectives by shying away from the fuller implications of Lowell's past for its present and future. The one-directional narrative I encountered on this and other park tours avoids the larger—and, for me, the crucial—question posed by Lowell's history: Does the new Lowell experiment offer anything that could help the city withstand the inevitable next turn in the cycle of capitalist development and loss? Paul Marion, a long-time local cultural activist who will reappear in Chapter 7, raised precisely this question in one of our interviews: "Lowell shows us all of the flaws in the capitalist system. The system, left to its own devices, left to pure self-interest, you know—to me, that's one of the great challenges of this whole Lowell reclamation project, is can we within this community find some way to stabilize the kind of economic whims based on what we've learned the hard way?" But the very mechanisms by which we might best learn the lessons contained in Lowell—its public historical productions—are themselves charged with contributing materially and symbolically to the latest phase of the city's economic life, placing them in an ambivalent position that can be felt in expressions like the ranger's one-directional narrative. Because the national park's tours are cultural performances embedded in an overall project that is, at its heart, supportive of notions of progress and improvement, it is very difficult for those productions to question the imperatives of economic growth or how the historic tensions between capital and labor are playing out within new relationships of production and consumption—including, increasingly, the consumption of cultural experiences themselves.

Destabilizing the Linear Narrative

The second half of the Run of the Mill tour takes place on land. After the boat returns to the Swamp Locks, visitors reboard the trolley and ride to the Suffolk Mill, the park site devoted to interpreting the workings of waterpower. Unlike the main park exhibits, this facility is somewhat outside the core downtown area. It is not staffed on a regular basis, but is open only to scheduled tour groups. Inside the Suffolk Mill exhibit, visitors learn about the system of waterwheels, penstocks, turbines, gears, and line shafts that transmitted power from the canals to the textile equipment of the early Lowell factories.[6] After viewing an 8-ton wooden waterwheel with an 800-pound leather belt, still in its original site in the building, tour groups move to an area where a single loom (now powered by electricity) is set up as a demonstration machine. Switching on the noisy, clacking loom, the rangers show how cloth is woven and recount the various dangers and difficulties of the job, as well as some of the technical improvements that resulted in fewer workers being required to tend more and more machines. Although the written tour outline focuses largely on mechanical information, rangers seem to welcome this moment as an opportunity to invite visitors to enter imaginatively into the experience of factory work. In Chapter 6, I explore the nature and implications of this imaginative leap more fully. Here it is enough to note that for the most part, rangers' descriptions of the weavers' jobs stay within the same linear narrative pattern that I have commented on above. While acknowledging the demands, monotony, and occasional danger of work in a textile factory, the park rangers generally also make it clear that the worst horror stories about this kind of labor belong in the past, and that working conditions overall have improved over time, so that present-day American textile workers at places like Collins and Aikman have it "a lot different from what the mill girls had."

But the ranger who led the August 2001 tour added a meditation of his own, which suddenly disrupted the linear narrative and folded past and present in on each other in a highly provocative—and, for the national park, unusual—way. At the end of his explanation at the loom, he paused for a moment, then said,

> I want to say, this machine isn't just history. When we built this historical park we had to travel around the world to buy looms. Looms like this are operating as we speak somewhere around the world. It's kind of neat to think about that. And there's no right or wrong answer, there's no easy answer to it, but we can go to Wal-Mart or A. J. Wright or any store, really, and buy really cheap clothing. And what's the alternative? Paying a lot for your clothes? We all work, we all try and pay the best we can for our cloth. But the reason we can get cheap cloth is because someone around the world is working on these looms, and looms not unlike what we have today. A few years ago, Kathy Lee Gifford was in trouble for using child labor on machines *just like this*. So it's just something to think about.
>
> One other thing I like to sort of think about is the word "labor." It means "to suffer" in Latin. And when you think about the suffering that goes into making cloth, back in history and even to the present day, it's just something to think about. We wear the clothes, sometimes we don't think especially how hard the person who built or made the clothes worked to produce that. And all the labor, all the suffering that went into building this city, and the results, both good and bad. Just think about that a little bit. And I'll be talking about more of the positive consequences on the way back. But on a hot, sticky day, with this loud machine and the lint flying in the air, it's pretty easy to picture how miserable it would be to work there.

It was a remarkable moment, one that went a long way toward undoing the process of commodity fetishism by which, in Marx's well-known analysis, capitalist systems of production mask the actual social relationships between those who produce goods and those who consume them. Judging by the startled looks on the faces of many of the other people on the tour, I was not alone in feeling an unexpected and not entirely welcome awareness that the clothes on my own body had been made by another laboring human body—probably that of a young woman— whose life was far less privileged and comfortable than mine. That moment around the loom, at the end of a long tour on an uncomfortably hot summer day, suddenly brought our own choices as consumers into the interpretive framework, and asked us to confront the phantom figure of the Malaysian or Pakistani mill girl who was laboring—suffering—so that we could buy a T-shirt for a small fraction of what it would have cost to produce in a developed country.

MacCannell has argued that such confrontations are incompatible with the tourist experience, which is threatened by anything that exposes "the structural arrangement that set [the tourist] into a touristic relationship with a social object, in this case, *work*" (1999:68). In fact, the park ranger did seem to sense that what he was doing was potentially dangerous. His words were carefully softened by assurances that this was "just something to think about," and that he would in due course be telling us the positive side of the story as well. When I asked him after the tour about his decision to try to bring home this idea to his audience in such a direct way, going so far as to name specific and familiar retailers, he was evasive and reluctant to elaborate, as if he had breached some protocol and did not want further attention drawn to it. I witnessed no similar moments during the other mill and canal tours I took during my two years of fieldwork. Yet the visitors on this tour, while clearly startled, did not seem offended. If there was risk in breaching the touristic distance, there was also potential reward—not a direct storming of the barricades to demand a redress of the inequalities of global capitalism, but perhaps a series of small recognitions of our own privileged places within it, which might eventually combine to produce action and change. This is precisely the goal of progressive public history—to seize such small opportunities and compound them into larger visions of the processes we are all a part of.

But that promise was only partially realized on the Run of the Mill Tour I have been describing. The moment around the loom was striking, but it was also isolated from other insights that the tour might have provoked, and from the physical presence of the less privileged. We were not forced to confront the phantom mill girl evoked by the ranger, except in an uncomfortable momentary sensation of realizing that her hands had tended the machine that wove the cloth that covered our bodies. The encounter with the Asian women at the Collins and Aikman factory was closer—they waved at us and we waved back, and at least some of us on the tour boat felt uneasy about the discrepancy between our circumstances and those of the people on the factory floor. One park visitor, responding to my survey, commented on a similar moment on the canal tour she took: "[Lowell] still has 'a way' to go, with an unair-conditioned mill still in operation. My mother worked in a spinning room when I was growing up. It saddens me to know that people still do that in such conditions. (And yet, a worker waved to us on the canal boat!) How could I enjoy/appreciate Lowell if my family was still mill workers in this year of 2002?" But her unease was framed as a concern that not enough improvement had yet been made, rather than as a questioning of the larger cycle that these workers are caught up in. Like the ranger who led the Run of the Mill tour, she demonstrated a linear sense of progress over time, instead of noting the striking parallels between various kinds of past and present "mill girls" encountered on the tour—the Yankee women of the early nineteenth century, the workers at Collins and Aikman, the young Burmese or Nicaraguan women who produced cloth or clothing that would find its way onto the racks of Wal-Mart stores.

In fact, as many studies have pointed out, patterns of work and employment in the textile and garment industries today very closely replicate the cycle that has continued to play itself out in Lowell (Clairmonte and Cavanagh 1981, Dickerson 1998, Fuentes and Ehrenreich 1983, Stearns 1993:27,123). These trades have often served as entry-level industries for newly industrializing areas and have historically relied on a workforce largely of young women. Often these workers are drawn from agricultural areas disrupted by various kinds of upheaval (as with the southeast Asian wars of the 1970s), by deliberate state policies of industrialization and relocation (as in the land clearances of late-eighteenth-century Britain and some parts of present-day southeast Asia) or by a decline in the profitability of family farming within a changing economy (as with the original Lowell mill girls). The ranger leading the Run of the Mill tour briefly destabilized the linear narrative by revealing the unseen connection between his audience and the invisible worker who produced the cloth for our clothes. But he stopped short of making a similar connection with the waving workers at the Collins and Aikman factory, who were employed on a hot summer day making fabric that would cover the seats of the cars we drive. He did not point out that manufacturing jobs in Lowell—like low-end jobs in the growing service sector—still rely heavily on the labor of immigrants, often women, who usually have few good options for earning money. He did not say (and probably did not know) that just a few blocks from the Collins and Aikman building was

FIGURE 5. Only blocks from the route of the national park's "mill and canal" tours, immigrant women still work long hours in Lowell's few remaining textile-related jobs, but their physical presence is not allowed to complicate the linear narrative told by the park's interpretation. CATHY STANTON.

a factory where immigrant women worked long hours sewing cloth bags and other items for nationally prominent catalog-order companies (fig. 5). These workers, according to an acquaintance who took me there one day, were mostly Cambodian and South American immigrants, many of them in the country illegally. They were supplied by temporary agencies who took a large share of their wages and provided no benefits or protections in return, beyond acting as a mediator between companies in search of cheap, compliant labor and unskilled workers in need of a way to survive in the United States. As sweatshops go, this one appeared to be well-ventilated, well-lit, and reasonably comfortable—but its very existence still poses a considerable challenge to the story of progress and rebirth told by the national park. Where visitors are brought into direct contact with the ongoing realities of industrial work—the unair-conditioned factory, or the vicissitudes of global competition, mergers, and bankruptcies—those realities are folded into a story that has a happy ending for workers, for the city, for capitalism as a whole. Potential disruptions to that story are kept at arm's length, in the rare cases—as with the ranger's evocation of the contemporary mill girl—when they are allowed to enter the narrative. More often, they are invisible as well as silent.[7]

The Run of the Mill tour, like many of the park's other productions, masks or evades other similar realities in much the same way. On the trolley ride between the Suffolk Mill and the Visitor Center, the ranger leading the August 2001 tour pointed out the Tsongas Arena, one of the flagship developments of the "revitalized" Lowell. The arena sits in a part of the city that was formerly part of the "mill of miles" along the Merrimack, but which was largely razed during urban-renewal efforts in the 1950s and 1960s. Named after the locally born U.S. senator who was the political godfather of the reborn Lowell, the Tsongas Arena is home to a minor-league hockey team, the Lowell Lock Monsters, which the ranger described as "another one of the small businesses that's here in Lowell replacing the big cotton mills." While commendably acknowledging that entertainment has become an important part of Lowell's new economy, the ranger left much unsaid about this particular "small business" that could have given visitors some sense of how that economy actually works. The Lowell Lock Monsters are owned by Elkin McCallum, also the owner of Joan Fabrics and a part of a circle of wealthy local businessmen closely associated with Paul Tsongas.[8] Tsongas championed the arena and the hockey franchise, as he did the national park, as part of a wider vision of a culturally vibrant city able to attract investors, workers, and residents linked with Massachusetts's prosperous knowledge, service, and information sectors rather than its declining manufacturing economy. In pursuit of that vision in the 1980s and early 1990s, he helped to mobilize (in ways that are discussed in Chapter 5) a network of influence that included businessmen and real estate developers like McCallum, bankers, the powerful local newspaper, politicians and planners at the city, state, and federal level, and many of the city's cultural institutions. The component parts of this network, and the former Tsongas staffers who are now fully integrated into it, continue to determine and dominate much that happens in the city. In the case of the Lock Monsters, Tsongas was active in obtaining the franchise, pushing through the arena plan despite considerable local opposition, and encouraging three businessmen from his circle of supporters to buy the team. As Ward points out, cities trying to sell themselves as vibrant centers within the postindustrial economy often attach great symbolic importance to acquiring and building facilities for professional sports teams—a tactic that not only attracts visitors but can also help to "brand" a place and prove useful in enlisting local support for the overall projects of planners and developers (Ward 1998:231, 235). This seems to be the case with the Lock Monsters, where key local players continue to support the hockey team despite the fact that it has consistently lost money. Thus, McCallum bought out his two less enthusiastic partners in 2002 to ensure that the team remained in Lowell (Lock Monsters 2002), and the city government, during a state budget crisis that was cutting deeply into civic revenues, reduced the team's rent at the city-owned Tsongas Arena by a quarter million dollars per year (Lafleur 2003). The hockey team is a loss leader, the kind of investment that is clearly expected to pay off in the gradual reinvention of this old textile city.

The park ranger leading the Run of the Mill tour did not include any of this information in his narrative. As we passed the Tsongas Arena on the final trolley leg of the tour, however, he did mention the very similar network of financial and cultural influence among the Boston Associates in the early nineteenth century. Making good on his promise to tell his audience about "some of the positive consequences" of the founding of the Lowell mills, he noted:

> The Lowells and the Lawrences and the Cabots, these leading families, these Boston Associates who would later be called the Boston Brahmins . . . got their money from shipping and when they made money here, what they did was they invested it in charitable organizations. The big charities that they gave their money to: Harvard University, Massachusetts General Hospital, McLean Mental Hospital, the Boston Symphony Orchestra. They would give this money to these organizations, but then they would get on the board of trustees, and when it came time to investing the endowment that they had at Harvard or Mass General, lo and behold, they would choose to invest their money right here in Lowell. So it works in sort of a symbiotic relationship. Sort of a credit union for the elite.

In such a system, as Dalzell states, it is difficult to tell "where self-interest left off and philanthropy begins" (1987:136). The same could easily be said of the dealings of the influential group I came to think of as the Lowell Associates—the men (virtually all of the group are male) who have spearheaded the city's ongoing shift into a postindustrial era in ways that have very often made it difficult to distinguish between wealth and commonwealth. Like the original Boston Associates, these men have maintained that what is good for business is good for the city, and many have been willing to invest in unprofitable ventures—hockey teams, in the twenty-first century, rather than boardinghouses—in order to contribute to the creation of a healthier business environment. Again in Dalzell's words, "For better or worse, the world the [Boston] Associates made is with us still" (1987:231). But that continuity is masked in many subtle ways, just as the ranger leading the August 2001 Run of the Mill tour masked the connections between those of us on the tour boat and the waving women of the Collins and Aikman factory, or the mechanisms—including the national park itself—that the city has used to try to reinvent itself in a postindustrial age.

In the 1970s, progressive historians and planners were able to tell a story about Lowell that effectively raises challenging questions about the nature of capitalism. The spatial legacies of the city's early development—the mills, the boardinghouses, the canals—combined with ample public funding and the inventive spirit of the times to support an interpretation of capitalists and mill workers that remains among the most thought-provoking material at any industrial history site. And the park's interpretative offerings are compelling enough that they can create some small opportunities to follow where those questions might lead—for example, the extraordinary moment around the Suffolk Mill loom on the August 2001 Run of the Mill tour. But the existence of these openings has not been enough to foster a larger, shared debate about the lines of connection between early and later Lowell history. In this, they reflect a characteristic facet of culture-led redevelopment: although these projects ostensibly seek to make the workings of history "legible" in contemporary landscapes, they ultimately contribute to the creation of more opaque environments in which centers of actual contemporary power are increasingly hard to locate or challenge. As Bella Dicks puts it, "What they offer are places rich with cultural images, snapshots and identity-tags all busy communicating lifestyles and histories, but where the social, political and economic relations of the city today become obscured and unreadable" (2003:73). Even when the officially sanctioned narratives are unusually critical and challenging, then, as they are in Lowell, these "communicative spaces" are highly selective about what they actually communicate. And despite the good intentions of many of the people who shaped these landscapes, they do not provide maps for actual participation in or conversation about the relationships of power and modes of production in the world we live in now.

CHAPTER 4

A Walking Tour of the Acre

The Lowell neighborhood known as the Acre was originally an acre of land reputedly donated to Irish laborers in the 1820s so that they could build a church. It now encompasses more than 400 acres and is home to many thousands of people. It borders the downtown (to the west) and has been in many ways a kind of shadow side of the redeveloped business district. The Acre is and has always been Lowell's poorest neighborhood, long a gateway for the city's newest immigrants and refugees and now the site of its most extensive public housing projects. One of these, at a convergence of streets once known as the Greek Triangle, was pointed out to me by many people as the center of Lowell's substantial illegal drug trade. Merrimack Street, Lowell's main commercial thoroughfare, connects the downtown with the Acre, while Dutton Street, along which the park's trolley line runs, draws a line between the two that most park visitors—and some city residents—are reluctant to cross. On one of the tours I describe here, a man who had just moved to the city and was learning about it via the park's tours and exhibits, noted, "I was told when I moved here, stay out of the Acre." National park rangers lead occasional walking tours of the Acre—usually once a month from spring through fall. Like the park's mill and canal tours, these offerings take visitors beyond public historical space and into the lived reality of the city. In doing so, they fulfill the notion of Lowell NHP as a "living park" whose exhibits include not only text panels and museum artifacts but also the city of Lowell itself, the changing face of which reflects the social, cultural, economic, and technological stories the park was designed to tell.

In Chapter 3 we saw how a group of waving textile workers became part of a regular mill and canal tour, and how the ranger used the incident to reinforce a linear narrative that ultimately served to mask the visitors' own privileged positions in the globalizing economy. Similar encounters occur constantly in the Acre tours, but there the inequalities are more glaring and more difficult to mask. One visitor from California was shocked by the seediness of the neighborhood. "Are there *other* places like this in New England?" he wanted to know. On another Acre tour, a visitor who had grown up near Lowell told a story about how her Franco-American parents had always promised her that someday they would go to Little Canada, a neighborhood that bordered and to some extent overlapped with the Acre, to buy Easter candy. Little Canada had seemed a magical place to her—until they finally made the trip: "And then we went to this area that looked really poor and dark, narrow houses, little dark doorways—oh, *this* is Little Canada?" One of the national park rangers who guides these tours told me, "A lot of the rangers are uncomfortable leading tours in the area. They won't do it. . . . They're not comfortable walking through, leading people through, where people live."

"Yet," the ranger added, "that same person goes through Belvidere [the most upscale of Lowell's neighborhoods]." What unsettles the park's almost entirely middle-class visitors, as well as many of its rangers, is clearly the poverty of the Acre and the socioeconomic distance between their own lives and those of Acre residents. "It's a moral struggle for me," one of the rangers admitted. "Because it's—you know, I would go around, I see the houses with the screens torn and the million kids pouring out, and—would I want to live there? No. . . . It's tough, it's a tough life. It's very tough. And it makes you ask, 'What are we doing there?' It really does."

In this chapter I demonstrate how this uneasiness—coupled with a unifying discourse about ethnicity that was established during the early days of the Lowell experiment—shapes the park's attempts to interpret ethnicity, immigration, and present-day life in the Acre. I took five walking tours of the Acre in 2001 and 2002, led by three different rangers whom I interviewed individually during the course of my research. I videotaped and transcribed each tour, talked with visitors, and, on the final two tours, conducted a more formal survey of visitors and asked them to mail me a follow-up questionnaire.[1] I also lived in the Acre for half of the time that I was resident in Lowell.

The Acre and Lowell's Immigrants

The Acre's persistent poverty makes it a site of shame and anxiety for many people in Lowell. But at the same time, as the point of entry for many immigrant and refugee communities, the neighborhood plays an important role in a city that actively promotes its cultural diversity and immigrant history. In the spring of 2002, as part of a documentary project by a visiting photographer,[2] Lowell Mayor Rita Mercier was photographed with a banner she had created, which read, "Everybody comes from the Acre" (fig. 6). The mayor was articulating one of the main tenets of local identity in Lowell: "true" Lowellians trace their roots to the city's ethnic and working class neighborhoods, of which the Acre is emblematic. Indeed, the majority of the city's residents can claim this characteristic. Industrial places and impoverished immigrants have a long and symbiotic history in America, and Lowell, like most manufacturing centers, has been home to many immigrant groups, beginning with the Irish day laborers who were hired to build the mills and canals and who first settled the area now known as the Acre. By 1860, half of Lowell's population was Irish, and the immigrants had begun to move into the jobs of native-born factory workers who had left after becoming disenchanted with the changing nature of mill work in Lowell (Dublin 1993:138–39). By the turn of the twentieth century, French Canadians were the largest ethnic group in Lowell (Marston 1991:216). Pushed from Quebec by the declining productivity of their farms, and pulled to the United States by the promise of industrial work, they settled throughout the region, to the extent that "a map showing the major rivers of southern New England or this area's chief cotton textile mills is at the same time a chart of Franco-American demography to this very day" (Brault 1986:54). In the first two decades of the century, large numbers of Greeks—first single men, then family groups—came to the United States as part of a far-reaching diaspora in the wake of financial and agricultural crises in Greece (Moskos 1999). Many established themselves in Lowell's Acre, where unofficial boundaries had come to

FIGURE 6. Reflecting many Lowellians' sense of being rooted in the city's ethnic and working-class neighborhoods, then-mayor Rita Mercier stands with a sign she created for a visiting photographer in 2002. BILL HAYWARD/THE AMERICAN MEMORY PROJECT.

delineate one ethnic enclave from another. (I met one man of Polish background who told me that because Poles did not typically live in the Acre when he was growing up there in the 1950s and 60s, he spent much of his childhood fighting with Greek boys who considered him a trespasser on their turf.) Significant numbers of Poles, Portuguese, and other immigrants also settled in Lowell, but the "big three" among the city's Euro-American ethnic communities remain the Irish, French Canadians, and Greeks, who have dominated local politics and business for many decades.[3]

With more restrictive national immigration policies and a sharp decline in the local textile industry beginning in the 1920s, Lowell was no longer a magnet for immigrants. The city's population peaked at 112,759 in 1920 (Lipchitz 1976:101). By 1970, it had dropped to 92,418.[4] Starting in the 1960s, Latinos from Puerto Rico and Colombia began to move to Lowell, reflecting the easing of quotas on non-European immigrants with the Immigration Act of 1965 and the ensuing arrival of many migrants from throughout the United States's sphere of economic and political influence. Latinos in Lowell numbered approximately 8,000 by the mid-1970s (P. Blewett 1976:200). By 2000, as they were joined by Dominicans and others, that number had grown to 14,734. A notable minority among this population are the Colombian textile workers who were recruited by the owner of one of Lowell's remaining mills in the 1970s. In a strange reverberation of the industrial production cycle, these workers found—as Lowell's original mill girls had found on their home farms—that their work enabled them to survive but not to accumulate any cash in a system that increasingly required capital for economic advancement. Trained in government-sponsored programs, the Colombian weavers were familiar with the antiquated equipment still in use in Lowell, and they eagerly responded to the invitation of American textile companies who were having difficulty retaining skilled weavers in the uncertain climate of a "sunset" industry. The industry's continued decline, along with immigration problems, however, meant that the Colombian weavers' sojourn in Lowell was a short one (Glaessel-Brown 1991).

Much more long-lasting and significant has been the migration of southeast Asians to the city. The 1980 United States Census counted 604 Asians in Lowell, a figure that jumped to 10,564 in 1990 and 18,781 in 2000.[5] Cambodians make up the great majority of these new residents, with smaller numbers of Laotians and Vietnamese. These people are part of the approximately one million southeast Asian refugees, including 150,000 Cambodians, who entered the United States between 1975 and 1996 (Hopkins 1996:2). Most of these newcomers arrived after the passage of the 1980 Refugee Act, by which the U.S. government committed itself to a policy of resettlement (Robinson 1998). Many refugees were resettled in Lowell in the early 1980s, because the depopulated and long-depressed city offered a great deal of cheap housing; at that time, there were also large numbers of unskilled assembly-line jobs available in the then-booming electronics industry. Although the Wang boom noted in the previous chapter did not last, the nucleus of a Cambodian community that formed during those years has been strong enough to attract considerable secondary migration. Lowell is now the second-largest center of Cambodian population in the United States, after Long Beach, California. The community supports two Buddhist temples and several Christian congregations, and the children of former refugees now make up about one-third of the students in Lowell public schools.

Substantial numbers of Brazilians and Africans in recent years have continued to swell Lowell's immigrant population. The demographic changes in Lowell over the past four decades reflect trends in the country as a whole, where immigrant inflows (particularly from Asia, Central and South America, and the Carribean) account for the net population growth in many regions and have helped to repopulate urban areas that lost population to the "white flight" and suburbanization starting in the 1950s. The official 2000 census count for Lowell is 105,167, but if we accept social-service workers' assertions that this does not include many undocumented or illegal migrants, it may be that the city's population is once again approaching its 1920 peak figure, with immigrants and their children once again making up a majority of the total as they did a century ago. The Acre is no longer necessarily the "revolving door" for new arrivals, who are now more widely dispersed throughout the city's neighborhoods. The Acre's current demography is weighted toward Latinos and poor whites, the majority of whom live in public housing projects. I also encountered scattered pockets of older, long-standing residents—Franco-Americans in the boardinghouse block where I lived, and Greek Americans in a small apartment building on Merrimack Street. A few stores catering to southeast Asians draw some business into the Acre, but the real concentration of southeast Asians is now found in the Lower Highlands to the west. Nonetheless, the Acre remains symbolically the most important of Lowell's ethnic neighborhoods, making its poverty not purely a source of shame, but also a badge of authentic localness, to be worn—or at least pointed to from a safe distance—with pride. A former Lowell mayor, Tarsy Poulios, told *Time* magazine in 1993, "The Acre is the bottom of the social ladder. The last group that comes in is always on the bottom rung. But you can climb that ladder. You just have to prove your worth to the group ahead of you to be accepted" (Blackman 1993:34). As the lowest rung on that ladder, the Acre is an important foundation for the story that the city tells about itself in its official cultural productions—a story largely constructed, as shown later in this chapter, during the early years of the redevelopment project itself.

Walking through the Acre

The tour script developed by one of the Lowell NHP rangers for the Acre walking tour, and the route followed by most of the tours I took, traces a loop of slightly more than a mile through the Acre that starts and finishes at one of the park's downtown mill buildings. Two of the three rangers began by speaking to visitors in Mack Plaza, the usual orientation site for park tours. Instead of giving the standard explanation for Lowell's creation, however, they focused on a public art installation in the plaza called *The Worker*, which depicts an Irish laborer moving granite blocks.[6] The rangers used the figure as a springboard for discussion of the first of Lowell's immigrant groups. The tours then took visitors along Market Street, one of two main east–west thoroughfares that cross the Acre, where the rangers pointed out such features as the Whistler House (an art gallery in the 1834 birthplace of artist James McNeill Whistler, whose father was an agent for the Proprietors of Locks and Canals), a row of Greek restaurants and dilapidated former coffeehouses, and the public housing developments that were built starting around 1940 (P. Blewett 1976:210). A central feature of the tour, in terms of the time allocated to it and its importance to the rangers' interpretive themes, was a space called Ecumenical Plaza, which spans the Western Canal between the Holy Trinity Greek Orthodox Church and St. Patrick's Catholic Church. This small area was created as a pedestrian bridge during the 1970s, an early project in the prenational-park phase of Lowell's redevelopment experiment, which I discuss in more detail below. On two of the tours I took, the group went inside St. Patrick's; on one tour, we visited a small local history museum created by people in the parish and spoke with the priest, who told us of the church's current membership:

> old Irish who have moved away and come back, because of their feeling
> for the church. And . . . we're the only Catholic church in the city that has
> an organized ministry to the southeast Asians. So we have a very strong
> Vietnamese community and a Cambodian community. And we have
> quite a few Hispanics, [although] we don't have that many because the
> Hispanic church is right up the street. And poor white, basically.

Two of the five tours I took featured essentially just one other major stop: the handful of southeast Asian businesses on Merrimack Street, the Acre's other main cross street. One of the rangers took visitors inside the Battambang Market, a busy Cambodian grocery store. The other three tours went slightly farther afield in order to touch on the history of Little Canada, the French Canadian neighborhood that occupied much of the territory just west of the Acre until it was largely razed during urban renewal in the 1960s. Each of these three tours stopped at the former St. Jean Baptiste Church, an immense stone structure erected in 1896 by the then well-established population of French Canadian immigrants. On two of the tours, we found the church doors open and went inside to explore the building and talk with the Oblate priests who ministered to the large Latino Nuestra Señora del Carmen parish. The rangers started back to the Visitor Center from various places in the Acre. One of the rangers finished her tours in front of the new City Hall, also built in 1896, interpreting its monumental architecture as a statement about the growing power of the city s ethnic communities and workers in relation to the earlier control of the Yankee capitalists who had founded the city.

The three rangers who led the Acre tours were somewhat unusual among the national park's frontline interpreters. The one who had generated the tour script was the only Lowell NHP ranger to have been trained in an academic public history program. A second actually lived in Lowell, the only ranger among my frontline informants who did. The third had recently moved out of the city but had lived there for several years and had family in the immediate area, making him more "local" than most of his colleagues. The tour audiences were also somewhat different from those I encountered on the park's mill and canal tours. The Acre tours routinely seemed to attract people with some existing connection to the city or the national park: local residents or newcomers to the area, returning natives or descendants of natives, park volunteers, former teachers or students from various levels of Lowell's educational system. The tours, with their flexible itineraries and opportunities to see and speak with people in the Acre, appeared to open many possibilities for encounters among cultures and between local people and visitors, as well as between celebratory and critical approaches to understanding immigrant and ethnic history.

Yet the five tours that I took revealed how the park's interpretation works against the potential for these tours to function as a genuine space of encounter—what Dean MacCannell has termed an "empty meeting ground," on which radically different people may converge and find themselves challenged and changed by the experience (MacCannell 1992). Like the Run of the Mill tour, which was based on a linear, progressive logic that created false continuities and masked uncomfortable connections, the Acre tour created a false conceptual unity while failing to bridge or account for various levels of social disunity and disconnection—between the park visitors and the people they were observing, or between and within Lowell's ethnic communities themselves. The park's tours of the Acre tell a neat, evolutionary story of achievement, improvement, continuity, and orderly succession from one immigrant group to the next and from one socioeconomic stage to the next. In the words of one of the rangers, "Just like the Irish, the French Canadian, and the Greek, the southeast Asian community came here as well with nothing but their dreams. . . . And today they are, like the Irish, a thriving ethnic community right here in Lowell, contributing tremendously to what we know today as Lowell." Another phrased it this way:

> What I'd like to bring you is a sense that this community is still alive. It's still intact as an immigrant community, as a revolving door, a first step in a new country for these immigrants, starting with the Irish, then the Greeks, the Hispanic, and now southeast Asian, that it's there, it's intact. There are pieces of community, what we would call an intact community, still there. It's not just history, it's not just something I'm going to tell you about that happened long ago. It's ongoing, still continuing to this day. And that's part of what makes Lowell such a great place to visit, to learn about.

In this multiculturalist vision, Lowell's ethnic communities are depicted as bounded, homogeneous entities, which can mingle on an equal basis with others and yet remain "intact" within the larger entity "[that] we know today as Lowell." Such an approach draws a veil over many aspects of ethnicity and immigration in Lowell. First, the neat chronology presented by the park greatly oversimplifies the layers of overlapping and secondary migration, ongoing homeland allegiances and returns of some migrants, changing public immigration policies, and very uneven successes and socioeconomic progress among Lowell's various immigrant groups. Ironically, the only specific Latino immigrants mentioned in the Acre tours I took were the Colombian textile workers who came to the city in the 1970s. Their experiences were highly unusual among Latinos in Lowell, who have not historically worked in the textile mills. But because the Colombians fit within the sequential story of industrial development and immigrant progress told at the park—and thus within the larger celebratory narrative about opportunity and socioeconomic mobility among American immigrants—they have often been used to stand in for the city's Latinos in many productions at the park (for example, in the immigrant exhibit in the Patrick Mogan Cultural Center, discussed in Chapter 7). Thus one of the park rangers could state during a tour of the Acre: "Latinos were recruited to come work here during the late 70s, 1970s . . . because they were one of the few people that really knew how to fix and operate this very, very old machinery that was still being used in Lowell at the time. . . . And just like the early Irish, or French Canadians, you get a small group of them here, and then their brothers and sisters and cousins and extended family come, and eventually it develops." Ethnic communities, then, are shown to be not only natural entities but also naturally self-reproducing, without reference to government or business policy or specific "push" or "pull" factors.

The rangers' approach also presupposed a level of cohesion and unity that simply does not exist (and probably has never existed) within Lowell's ethnic "communities." The "southeast Asian community," for example, is deeply divided along class, regional, language, political, national, religious, generational, and ethnic lines. To give just one example, the Cambodian small businesses that the park rangers point to as exemplars of ethnic enterprise and progress are, in many cases, owned by ethnic Chinese from either Cambodia or Vietnam, who have little in common with (and are sometimes resented by) the ethnic Khmer who constitute the great majority of Lowell's Cambodians (see Smith-Hefner 1995 for a discussion of this relationship). Similarly, while immigrants from Latin America and Africa have made some attempts to present a pan-Latino or pan-African identity in Lowell, such collectivities tend to be highly problematic and unstable, reflecting the tremendous heterogeneity and flux within these groups. The unifying discourse about ethnicity employed by the rangers is much more a reflection of the politics of the redevelopment experiment itself than of the realities of ethnic politics in the city.

Rangers leading the Acre tours routinely referred to the political achievements of members of different ethnic groups—including national politicians like John F. Kennedy and Paul Tsongas as well as local leaders—as evidence that all of the city's groups were making their way up the ladder in an orderly manner. As one phrased it, "The [Lowell] city council today, when you look at it, you . . . have represented there, you have Irish, you have French Canadians, you have Greek, you have southeast Asians, you have Latino, you've got all walks of life in Lowell represented in the city government." Another noted, "The first southeast Asian elected official [in the U.S.], Rithy Uong, is on the city council here in Lowell. So that community, too, is starting to understand that, hey, if we want to be represented, you have to go out and vote, you have to get that done."

The political career of Lowell city councilor Rithy Uong , elected in 1999 and twice reelected since then, would at first appear to reinforce local claims of inclusive multiculturalism and immigrant incorporation into the city body. However, to speak of Uong as being representative of all Lowell Cambodians, or *only* Cambodians, is to greatly oversimplify his constituency. Comparatively few Cambodians in Lowell participate in electoral politics, having learned to distrust and fear political activity during the Khmer Rouge and resettlement periods (Lefferts 2002; also see Watanabe and Liu 2002 for a discussion of voting patterns among Asian American voters in Massachusetts). Uong won his seat on the city council largely with the support of affluent white liberal voters and backers, along with a multifaceted and multiethnic coalition of Cambodians and people from other groups, including Latinos. There is no doubt that many in Lowell see him as representative of Cambodians and, to a lesser extent, other immigrant groups. But his presence reflects not so much a high level of social or political integration by those groups as a high level of commitment among many voters for the now well-publicized notion of Lowell as a peacefully multicultural place. Uong had just recently been elected when I began my fieldwork, and many of the liberal Euro-American Lowellians I met told me they had supported him because, "It was just time," or "It was the right thing to do." Meanwhile, despite the first ranger's assertion, no Latino had been elected to public office in Lowell by 2002, and the large Latino population remains strikingly unintegrated into the city's civic and political life. Many Euro-American Lowellians see Latinos as unwilling to assimilate into the mainstream culture, to climb the ladder of success, or—paradoxically—to define and "perform" their own culture in Lowell's heritage arena as other groups have done.[7] The park's interpretation sidesteps these realities, however, repeating former Mayor Poulios's confident assertion that every ethnic group "can climb that ladder. You just have to prove your worth to the group ahead of you." The rangers questioned neither the hierarchy implied in this vision nor the uneven success rate of the groups climbing the metaphorical ladder.

In some ways, then, the park's tours of the Acre created a false continuity and coherence. In other ways, these tours, like the Run of the Mill tour, worked to divide past from present, and to separate those taking the tour from those whose lives were being displayed. A central mechanism for doing this was to acknowledge conflict and struggle—subjects that progressive public historians insist must be a part of any historical presentation—but to keep them safely in the distant past, rather than letting them inform the celebratory story that is told about the present. In this approach, prejudice and ethnic division are shown as obstacles that immigrants have historically overcome rather than facets of present-day life in the city, much less an unadmitted presence on the Acre tours themselves. The rangers discussed these topics only in relation to the earliest Euro-American immigrant groups, with particular emphasis on the Irish. At the stop at Ecumenical Plaza, all three rangers described the "Battle of Stone Bridge" that occurred there in 1831, when a group of resentful local Yankees attacked Irish laborers who were building a Catholic church on the site of the present-day St. Patrick's. One ranger heavily emphasized the dubious story of the "No Irish Need Apply" (NINA) signs that supposedly confronted Irish immigrants looking for work in nineteenth- and twentieth-century America—a claim to "victim" status that Irish Americans have long used to bolster their assertions of political strength in the United States.[8] Another encouraged visitors to interpret the statue of *The Worker* in Mack Plaza as showing an Irish laborer struggling, not just with the weight of the granite blocks he was moving, but also against "the prejudice . . . these Irish and the immigrants who came later would have to face." Although all the rangers alluded at some point to conflict and discrimination in relation to later as well as earlier immigrants, the only specific cases they mentioned involved the earliest Irish.

Such a view obscures historical evidence that contradicts the oversimple story. None of the rangers noted that, in the 1830s, there was an innovative collaboration between Lowell's new public schools and the Catholic educational system developed by Irish immigrants (Mitchell 1991:124–5). This approach also masks more recent ethnic tensions and struggles. The huge influx of southeast Asian refugees in the 1980s created enormous stresses on the city's educational and social service systems, especially after the economic bubble of the Wang period began to deflate at the end of the decade.[9] The overcrowding and segregation of immigrant children in the Acre's schools led to a state-ordered busing program that met with considerable resistance, culminating in the 1987 drowning of a thirteen-year-old Cambodian boy who was pushed into the fast-flowing Pawtucket Canal by a white boy waiting for the same school bus (*New York Times* 1987). The city school department responded with a ground-breaking bilingual education program, but opposition to the plan was made clear in the overwhelming 1989 victory of a nonbinding ballot question declaring English Lowell's official language (*New York Times* 1988, 1989a, 1989b). "Let's teach the three R's and forget about social engineering," declared the Greek American school committee member who sponsored the ballot measure. "Bilingual education is a disservice to these kids because it keeps them from learning English like other immigrants did" (*New York Times* 1988).

The Acre tours also worked to separate park visitors from those whose stories are being told—disjunctions that were all the more jarring because the people whose lives were being interpreted were in many cases physically present while the tours were taking place. As I have already shown, visitors and many park rangers are made uneasy by the presence of Lowell's impoverished "others." This uneasiness was most strikingly exemplified by two Greek American women who had spent their entire lives in the Acre. They had decided to take one of the national park's tours of the neighborhood because, as one of them told me, "There've been all these changes recently, and I wanted to understand those." It was clear that she knew little about most of her current neighbors and felt uncomfortable experiencing their otherness directly, so she had chosen to learn about them through the safe mediation of the national park and the rubric of celebratory multiculturalism within which it operates.

Most people on the Acre tours, then, appeared to be stepping outside their comfort zones merely by venturing into the neighborhood, even with a uniformed guide. In that sense, it could be argued that the park's Acre tours help to facilitate at least a rudimentary level of encounter with cultural and class otherness. However, my own analysis is that these tours actively work *against* the possibility of such encounters, by glossing over any acknowledgement of present-day conflict and unease, and by minimizing or avoiding actual face-to-face interactions with the "natives" in the Acre. In part, this appears to be a reflection of the rangers' own ambivalence, as shown in the words of one of the three tour leaders:

> I go walking in the Acre a lot, because I like it. I like to hear the noise and the bustle. I don't go in the stores too much. I know there's some rangers who like to take people into the stores. . . . I'm not too comfortable with that. I've gone in a few times in uniform just on my own. And the Greek variety store, "Come on in, we'll give you a . . . discount, come on in, bring 'em in." You'd never get a tour out of there! But that's cool to see all the different types of foods and things that are being imported. But the Asian market—I've gone in there, and I know I make them uncomfortable in uniform. I don't think they understand why I'm there. I've never gone up and said hi, which I should perhaps do, but I'm uncomfortable, too. Because they really sense it. I don't know if they think I'm an inspector, checking out their goods, or what. But there's some cool stuff in there! It's fun to go and look, but I really get, I really sense attention when I'm there. And I've never actually gone in not in uniform, so I don't know. Because—I don't know why I haven't.

This ranger expressed a range of reactions that typified the uneasy relationship between established and newer cultures in the city: a fascination with the alien and the exotic combined with a leeriness of too direct an experience of it, and a reluctance to let its "noise and bustle" erode the representational authority of the city's professional and designated interpreters and culture brokers ("You'd never get a tour out of there!"). Although one ranger told visitors that "we're going to be walking right through people's neighborhoods, and we may see some very interesting, very colorful things, we'll certainly see ethnically diverse children out playing," he moved his planned tour starting point away from Mack Plaza to escape what he called "the competition of the fountain"—meaning the noise made by the "ethnically diverse" (in this case, Latino) children who were playing in it on a hot summer day. Although he seemed more at ease with a direct encounter with otherness when he led his tours into the Battambang Market, he told me that he had never introduced himself to the store's owners or spoken to them about his inclusion of their business on his tour route. Nor did any of the rangers have other personal contacts in the neighborhood, except for the priest at St. Patrick's. In fact, the two priests—like the rangers, white middle-class professional outsiders who mediated among cultures and groups—were the only two people in the Acre with whom rangers and visitors actually spoke during the tours I took. There were many opportunities to broaden the contact between the visitors and the neighborhood: perhaps by speaking to the Greek, Cambodian, or Latino store owners, or to the Vietnamese parishioners who were helping to renovate a basement room at St. Patrick's on one of the tour Saturdays, or to the neighborhood children who occasionally hung around the edges of the tours, as, on one day, a young Latino boy sat on a wall in Ecumenical Plaza directly behind the park ranger who was expounding about the clash that had taken place there between Yankees and Irish in 1831. But these moments were never seized, and it seemed that to the rangers, they represented potential dangers, rather than opportunities:

> *Does real life or stuff that's happening in the Acre ever disrupt the tours or has it ever just gotten into the tours?*
>
> Not for me, no, I've never had a problem with that. Generally people are very friendly, I say hello, nod and say hello, how are you doing, walk by, you know. That goes a long way to deflecting anything that might be trouble. But I've never had a problem.

Despite the living presence of residents of the Acre, the overt acknowledgement of ethnic tension and conflict in the past, and the unusually porous boundary between those taking the Acre tours and those being interpreted, then, the voices of Lowell's "others" are not heard within these particular cultural performances. This displacement or muting is not an uncommon feature of culture-led redevelopment projects, which, as Bella Dicks notes, "may seek to represent, and even celebrate, resistant and disorderly culture in public displays, but are less willing, it seems, to accommodate the people who create it within the physical space of the city" (2003:84). The result in Lowell is a dampening of public history's potential contribution to interpreting and understanding the continuing poverty of places like the Acre and the complexities of ethnic identities and coexistence in the city and elsewhere.

It is possible to understand the rangers' retreat from critique on more than one level. As I show in Chapter 6, public history interpreters and their audiences share personal characteristics that make them inherently unlikely to challenge the teleological narratives supported by Lowell's redevelopment project. But the uncritical story about ethnicity reflected in the Acre tours also has a specific historical genesis, one that I conclude this chapter by examining.

Patrick Mogan and Unifying Ethnicity

Lowell's new experiment—the broadly supported plan to turn the city's past into an educational, social, and economic asset—began to cohere in the late 1960s and early 1970s in various forums in the city. By that time, civic leaders had been struggling for decades to reverse the decline caused by the slow exodus of capital from the industrial northeast. Like other deindustrialized places, Lowell tried, without lasting success, to attract new industry. It also followed the "urban renewal" trend of the 1960s, a decade that saw the razing of much of its industrial landscape including its oldest textile factory, the Merrimack Mill, and most of the original boardinghouse blocks around the city. The demolition of one row of Merrimack Mill boardinghouses on Dutton Street in 1966 sparked some resistance from a loose coalition of historic preservationists, property rights advocates, and critics of urban renewal who came together to try to save the historic structures (fig. 7). In her study of the origins of the national park, Ryan points to this campaign as the first stirring of a preservationist ethos in Lowell (1987:34–64). At the same time, the destruction of the French Canadian neighborhood known as

FIGURE 7. The demolition of a row of Merrimack Manufacturing Company board-inghouses on Dutton Street in 1966, shown here, was an important catalyst for a new historic preservation consciousness in Lowell. JOHN GOODWIN/LOWELL NATIONAL HISTORICAL PARK.

Little Canada, which bordered the Acre, aroused public resentment and led, as in other places, to the eventual adoption of less draconian policies for dealing with the problems of urban decay and poverty.[10] On a federal level, the backlash against urban renewal and the growing interest in preservation found expression in the National Historic Preservation Act of 1966, whose framers argued that "the historical and cultural founda-tions of the Nation should be preserved as a living part of our commu-nity life and development in order to give a sense of orientation to the American people" (1992[1966]:1). This "sense of orientation" echoes the influential arguments of Kevin Lynch and others that "legible" and comprehensible places could foster a sense of social coherence and cohe-sion, a view that continues to find expression in the conscious and wide-spread creation of "narrative places" and "documentary landscapes." Locally, although many in Lowell saw the old textile mills and run-down ethnic neighborhoods as symbolic of decline and exploitation, other people were beginning to believe that the city's past and its ethnic diver-sity could become the foundation for a new and positive local identity.

Foremost among these people was the then assistant superintendent of schools Patrick Mogan, who came to be seen, along with U.S. Senator

Paul Tsongas, as a godfather of Lowell National Historical Park and the wider culture-led redevelopment project. Unlike Tsongas, Mogan was not a native Lowellian, although he married into a prominent Lowell family. An Irish American himself, he identified strongly with Lowell's ethnic communities and believed that much had been lost in the immigrants' rush to assimilate to American culture. Just as the 1966 National Historic Preservation Act saw a sense of the past as a means of "orientation" for Americans, Mogan viewed cultural rediscovery and celebration as a way of grounding people in place and time so that they were better able to make decisions about their collective future. Paul Marion, a protégé of Mogan who has played several important roles in the redevelopment project, phrased it this way in one of his interviews with me:

> I think it's about knowing who you are. And I think if you have a better sense of who you are and where you came from, you're going to be more whole as a human being. It's about not being alienated. . . . And if you see both tangible and intangible elements in the culture, in the history, as reflections of . . . people who have come before, I think your impulse is to respect that. So a building isn't just a building. . . . [T]hese things connect up to the experience of one's own life and the life of the people that you're connected to.

This outlook reflected the broader "roots" phenomenon of the 1970s, which saw large numbers of Americans searching for stronger connections to their individual and collective pasts. The celebration of the national Bicentennial in 1976 served to focus new attention on history and heritage at the national, state, and local levels. During the same period, consumer culture reflected and played a role in fostering an increased interest in genealogy and cultural heritage, via such productions as the hugely popular 1977 television miniseries based on Alex Haley's *Roots* and the increased creation of products and events for ethnic niche markets (see Halter 2000 for a discussion of this "marketing of ethnicity"). Public policy supported the heritage boom through federal legislation like the Ethnic Heritage Act (1974), the creation of the American Folklife Center (1976), and, on the state level, the 1974 formation of a governor's task force in Massachusetts to coordinate the promotion of ethnic celebration and heritage (Ryan 1987:118). Lowell already had a history of celebrating and displaying its various ethnic groups, most notably in the ethnic festivals sponsored by the International Institute, a

YWCA-affiliated settlement house that opened an office in Lowell in 1918.[11] In the early 1970s, under the leadership of the owner of a Greek restaurant along the Merrimack River bank, a committee formed to run an annual regatta that incorporated ethnic food, dancing, and music. This annual event expanded into a series of regular weekend ethnic festivals that were eventually moved to downtown Lowell, providing an organizational structure and a model for the hugely popular Lowell Folk Festival, which began in 1988 (Ryan 1987:171–73).[12]

As a high-level educator, Patrick Mogan first sought to integrate this focus on heritage into the curricula of Lowell's public schools, but before long he began to promote a much more ambitious plan for the revitalization of the city itself. Mogan was perturbed by the tendency of ethnic discourse to concern itself with the agendas of specific groups, a characteristic that he saw as contributing to the balkanization of Lowell politics and culture along ethnic lines. The Yankee elites who had dominated city government in the heyday of the textile mills had become less of a political force by the first two decades of the twentieth century, as voters and politicians from the immigrant groups—particularly the Irish, French Canadians, and Greeks—tipped the balance of power. Over time, these groups and the mainly Yankee downtown business leaders had established an equilibrium that continues to make itself felt in local politics today. But by the 1960s, with Lowell's economic pie steadily shrinking and no clear solution in sight, the entrenched factions were gridlocked, defending their existing territory but unable to unite behind any plan for revitalization. Mogan also rejected another element of the 1970s ethnicity boom: the fact that for many Euro-Americans, it began as a reaction against the claims of non-European groups (blacks, Indians, Latinos) for greater political and social equality. This counter-claim asserted that whites, too, had suffered discrimination and poverty at the hands of dominant groups (di Leondaro 1998:83–94, Halter 2000:4–5). Indeed, many depressed urban places like Lowell were able to mobilize this claim in the 1970s as a way of securing state and federal resources to aid their economically struggling communities—an intriguing parallel to the use of "victim" status by Irish Americans noted above. Such rhetoric had particular resonance in impoverished working-class places like Lowell, where it sometimes contributed to nativist and racist backlash against recent immigrants and nonwhites. But it was precisely these characteristic qualities of ethnic discourse—its use of past wrongs as a rallying point and its focus on narrow agendas—that Mogan hoped to neutralize in Lowell. He saw such tactics as negative and divisive, and he was in contact with progressive activists in national organizations who were similarly trying to mobilize white ethnic pride without further exacerbating interracial and interethnic tensions (Ryan 1987:115–16).

What Mogan sought was a way to build consensus around a single, culture-oriented plan, so that city planning and revitalization could move forward more effectively. As the new Lowell experiment began to take shape, he consistently resisted attempts to depict ethnic conflict or to dwell on past wrongs and exploitations. This position put him somewhat in opposition to the new social historians whose research was also helping to shape the public representations of Lowell's past that began to appear in the 1970s. Their discussion of past difficulties was generally welcomed by Lowell audiences, because it gave a public voice to the accomplishments and struggles of many of the city's residents, but Mogan himself never embraced this more critical approach. He was known to dislike the Lowell Museum, a local precursor to the national park, declaring it "morbid" because it looked at some of the less-upbeat aspects of Lowell's ethnic communities (Ryan 1987:315). An energetic and idiosyncratic visionary, Mogan proposed many plans over time. But his central and most lasting proposal focused on the idea of an "urban cultural park," which he saw as a learning laboratory for students, a potential attraction for tourists, and a venue for celebrating local culture and heritage (fig. 8). In his mind, this was a potential starting point for changing Lowell's image in the minds of both residents and outsiders— a way, as he was fond of saying, of helping the city "become a good address again." In many ways, Mogan was in tune with brand-promoters and place-marketers who recognize that the image may to a very large extent precede the reality. Although acknowledging that few people wholly accept the cohesive visions of public life often proposed by planners, developers, and public officials, Sharon Zukin nonetheless points out that "visions persuade if they suggest an escape from the chaos of social decay" (1995:280). Such was the case with Mogan's proposal for a revitalized Lowell based on the city's ethnic cultures and industrial history. In the absence of other viable plans or any clear consensus among city leaders, Mogan's ideas began to gain a hearing.

Although many of his specific proposals were highly impractical, even eccentric, Mogan's overall emphasis on the celebration of local ethnic

FIGURE 8. Assistant Superintendent of Schools Patrick Mogan was one of the first promoters of the idea of creating a national park in Lowell. In this 1972 photo, Mogan is on the right, with State Representative Cornelius (Connie) Kiernan and U.S. Representative Bradford Morse looking on. CENTER FOR LOWELL HISTORY.

culture was strategically very adroit. There was (and is) still some bitterness in Lowell about the textile-mill era, and the public battle over the demolition of the Dutton Street row houses had demonstrated that many people were hostile to anything that smacked of glorifying the Yankee capitalists who had owned the mills. However, as Ryan notes, "It became far more acceptable to remember the industrial greatness of early nineteenth century Lowell when it was attributed to Lowell's ethnic populations than it had . . . when capitalists and Yankee workers were given the credit" (1987:118–19). Mogan's emphasis on the positive aspects of ethnicity created some new common ground on which many of Lowell's powerful players—City Hall, bankers, the local newspaper, the Proprietors of Locks and Canals, who still controlled the canal system and much downtown real estate—could begin to consider what had originally seemed like an outlandish idea. Robert Weible, the first historian at Lowell NHP, noted in 1984 that the city's ethnic heritage was "the historical glue that held the cultural park concept together," and ascribed this to the fact that "ethnicity and cultural pluralism were noncontroversial and popular in the seventies," making ethnicity "a subject that could be quite easily celebrated, an entertaining theme that could be used to inject life and pride into the community" (Weible 1984:31–32). The reason these topics could be uncontroversial and potentially unifying in Lowell, however, was that leaders from the Euro-American ethnic groups no longer needed particularist strategies to assert their presence in Lowell's political and social realms. They had been in power for many decades (M. Blewett 1976); their common problem now was that the overall power base was diminishing as the city continued to decline. Mogan managed to convince them that a unifying discourse about ethnicity—as opposed to more narrowly strategic and specific ethnic discourses—would ultimately be in everyone's interests. The eventual coalition of park supporters was so successful in presenting a unified front that members of a Congressional field visit to Lowell in 1974 commented on the startling lack of dissent, prompting one Lowell official to joke that perhaps they should recruit someone to speak out against the plan at the next hearing, just to lend a greater sense of realism (Ryan 1987:188).

As the plan developed, Mogan's emphasis on ethnicity dovetailed with both critical historical perspectives and economic development agendas, two approaches that in other aspects were fundamentally at odds. Despite Mogan's personal disapproval of interpretations that included emphasis on conflict or tension, the new social historians associated with the project as consultants and researchers were able to connect the plan with their own more critical focus on ethnic, immigrant, family, and labor histories. At the same time, people whose primary concern was economic development were able to support the Mogan vision because it allowed for the creation of a narrative in which a difficult or exploitative past would be replaced by a better present and future (Ryan 1987:357–58), a perspective we have already seen at work in the Run of the Mill tour. Because it was linked with Lowell's specific cultural and physical landscapes, Mogan's plan also offered a useful marketing strategy for those who hoped that tourists, new businesses, and residents would be attracted by a re-imaged and unique Lowell identity. As Stephen Ward notes,

> Far more than . . . in industrial promotion, where most places told very
> much the same story, all post-industrial marketers took great pains in
> weaving their own unique mythic vision of place. . . . As always, history
> provided a convenient way of doing this. Key heritage projects were one
> popular way of sending the 'right' message about the past. . . . Another
> approach to asserting distinctiveness was selective history, used to define
> special place qualities. (1998:210)

The two divergent agendas—educational and economic—found a meeting place in Mogan's emphasis on present-day ethnic culture in Lowell,
a component that became firmly embedded within the structure of the
redevelopment plan as it evolved during the 1970s.

Mogan and his allies worked energetically to secure funding and designation from outside Lowell for the city's culture-led revitalization
plan. On the state, regional, and national, levels there was considerable
support available in this period for projects that addressed urban poverty, social and racial disparities, and the plight of deindustrialized and
other struggling places. Within Massachusetts, one of the culture-based
responses to the loss of industry was the creation of a system of "state
heritage parks" in declining mill towns. In 1973, Lowell submitted a
successful proposal to be included in this system, and Lowell Heritage
State Park was created in 1974. The state park initially included an
exhibit on waterpower in a building near the present national park Visitor Center and a riverfront esplanade outside the downtown area. Like
the Lowell Museum, it was an important precursor to the national park,
but its historical component has dwindled over time and it no longer has
a presence in the city's public historical scene.[13] Mogan aimed beyond
the state level, however, and in 1970 he began to promote the notion of
creating a national park in Lowell. Two federal initiatives provided key
underpinnings for this idea. The first, the Model Cities program, was a
Great Society initiative aimed at reducing urban poverty, crime, and
decay. In the late 1960s, Mogan had worked to secure Model Cities
funding for Lowell and had directed its educational component. Originally, the Lowell Model Cities effort concentrated on the Acre, whose
chronic poverty typified the social and economic ills that Lowell had
been struggling with since the 1920s. Although Model Cities brought
educational and economic development interests closer together over
time, the initial focus on poverty faded as the program became a springboard for the broader Mogan-inspired vision of Lowell as an "educative

city," a tourist destination, and a cultural marketplace—precisely the kind of "visitable" place now being fashioned in so many parts of the world.

The second federal contribution was a 1970 announcement by the U.S. Department of the Interior that it intended to create a series of new national parks and recreational areas near major urban centers. This represented a shift away from the traditional National Park Service focus on wilderness and was, to a large extent, a reflection of national concern over the inequality and volatility of impoverished inner cities. In New England, this concern was blended with worry over what to do with the region's depressed manufacturing centers. Both Paul Tsongas, then a rising young politician from Lowell, and Massachusetts Governor Michael Dukakis were strong supporters of governmental efforts to ease the effects of deindustrialization. The group associated with Mogan—particularly a coalition called the Human Services Corporation, formed in 1971—skillfully mobilized newly available state and federal funding throughout the 1970s for feasibility studies and other projects that laid the groundwork for the proposals eventually submitted to Congress.[14] Small ventures—the Ecumenical Plaza spanning one of the canals between the Greek Orthodox and Irish Catholic churches, a regular series of ethnic festivals along the river and in downtown Lucy Larcom Park—served to create a sense of momentum and an integrated network of people and institutions working to promote culture and history as viable elements of a new revitalization plan for Lowell. This group commissioned outside consultants to produce conceptual plans for a dispersed urban park that would combine a focus on Lowell's early industrial history with a celebration of its present-day ethnic communities—which, in the early 1970s, primarily meant the well-established Euro-American groups.

Ironically, this focus on ethnicity was one of the elements that caused the National Park Service to balk at first at the idea of creating a national park in Lowell. As a federal agency, the Park Service cares for sites deemed to be nationally significant, and many in the agency saw Lowell as just one among countless ethnically diverse decaying mill towns in the United States. The city's early "golden age"—from the 1820s to the 1840s—*was* nationally significant, given Lowell's high profile and its status as a model for later industrial cities. But the Park Service contended that not enough of Lowell's original built environment remained to serve as a coherent depiction of that period of its history. Park Service officials eventually softened their stance, particularly after reconsidering the role that the intact canal system might play in the park's interpretation. But this solution did not particularly suit the local coalition championing the park plan, who wanted a national park dedicated to a history they themselves felt a sense of ownership in. The new social historians involved in the project offered some consolation: they were actively working to see that labor history would be included in the park's interpretation. But from the point of view of Mogan and his allies, the early nineteenth-century mill girls were the wrong laborers. The coalition that had been so carefully put together would not continue to adhere around a narrative or a park that ignored the histories of present-day Lowellians. And the coalition, as much as the park itself, was crucial to overcoming the inertia within the depressed city and showing that something new and successful could be accomplished. In discussions with the Park Service, and later in Congressional hearings on the park's enabling legislation, Tsongas, Mogan, and others argued vociferously that it was the combination of factors—Lowell's remaining industrial landscape plus its present-day ethnic composition, which they described as a living artifact of the industrial age—that made the city worthy of preservation and interpretation. This reasoning eventually persuaded Congress and the Park Service, and the bill creating Lowell National Historical Park was passed and signed into law in the spring of 1978. Lowell, the legislation stated plainly, was "historically *and culturally* the most significant planned industrial city in the United States" (U.S. Congress 1978:1; italics added). This cultural aspect has been so thoroughly embedded in the park's mission that a Lowell NHP ranger leading a walking tour of the Acre in 2002 could confidently rewrite history by telling his audience, "That's part of the reason why the National Park Service liked Lowell, is this stuff is still here. We didn't have to invent it, we didn't have to create it, we didn't have to design little props and sets. We can just take people and show it to them, it's right here."

Nonetheless, the dichotomy between local celebratory ethnicity and the more critical historical approach of public historians in the Park Service has remained, and is examined more thoroughly in Chapter 7. As we have already seen in the Run of the Mill tour, Lowell NHP interpretation continues to emphasize the nineteenth century rather than the twentieth. One park ranger summed up this continuing dichotomy when he told me, "I think most people in the town think about the last hundred years, rather than the first hundred years. You know, they're thinking about the 1930s, 1940s, 1950s. We're talking about the 1820s and 1830s." The dichotomy is reflected in the five themes around which, as I have already noted, early Lowell NHP planners decided to build the park's interpretation: waterpower, technology, labor, capital, and the industrial city. The last of these reveals the influence of voices of those inside and outside the park who insisted that the city was not reducible to its mills, and that its people had to be shown as more than just workers. But as an interpretive theme, "the industrial city" has always been something of a catchall that Lowell NHP has found problematic to deal with. Waterpower is interpreted via the river and the still-operating canal and lock system; technology is strikingly demonstrated in the Suffolk Mill exhibit and the working weave room of the Boott Cotton Mills Museum. Labor and capital are treated throughout the park's exhibits, showing the interests of the left-leaning, labor-oriented planners and historians who shaped these productions.[15] But "the city" has never been fully integrated into the park's interpretation. Initial plans for a city exhibit in the park-owned Old City Hall never materialized, and the representation of the city's people in the Working People exhibit, as we will see in Chapter 7, revealed deep cleavages between the two kinds of discourse about the city's past. The recently revamped Visitor Center exhibit does acknowledge the city's many neighborhoods, including the Acre, but during the planning process for this exhibit, it was clear that the park remains largely undecided about whether or how it should actively interpret these neighborhoods in its standard interpretive offerings. Its regular series of Exploring Lowell tours, including the tours of the Acre, come closest to an attempt to do this. But the Acre tours take rangers outside officially defined public historical space and into a symbolically charged area that is still a source of both pride and shame for the city, and where the poverty that initially prompted Patrick Mogan's original insistence on celebratory ethnicity is still very much in evidence.

Faced with that poverty and with the questions of privilege and inequality raised by such encounters, the rangers leading the Acre tours instinctively seemed to fall back on the positive, unifying role first envisioned by Mogan for the national park. One of the Acre tour rangers stated this explicitly after a visitor asked about the role of Paul Tsongas in Lowell's redevelopment: "Paul Tsongas . . . pushed really hard in

Congress to get the federal government to inspire private investors and local organizations to work all together. So the Park Service comes in—I feel like we're almost like a figurehead, almost like a cheerleading section."Another, discussing with me her feelings of discomfort at interpreting the poverty of the Acre, noted that,

> I want to do it in a positive way. These are people who are obviously struggling, and it's clear that they don't speak the language very well. When they come by with a shopping cart full of soda bottles that they've picked up, I mean, what do you say? I mean, it's—what runs through my mind is, "Keep it positive." Perhaps not for the visitor so much, but for the people who live there, to let them know that, you know, this isn't a bad place. There's some good things that happen here. So that's what goes through my mind. I will never go in there and say something negative. It just—it gets enough negative itself.

The Acre—so symbolically and culturally dynamic, so linked with the redevelopment experiment since its beginning, so physically close to the restored downtown, and yet so socioeconomically distant from it—presents an ideal ground for encounters that might cut across lines of class and ethnic otherness. Given a different kind of public historical interpretation, it could be a place for, in James Abrams's words, "the free expression of radically plural public cultures" (1994:34), where, as Dean MacCannell has put it, visitors and tour leaders alike might face "the possibility of recognizing and attempting to enter into a dialogue, on an equal footing, with forms of intelligence absolutely different from [their] own" (1999:xxi). But the park's ability to look more candidly and critically at present-day ethnic and socioeconomic relationships in the city—the very contribution that public historical approaches might most viably offer to public discourse in Lowell—is consistently undercut by the perceived need to emphasize the positive at all costs, a perception inherited in large part from the unifying approach to ethnicity constructed during the early days of the city's redevelopment project.

In an ironic way, the voice of at least one cultural "other" has found a place in the national park's tours of the Acre. Two of the three rangers whose tours I observed told visitors on the tour how Lowell had been selected as one of twelve national "host cities" for southeast Asian refugees in the 1980s, where social services could be concentrated and delivered more effectively. One ranger connected this with Lowell's search

for federal help with its revitalization beginning in the 1970s; in his telling, the refugees had been a conduit for massive government funding
that had helped to bring new life and new business to the city. Another
of the rangers went further, linking Lowell's host city status with the
picture of ethnic cooperation and coexistence promoted by the city's
heritage establishment:

> Now, I've never actually heard an official reason as to why it was chosen,
> but I want to believe it's because of what we're going to talk about, that
> over the years all of these immigration waves of Irish and Greek and
> Portuguese and French Canadian, we never really had a major riot here
> in town that was based upon ethnic divisions. We'll talk about a few small
> ones, but in general, relations have been pretty good. And I want to
> believe that that's why they picked Lowell, it's because it was a place that
> they saw immigrants being able to fit in over the years, Irish, French
> Canadian, Greek, et cetera, et cetera.

I was puzzled by the host city story, since the U.S. Office of Refugee
Resettlement had in fact, pursued a policy of dispersing southeast Asians
as widely as possible across the country, precisely to avoid overloading
any one area's services. The eventual concentration of southeast Asians
in specific places has been almost entirely due to secondary migration
and the insistence of new refugees on being settled near family members, rather than to government policy.[16] Eventually it became clear that
the source of the story was a Vietnamese friend of one of the rangers,
who, like most refugees, had been offered some choice of locations for
resettlement based on the availability of sponsors in those places. Her
experience had found its way into the ranger's narrative about Lowell,
to be expanded on by the second ranger who had used it to reinforce the
city's claim of exemplary multiculturalism.

Interestingly enough, this story overlapped with a rumor that I
heard occasionally among Lowell's Cambodians. Some people believed
that the city had somehow profited from their presence, suggesting
that comparatively little of the large amounts of public funding devoted
to public assistance for the Cambodians found its way into refugees'
own hands. Some resented being frequently studied by white American researchers who received funds while the Cambodians participated
for free; others clearly recognized that their arrival in Lowell represented economic opportunities for landlords, social service workers,

and employers in search of low-cost, unskilled labor. Although most people downplayed these rumors if asked about them directly, and much of the resentment seemed to be rooted in a lack of understanding of the unfamiliar social systems they were caught up in, there was nevertheless a good deal of sense in the perception that the Cambodians were a resource for Lowell that some in the city were using for purposes that sometimes exploited, rather than benefited, the Cambodians themselves. As Gayatri Spivak has put it, rumor is never error but basically errant.[17] It seemed to me that the Cambodian rumor was articulating in an errant, roundabout way, a phenomenon that I have been trying to delineate in this chapter: that immigrants' culture, their history as refugees, and even—in the case of a production like the Acre tour—their homes, businesses, and bodies, are in some sense grist for Lowell's heritage mill, which makes use of the newcomers but does not invite them to share in producing the representations on display. Like the rangers' account of the refugee host cities, the Cambodian rumor pointed out that Lowell had in some sense benefited from the arrival of the southeast Asians, not in a direct financial way as many Cambodians believed, but, as in this instance, because their presence allowed cultural producers in the city— including those at the national park—to continue telling a unifying story of ethnicity and socioeconomic progress. During my time in Lowell, I saw highly diverse groups of people in many areas of the city's public life—government, education, health and social services, religion— who were deeply committed to wrestling with the difficult realities of cultural encounter and change, and who had forged solid relationships that crossed class and ethnic or cultural boundaries. But the heritage sector was strikingly isolated from these processes, and from the present-day immigrants whose stories had been worked into the template of celebratory ethnicity that was constructed during the genesis of the redevelopment experiment in the 1970s.

CHAPTER 5

Historic Preservation as Economic Development

In August of 2001 I took a special tour offered by the national park, entitled "Historic Preservation as Economic Development." The tour was led by Peter Aucella, the park's assistant superintendent, who began the tour by describing his own background:

> I'm one of those guys who had a political science degree and you always wonder what happens to them after poli sci. . . . Over the years I've worked for the state transportation planning agency, the U.S. Department of Housing and Urban Development, the city of Malden, Massachusetts, doing community development. . . . After that I was an economic development aide to U.S. Senator Paul Tsongas when he was in the Senate. He had an economic development team—I used to spend a lot of time working in communities throughout the state. After that I came up to Lowell as the director of planning and development for the city, then moved over to be executive director of the Lowell Historic Preservation Commission, which . . . was a federal commission, created when the park was created. It no longer exists, it had a set life, and . . . our goal was to try to play a little different role than a national park normally plays.
>
> When a national park comes into a community, they acquire some property, they set up exhibits, they give tours. What the National Park Service needed to do in Lowell was much different, much broader, because it needed to set the tone for the historic preservation of a very deteriorated community, it had to set the standard for preservation. . . . Buildings are called "rehabbed" whether they're done poorly or well,

okay, and our goal is to get it done well the first time. Very often it takes the same money to do it right as the money people sometimes spend to do it wrong. So the Preservation Commission had some financial incentives to get some buildings done and get the ball rolling, so to speak.

For the last five years or so I've been the Assistant Superintendent for Development here in Lowell National Historical Park, and I've had two side projects, which are in the Preservation District and relate to tourism, but are not your standard national park stuff. And that is, I was in charge of helping the city build the Paul Tsongas Arena and the LeLacheur Park baseball stadium, as executive director of the city's Arena and Stadium Commission. Literally, the Park Service loaned me to the city to do those projects, and now I'm back doing the preservation stuff I'm supposed to be doing.

Aucella s introduction provides a useful thumbnail sketch of the areas I explore in this chapter through the lens of Aucella s own guided tour: the role of Paul Tsongas and his protégés in Lowell s revitalization project, the creation of the national park and its sister agency, the Lowell Historic Preservation Commission, and the close relationship between these entities and the city s overall strategy for pursuing a new postindustrial identity and economy.

Like the other tours I describe in this section, this one began at the national park's Visitor Center. Rather than being concerned with industrial history or ethnic culture, however, it focused on Lowell's built environment, and specifically on the rebuilding and renovation that has been taking place within the city in the past three decades. Aucella began with the Market Mills complex that houses the Visitor Center itself. Market Mills was the first major renovation undertaken in a former textile mill site in Lowell, and as such it made an important statement. As we saw in the previous chapter, a local coalition emerged in Lowell during the 1970s around the idea of revitalizing the city by preserving and interpreting its industrial history and ethnic cultures, rather than trying to erase or downplay them. In 1978, the efforts of this coalition resulted in the creation of Lowell National Historical Park and the Lowell Historic Preservation Commission, which were jointly charged with taking the lead in implementing the culture-led plans that had evolved in the preceding decade. Starting with a skeleton staff, the national park immediately established a temporary storefront visitor center and began offering mill and canal tours similar to the one described in Chapter 3 (fig. 9). But the twin agen-

FIGURE 9. U.S. Senator Paul Tsongas speaks at the ribbon-cutting ceremony for the first Visitor Center at Lowell National Historical Park in September 1978. Beside him is Lowell NHP Superintendent Lewis Albert. LOWELL NATIONAL HISTORICAL PARK.

cies also moved quickly to promote the kind of physical transformation that the revitalization plan had promised.

The Historic Preservation Commission developed part of the Market Mills site; the other developer, a private company, was using federal tax credits to build elderly and low-income housing in the rest of the mill complex. The national park's Visitor Center became the anchor of the first-floor redevelopment. A number of other cultural and commercial entities—an art gallery run by a local artists' collective, a food court called "The Melting Pot" (later replaced by a series of individual restaurants and currently empty), the local-access television station, a day-care center—are sublessees of the park's master lease.[1] Of major importance in the renovation, Aucella told the tour group, was the fact that "when people came into this courtyard, they were blown away, because they had never seen a mill renovated, they had never seen nice units . . . and public spaces that were attractive in a mill complex. You've got to remember that there was pretty much a generation or more with bad memories of work in the mills." Aucella showed pictures of the largely vacant and fire-ravaged mill complex before its transformation, and noted:

One of the themes that's going to come up in this presentation is, what all
of us involved in the historic preservation have done over the years is basically strip off the junk, clean what's there, try to go with appropriate
windows, and get back to what the buildings were. So as we'll see in some
of the other pictures, it's basically sort of deconstructing the junk that's
on the outside and getting back to what the buildings were before.

The rest of the tour followed the same format—"before" photographs
contrasted with present-day buildings, along with behind-the-scenes
stories about plans and renovations—as Aucella led his small audience
(five people plus myself) through the downtown area. He pointed out
some of the few properties actually acquired by the federal government:
the Old City Hall, now leased to commercial users, the park's administrative headquarters in a former mill agent's house, and the cluster of
buildings surrounding an open green space known as Boardinghouse
Park at the center of the national park's main interpretive area.[2] The
Boardinghouse Park area includes the Patrick J. Mogan Cultural Center,
a former mill boardinghouse that was drastically renovated to return it
to its early nineteenth-century configuration (fig. 10). The building,
whose development is explored more thoroughly in Chapter 7, now
houses the park's "Working People" exhibit and the University of Massachusetts's local history archive, the Center for Lowell History. Boardinghouse Park itself was created as an outdoor performing arts space in
the heart of the historic area. It currently serves as the main stage for the
annual Lowell Folk Festival and the venue for a popular summer concert
series, among other events. Across the park from the restored boardinghouse is the immense Boott Cotton Mills complex, within which the
federal government owns two buildings. These house the park's major
museum exhibit, some of its own and its partners' offices, and the Tsongas Industrial History Center, a highly regarded educational institution
run by the park in partnership with the UMass/Lowell Graduate School
of Education.[3] The rest of the Boott Mill complex is privately owned,
and is being developed building by building. A 90,000-square-foot
building already completed by 2001 was filled almost to capacity with
"new economy" companies, while a second 180,000-square-foot space
was then being renovated for office and residential use.[4]

Aucella also pointed out many privately owned buildings along the
tour route, as well as parks and properties owned by nonfederal public

FIGURE 10. This area next to the Boott Cotton Mills became the center of gravity for Lowell's culture-based redevelopment efforts. The parking lot in the center of the photograph was transformed into Boardinghouse Park, an important outdoor performing arts space. The low brick building in the center right is one of the few remaining textile boardinghouse blocks in the city; it appears, drastically renovated to its original appearance and renamed as the Mogan Cultural Center, in figure 15. JIM HIGGINS.

entities. Next door to the Boott area, for example, he told visitors about the neighboring Massachusetts Mills, a 500,000 square-foot mill complex of which more than half is now renovated as market-value apartment housing.[5] Adjacent to this complex is Kerouac Park, created in the mid-1980s on the site of a cotton warehouse that was deemed unsuitable for redevelopment. After relocating two hundred warehouse tenants and taking down the building, the Historic Preservation Commission used the empty space to further two projects: first, the extension of the restored trolley line from its terminus at the Boott Mill to a new downtown hotel that was a pet venture of Tsongas and the commission staff, and second, a memorial to native son Jack Kerouac. The Kerouac commemorative— a series of polished granite columns carved with excerpts from Kerouac's writings—was one of eleven public artworks sponsored by private funders and overseen by the commission in the late 1980s.[6] Finally, in the same immediate neighborhood, Aucella pointed out the modern red-brick building that was once the training center for Wang Laboratories, and now houses a Middlesex Community College campus. "I always say [Wang] never hired architects, they only hired engineers," Aucella told his tour audience. "So we got a building that didn't have a whole lot of character, but because it was coming downtown they agreed to put brick on it." The community college has been expanding its presence in the downtown, an effort in which Tsongas's widow, now the school's Dean of External Affairs, has been active. At the time of Aucella's tour, the college was beginning to renovate an old federal building as part of the ongoing transformation of the area known as the Lower Locks. This section of downtown, located at the confluence of two canals and the Concord River, was viewed by Tsongas and the Historic Preservation Commission staff as an important anchor for the redevelopment project.

The August 2001 tour finished by circling back through the main business district, where Aucella told many more "before and after" tales about individual buildings along the central section of Merrimack Street. In contrast to many other New England cities, Lowell s downtown is indeed a showpiece of careful restoration and preservation. There are few holes left by fires or urban renewal to interrupt the variegated jumble of nineteenth- and early-twentieth century façades. They offer what Kevin Lynch and his many protégés have insisted cities need: a legible or comprehensible landscape that supports many stories about the past and the present. Christine Boyer has termed such cityscapes "city tableaux" (1992:184ff.)—each is a visually pleasing, architecturally coherent built landscape. In addition to anchoring residents' own stories, memories, and relationships, such landscapes help to create an image that can be managed and promoted as part of the larger rebranding agenda. As Stephen Ward points out, "The essential point about all these devices— the flagship developments, the use of design, the references to the past and the use of public art—was that the form and spaces of the post-industrial city had to be striking and imageable. Whether in the city marketeer's brochure or the lens of the tourist, the intention was to signal change in an arresting and eyecatching way" (1998:194).

Peter Aucella, gregarious, polished, and untiring, is the pitchman par excellence for this "reimaged" Lowell. To Aucella, historic preservation, the keystone of the Lowell revitalization plan, is essentially a simple and unproblematic endeavor. "Our job is just to bring it back—to bring back [the buildings'] original character," he said several times during the

August 2001 tour. Like Lowell's nineteenth century founders, Aucella and other planners at the forefront of shaping and promoting the city's renaissance operate from a cohesive, tightly managed vision that seeks to blend capitalist development with idealistic social engineering. In the rest of this chapter, I read Peter Aucella's tour very much against the grain, questioning the coherent and compelling view it presents. I begin my counterreading by setting the tour and its depiction of a revitalized Lowell within a broader context of economic restructuring and social change in deindustrialized places.

Deindustrialization and Restructuring

Textile production in Lowell peaked in the late nineteenth century. It diminished gradually into the 1920s, then took a precipitous dive when several companies decided to move their operations to the American South, where labor was cheaper and raw materials closer to hand. Thus Lowell, which had entered on the cycle of industrial capitalist development earlier than most American places, was also among the first to experience the devastating effects of deindustrialization. Historian Larry Gross reports that an estimated $100 million of New England capital shifted to southern factories between 1923 and 1927, and that by 1930, 45 percent of New England's 280,000 textile workers had lost their jobs, with many more working in marginal and poorly paid positions (Gross 1991:282–84). Some textile producers found new, smaller niche markets, while others tore down their buildings to save on property taxes or sold them to other types of manufacturers. Conditions worsened during the Depression; as late as 1938, 40 percent of the city's population was still on some form of government relief (M. Blewett 1976:182). Because rot had already set into the city's economic base before the Depression, Lowell did not bounce back afterwards as other places did, despite a short-lived boom spurred by government contracts during the Second World War. Marc Miller (1988) has referred to this as "the irony of victory"—the end of the war, a turning point on the road back to prosperity for most American communities, sounded the death knell for places like Lowell whose economic centers had already been largely gutted. Local unemployment levels continued to exceed those of the state and nation through the 1960s, reaching a level of almost 13 percent by 1975 (Gall 1991:397). Lowell was—and still is—more heavily industrial than most American communities, but for many decades most of its industrial jobs have been low-paying and fixed in sectors that are in decline in the region (Gittell and Flynn 1995:58). Growth, innovation, and investment had moved elsewhere over the course of the century.

What that might mean for the future was far from clear in the 1960s and 1970s. Several decades later, the effects of deindustrialization have become much more familiar. So have the kinds of strategies being developed to cope with it and the outlines of newer "postindustrial" places that are emerging as a result. Discussion is needed here of these twin terms—deindustrialization and postindustrialism—which are central to my analysis of Lowell. The process of deindustrialization, of course, includes the disinvestment, capital flight, and plant closings seen in Lowell and throughout the United States and many industrial countries in the second half of the twentieth century.[7] The shift away from manufacturing has continued throughout these places in recent years, spurred by the opening of new and cheaper labor markets around the world, new technologies that make capital ever more mobile, and domestic policies that have "liberalized" trade and investment while loosening many of the restrictions under which corporations operate (Bluestone and Harrison 1982, Osterhammel and Petersson 2005). The loss of American manufacturing has been particularly damaging in New England, especially in Massachusetts, because of the high concentration of older industries there (Bluestone and Stevenson 2000:13). However, even newly industrializing places with an abundance of low-cost labor are now feeling some of these same effects, as machines increasingly replace human labor. Robert Reich reports that while the United States saw an 11 percent drop in manufacturing jobs from 1995 to 2002, China, whose industrial production has increased tremendously, actually lost 15 percent of its industrial jobs owing to mechanization in the same period (Reich 2003). Technological and organizational changes that once took decades now occur much more quickly. And they continue to be supported in many parts of the world by fiscal and political policies that facilitate the free flow of capital and the quest for profit on an ever more global scale—a set of policies generally referred to as "neoliberalism." (See Harvy 2005 for a useful overview of this process.) As historian Mike Wallace points out, deindustrialization is not the result of "some mystical urge toward a service economy inherent in the capitalist order" (1996:93), but of specific choices and decisions on the part of leaders in business and government. Wallace also argues that we should not view deindustrialization or postindustrialism as new phenomena, but rather as parts of the same long cycle of development that has been reshaping virtually all parts of the world for the past two centuries. This reshaping is never total or undisputed, but it is difficult to argue with its overall impact; as historian Peter Stearns has written, "no factors even remotely rival industrialization's impact in explaining what has gone on in the world—and what still goes on as adjustments to the alteration of basic human systems continue" (1993:12). In this view, it is not simply that the United States is becoming deindustrialized while China is industrializing, but rather that the United States and China are becoming linked together in new and complex ways within the continued elaboration of industrial capitalism. Indeed, the Slovenian philosopher Slavoj Zizek (2000) has argued that, despite many claims to the contrary, the American industrial working class is not disappearing after all—it is alive and well and producing goods in China.

Although the core causes and processes of deindustrialization take place in the economic realm, its effects—the adjustments Stearns is referring to above—are felt throughout the whole social and cultural fabric of former industrial places. And this means that postindustrialism, like deindustrialization, cannot be understood in purely economic terms. Rather, as John Urry proposes, postindustrialism is more of a seachange in the distinctive social patterns of twentieth century industrial places. Urry argues that postindustrial societies "are best thought of as having once been not simply 'industrial' but 'organised' during the first half to two-thirds of this century and that what is now happening in such societies is that a mutually reinforcing set of disruptions of those organised patterns has been established" (1995:120). These patterns include the taken-for-granted status of nation–states as the primary organizing units for political, social, and economic matters, a status that many have argued is weakening in the face of the growing consolidation of power in the hands of multinational corporations. The similarly taken-for-granted notion of socioeconomic class—the tripartite industrial structure of working class, middle class, capitalist class—is also undergoing many changes, a topic I take up in Chapter 6. Among these adjustments, traditional models of labor organizing are being transformed—and in many places, including the United States, greatly weakened. And postindustrial societies, particularly those whose leaders favor strongly neoliberal policies, are also seeing a shift toward an asymmetrical economy in which wealth is increasingly concentrated among a relatively small percentage of the population at the top, an ever-larger percentage at the bottom is finding itself stuck in persistent poverty, and the middle classes find themselves on uneasy ground between the two. A growing inequality characterizes the global economy in general, but among developed nations, the United States is by far the most lopsided, with the most unequal income distribution and one of the highest poverty rates among "First World" countries (Mishel et al. 2001:11).

Most commentators on postindustrialism are in agreement that cultural productions of all kinds are playing a new and important role in this social and economic reorganization, both as products and as part of the processes by which these transformations are occurring. (For an early and influential discussion of this connection, see Jameson 1984). In more and more places, cultural productions and cultural performances—heritage areas and trails, museums and galleries, sports facilities, festivals, public art, and so on—are part and parcel of the repertoire of tactics by which postindustrial places manufacture their images and invite public participation and consumption. As Dean MacCannell notes, the state is increasingly involved in such cultural productions (1999:25), a phenomenon that has been very evident in Lowell and that will be discussed later in this chapter. MacCannell also proposes that the emergence of a certain kind of tourism that he calls a "work display"—for example, industrial history museums—is a clear sign that a particular place has left the industrial and entered the postindustrial: "The appearance of a mythology of work consigns it to a remote and formative period and marks the end of the industrial age. Work was once the locus of our most important social values and the exclusive anchor point connecting the individual and society. Now it is only one stop among many in tourists' itineraries" (1999:57). However, MacCannell, like Wallace, sees the industrial and the postindustrial as two parts of the same phenomenon, not successive stages in economic and social development. "The hope for a 'postindustrial' society," he insists, "is, in fact, only a touristic way of looking at work" (1999:65). As we have already seen in the Run of the Mill tour and will explore in more depth in the following chapter, such touristic productions allow those in the more prosperous niches of the postindustrial economy to reassure themselves that these sweeping economic changes are part of a natural progression. At the same time, work tourism can help to mask both the tourists' own privileged places within those changes and the uneasy possibility that even privilege may not exempt them from the pitiless logic of the system in which they are enmeshed.

Lowell's own remarkable transformation owes a good deal to its position on the edge of metropolitan Boston, one of the most successful postindustrial areas of the country. Indeed, as historian Stephen Ward says, "If it is valid to speak of a formula for the post-industrial city, Boston stumbled across it first" (1998:191). As a regional financial hub for New England's industrial economy as well as a manufacturing center in its own right, Boston was "a metropolitan area in distress and decline" by the 1970s (Bluestone and Stevenson 2000:1). Over the past three decades, however, the city has energetically reinvented itself, courting (and in many cases creating) new knowledge- and service-based industries that have emerged as the most dynamic sector of the regional and national economies. A central factor in Boston's success has been the presence of "a large and diverse corps of knowledge workers" associated with the area's many academic and research institutions, which have helped Greater Boston become a "knowledge sector powerhouse" that is highly competitive in the new economy (Forrant et al. 2001:3). In a shift from "mill-based" to "mind-based" industries (Bluestone and Stevenson 2000:18), growth in the region is now driven by such activities as biogenetic and other medical research centered around institutions like the Massachusetts Institute of Technology, financial management from the new skyscrapers of the downtown core, software development and support along the "Silicon Alley" of Route 128, and the creation of new weapons technologies by the area's many defense contractors. Cultural tourism plays a considerable role in Boston's appeal; the city offers the entire panoply of arts, history, sports, the waterfront, and other activities that contemporary cities use to create and promote their identities. With many historic buildings, neighborhoods, and waterfront areas, perhaps the first "heritage trail" (the Freedom Trail, created in 1951) and the country's first "festival marketplace" (Quincy Marketplace, renovated in 1976), long-established fine-arts institutions, an active historic-preservation tradition, and a generally cooperative city government, Boston has actively mobilized its past to aid its transformation into a prosperous postindustrial place (Ehrlich and Dreier 1999).

With good road and rail access to Boston, Lowell both sends commuters into the city and receives some of the spillover from Boston's redevelopment in the form of "new economy" firms and residents for whom Lowell is a slightly less expensive alternative or an appealing smaller urban area. Nearby high-technology and defense companies employ many local people, and, as with Boston and most postindustrial areas, the health and education sectors are also major employers and elements of Lowell's changing economy and identity.[8] Once a byword for decay and crime, Lowell has seen its reputation change slowly but strikingly in recent years, to the point that many in the region and beyond now regard it as an exemplar of the revitalized ex–mill town—what *Historic Preservation* magazine called "*the* relevant precedent emulated by gritty cities worldwide" (Freeman 1990:32). By comparison with other small textile cities in the area—New Bedford, Fall River, Holyoke, Nashua (New Hampshire)—Lowell has made an extremely successful transition into the postindustrial age.

Although some of its success can be ascribed to its proximity to Boston, that is clearly not the full story. Worcester, Lawrence, Brockton, and other deindustrialized midsized cities on the outer ring of the Boston metropolitan area continue to struggle with the kinds of stubborn social and economic problems that Lowell appears to be well on the way to resolving. The key to understanding Lowell's revitalization is the word "appears." What Lowell has done far more effectively than any of the other small cities mentioned above is to create, project, and then work toward fulfilling an image of reinvention and prosperity—in short, to reify its own claims of revitalization. In the words of Paul Tsongas, one of the primary architects of the new Lowell, "Renaissance is a mind-set." As I show below, the actual extent of this new prosperity is highly questionable. As is typical with postindustrial economies, its benefits are distributed very unevenly, and gains in one quarter are often offset by losses in another. The social problems associated with poverty and cuts in social services are still as deeply entrenched in Lowell as in other deindustrialized Massachusetts towns and cities. In many ways, in fact, Lowell is still a struggling ex-mill town beneath its redeveloped surface. But it is impossible to deny that community leaders have been remarkably consistent, dogged, and adroit in promoting the image of the revitalized city, or that the creation of that image has produced many tangible and intangible benefits which similar cities in Massachusetts have not been able to achieve.

From the beginning of Lowell's redevelopment, both cultural and economic planners saw that an improved image was a first step toward more substantive changes. "If Lowell's mills are to be redeveloped, the city's image of decline must be reversed," stated the authors of the Brown Book (Lowell Historic Canal District Commission 1977:23). Just as the city's founders and earliest promoters used the vision of a utopian manufacturing community to help market their textile products and justify their economic dominance, its more recent advocates and leaders have strategically presented a three-part tale of innovation, decline, and rebirth as a tool for fostering change. Cultural geographer John Brinckerhoff Jackson has noted the power of this narrative, which he sees as a driving force in contemporary preservation efforts:

> There has to be (in our new concept of history) an interim of death or rejection before there can be renewal or reform. The old order has to die before there can be a born-again landscape. Many of us know the joy and excitement not so much of creating the new as of redeeming what has been neglected, and this excitement is particularly strong when the original condition is seen as holy or beautiful. The old farmhouse has to decay before we can restore it and lead an alternative life style in the country; the landscape has to be plundered and stripped before we can restore the natural ecosystem; the neighborhood has to be a slum before we can rediscover and gentrify it. That is how we reproduce the cosmic scheme and correct history. (1980:102)

The idea of overcoming a decline or break—what Jackson calls "the necessity for ruins," and what we will see in the following chapter as Victor Turner's notion of a "breach" phase in social dramas—is essential to generating excitement that can be translated into concrete social and financial investments in the "corrected" city. During my two years of fieldwork, I saw considerable evidence that this narrative had taken root firmly in the minds of many Lowellians and an increasing number of people outside the city. Virtually all the residents and outsiders I spoke to about Lowell saw the national park and the city's historic preservation efforts as interesting and positive. Although not everyone was uniformly upbeat about the city as a whole, there was a very widespread sense that many good things were happening there. The park, the summer folk festival, the Tsongas Industrial History Center, the ballpark and hockey arena, and the more recent emphasis on visual art have all created an unmistakable "buzz" about Lowell. And this buzz—in combination with the city's proximity to Boston—has translated into an influx of new residents and small businesses as well as a distinctive identity that most residents appear happy to claim as their own. Lowell's "brand" or image—a small and gritty city climbing back from the brink of disaster by celebrating its distinctive industrial history and ethnic cultures— seems firmly established in the minds of many. The association of Lowell with the Yankee mill girls appears to constitute almost a brand within a brand; people who otherwise knew nothing about Lowell frequently mentioned the mill girls to me when I spoke of my research.[9] If that brand is not, after all, unique, it is compensated for by the fact that Lowell claimed it first (which may contribute to the difficulties that other comparable nearby cities have had in differentiating themselves in a more and more competitive cultural marketplace).

Lowell's "symbolic economy" (Zukin 1995:8–9) generates few actual jobs and much less revenue than the architects of the new Lowell once optimistically projected it would (fig. 11). Culture-based redevelopment strategies in themselves tend to create comparatively little direct revenue; Lowell National Historical Park, for example, employed about one hundred people during the time when I was doing my fieldwork, and as with workers in other sectors of the city's new economy, many of the people in those jobs lived outside Lowell itself. Nor does cultural tourism consistently generate large amounts of revenue for Lowell; because it is so close to the much larger urban center of Boston, Lowell is not a "destination" city, which means that most visitors come only for the day and usually spend little money outside the specific institutions they have come to visit. But planners and place-marketers have come to see that it is the indirect benefits of these projects that ultimately have the greater value. The experiences and knowledge generated within the cultural sector can be consumed as part of a lifestyle that contributes to reshaping and reframing urban space for uses and users associated with the new economy. The processes involved in this reshaping—for example, the emergence of New York's SoHo as a distinct neighborhood of loft-dwelling artists in the 1950s and 1960s—are often seen as spontaneously caused by grass-roots developments. But Zukin (1982) and others have demonstrated that, in fact, government, banks, and property holders are all instrumental in causing these changes. The zoning, investment, and designatory decisions that are made about deindustrialized urban places are intended to repopulate (and often first to de-populate) and revalue urban real estate. Such strategies are ultimately designed to support the

FIGURE 11. The cultural sector of the postindustrial economy generates comparatively few jobs, as shown by the visual contrast between figure 4 and this recent
photo of Lowell National Historical Park employees in the same Boott Cotton
Mills courtyard. JIM HIGGINS.

overall project of economic restructuring and revaluation and the courting of people and businesses linked with the new economy: knowledge
and service workers, tourists, and cultural producers of many types,
from artists to immigrants. The city's investment in culture pays off—
not in the short term, with windfall weekend events like the Lowell Folk

Festival—but when people who have visited for a festival or a boat tour or a baseball game decide Lowell would be a good place to buy a house, renovate a building, or relocate a business.

As we have already seen, the culture-led strategies pursued by places like Lowell often disguise the workings of history and power rather than rendering them legible. Christine Boyer points to what she calls the "double erasure" inherent in these strategies. The first erasure occurs when a place loses its primary reason for being—in Lowell's case, its identity as a manufacturing center. But the endeavors that most people think of as acts of rescue or preservation—the creation of museums, the restoration of historic buildings, the staged celebration of ethnic heritage—constitute, in Boyer's view, a second erasure, one that further removes places and events from the realm of everyday experience and places them in the realm of abstraction and representation. Once there, they are experienced in quite different ways by new groups of people. Boyer has chronicled this process in the instances of New York's Times Square and the South Street Seaport redevelopments (M. C. Boyer 1992, 2001), both of which have promoted uncritical, feel-good reinterpretations of the past, closely linked with consumer activity in the present. Lowell's repackaging has been less glossy, and its interpretation has included—largely thanks to the work of leftist public historians within the overall project—some unusually critical readings of the city's industrial past: the labor organizing of the mill girls, the close connections between the northern textile industry and the Southern slave economy, the class tensions inherent in industrial capitalism, and so on. Yet the basic rationale remains the same in Lowell as in Times Square. At bottom, these acts of representation—Boyer's double erasures—are about creating a striking and marketable image that can be used to make old places viable in a changed economy.

This point was made abundantly clear by an anecdote related to me by two of the first public historians to work at the park. In the early 1980s, a pair of local businessmen came to the park's new Visitor Center to look at its small theatre space as a possible meeting venue.

> And they sat through the slide show, and there's one line in the slide show that says something about "Lowell had become precisely what its founders had intended that it not be, a city based on the exploitation of a permanent working class." And . . . one of the guys, when that line came on, he jumped out of his seat. But the other guy was the one making the deci-

sions. So afterwards, when the thing was over, the decision-making guy said, "Yeah, sure, sure, sure, that's fine, let's go." And the other guy's going, "What about the exploitation?" [And the first guy said], "Nobody pays attention to that!" [Shortly afterward] We had [historian] Mike Wallace come up and speak at the Lowell Conference. . . . [He] fastened onto this notion that the business community was not critical. They had really a hands-off attitude, you know, and if they're dealing with labor or industrial accidents or environmental issues, fine, you know. And what he said, and it was very memorable, was, "Well, if you have Old Faithful in your backyard, then you're in favor of geysers." And if labor history sells, then go ahead and sell it.[10]

Within this stage of capitalist development, where culture itself is increasingly commodified and made into spectacle, critical views as well as celebratory ones can be put to use in aid of the overall reimaging and revaluation of a place. There is nothing inherently wrong with spaces and culture transforming themselves to meet new circumstances—that is how cultural and spatial processes have always worked. But it is crucial to ask what kind of new reality these processes are helping to create. When we consider the widening inequalities of wealth and opportunity characteristic of the new American economy, projects like Lowell's appear in a new light. The underlying logic of economic restructuring makes itself felt at all levels of cultural production in Lowell, manifesting itself in a variety of ways but always supporting the economic, cultural, and physical reshaping of the city as a postindustrial place.

Paul Tsongas and Economic Redevelopment

To understand more fully how this process has worked in Lowell, we must examine the career of U.S. Senator Paul Tsongas and the redevelopment mechanisms that he helped to create. Tsongas, the son of Greek immigrants who owned a successful dry cleaning business in Lowell, was elected to the U.S. House of Representatives in 1974 and to the Senate in 1978. He left the Senate in 1984 to battle cancer, returned to the national stage in an unsuccessful bid for the Democratic presidential nomination in 1992, and died five years later at the age of fifty five. Like Michael Dukakis, another Greek American politician from Massachusetts who had unsuccessfully sought the presidency four years before Tsongas's attempt, Tsongas built much of his political platform around the issue of deindustrialization and the need to encourage economic growth in former manufacturing centers. Both men argued that the high-technology-powered economic revival of the 1980s—the so-called Massachusetts miracle—demonstrated the effectiveness of their economic policies; both pointed to Lowell as an example of what could be done to revitalize depressed urban areas. Tsongas, in particular, identified himself very closely with the fortunes of his hometown and promoted its redevelopment strategies as a model for the rest of the country. "If Lowell fails, if it can't come back," Tsongas told the audience at the swearing-in ceremony of the Lowell Historic Preservation Commission in 1979, "then it can be argued that no city can come back" (Lowell *Sun* 1979). The championing of the city by both Dukakis and Tsongas raised its visibility considerably and turned its successes or failures into questions that engaged observers at the state, regional, and national level.

Given Tsongas's early death and the continuing presence of his widow and many of his former aides and allies in key positions within Lowell's symbolic economy, it is perhaps inevitable that he has tended to receive the lion's share of the credit for the creation of the national park and other projects in the new Lowell. In fact, most of the groundwork for Lowell's culture-based revitalization project was already laid by the time Tsongas took national office. As we have seen, by the early 1970s, educators, historians, social service workers, and politicians had formed a broad coalition in support of the national park plan, and had already secured Congressional designation of a historic district with a federally appointed commission to oversee its preservation and development. These accomplishments reflected the growing ability of civic leaders in Lowell to put aside internecine struggles while in pursuit of agreed-upon goals, an ability that many deindustrialized and impoverished places have never developed and that has given Lowell a distinct edge in its pursuit of outside resources for local purposes. As a Lowell *Sun* writer noted in 1997, "When Lowell needs something . . . it speaks in one voice." But he added: "For many years, that voice sounded like Paul Tsongas, and it will sound like Paul Tsongas for years to come" (Howell 1997). Tsongas made two crucial contributions to the city's evolving redevelopment plan. First, he was part of a well-positioned Massachusetts Congressional delegation that was able to orchestrate an intensive, well-organized, and skillful lobbying effort to secure a national park for Lowell (Ryan 1987:334–35). Tsongas himself had no compelling interest in history per se, and acknowledged that he would have been quite happy to pave over the canal system if it would provide an economic benefit to the city. But the campaign whose final phase he spearheaded made strategic use not only of history and ethnic celebration but also of the critical perspectives that had become part of the proposal via the contributions of historians and community activists. To counter the objections of those who worried that the park proposal was merely urban renewal in disguise, witnesses at Congressional hearings adroitly balanced praise for Lowell's golden age with what Ryan calls "a politically useful emphasis on the Park's remembering labor, the exploited immigrant, the average person, and Lowell's decline" (Ryan 1987:343). Such arguments were convincing enough to allay fears that the federal investment in Lowell would ultimately be aiding private interests as much as public ones.

Ironically, Tsongas's second major contribution was precisely to bring those private interests—bankers, propertyowners, real estate developers—fully on board the culture-based development plan. Pursuing the idea of "public–private partnerships" that has undergirded much urban redevelopment starting in the 1970s (see Ward 1998:194, Zukin 1982:163–72), Tsongas was influential in shaping three mechanisms that supported such partnerships in Lowell: the Lowell Development and Financial Corporation (LDFC), the Lowell Plan, and the Lowell Historic Preservation Commission. The LDFC, which Tsongas created in 1975, is a quasi-governmental agency that works hand in hand with local banks to channel loans to developers working on projects that support the city's revitalization plan.[11] Tsongas also convened a large group of Lowell business leaders in 1979 to form an organization known as the Lowell Plan, which functions as a kind of business-sponsored think tank for the redevelopment project.[12] In both of these projects, he allied himself with then-City Manager, Joe Tully, an aggressive politician who was highly skilled at what Peter Aucella refers to as "raw politics."[13] In the words of Aucella, who points to Tully as an important factor in Lowell's revitalization, "[Tully] did not necessarily bring, shall we say, this higher level of thought about urban municipal management. That wasn't what he was about. However, he could get stuff done, due to the sheer force of will." One of Aucella's favorite stories, which he told to visitors on his August 2001 park tour, concerns a downtown property owner who ignored pointed suggestions by

Tsongas and Tully that he should renovate his building in conformity with the master plan for the downtown area:

> The guy comes in and he says, "I'm not doing anything . . . with my building. I'm taking in rents and I'm not making enough money to make it worth my while to do anything, and screw you and your revitalization—I really don't care." So Tully, the next day, sends up a crew to the guy's house. They dig up the street and cut off the water line to his house. Then they go home for the weekend. So the guy says, "This is retaliation!" Which it was. Tully said, "I don't know what you're talking about. I'm an angel. I know nothing." . . . So a couple of days go by and he sends the crew up and they fix the water line. And everybody else that came in to see Joe and Paul Tsongas about revitalizing their building said, "Sure, we'll be there, sure. What would you like me to do?"

In Aucella's estimation, such strong-arm tactics were necessary to convert reluctant bankers and self-interested property holders to the larger public good represented by the revitalization plan. Some critics, however, have pointed out the potential dangers inherent in linking private and public gain quite so closely. Of quasi-public entities like the LDFC, Sharon Zukin has noted, "It is inconceivable that the local development corporations would quarrel with the private sector's development strategy, because in many ways they *are* the private sector" (1982:163). Peter Aucella outlined for me the original vision for the Lowell Plan, which was "for every group in town to do something. So the Boy Scouts, the Girl Scouts, you know, everybody, the Rotary, the Kiwanis, everybody do one project to enhance the community. . . . It's a great idea. I don't know—I couldn't tell you what happened exactly, I wasn't here then. But it sounds great. But it became anyway, the other part of it, became CEOs, thirty CEOs, meeting every month, and working on community issues and raising money." Like the LDFC, which is essentially a consortium of bankers, the Lowell Plan functions as the voice of business interests in the city. In Aucella's telling, this arrangement has worked to guarantee that the private sector is accountable to the public interest, as defined in various planning documents and preservation plans. It is also possible, however, to interpret it as a way for business leaders to mobilize public policies and funding in their own favor. As Rosalyn Deutsche puts it in her study of New York, "Redevelopment . . . was hardly a matter of the city enlisting the real-estate industry to fulfill the needs of residents. Rather, real estate and other capital interests enlisted city government to supply the conditions to guarantee their profits and reduce their risks" (1996:26).

This is precisely what has happened in Lowell. Since the financial, real estate, and business interests climbed on board—voluntarily or under coercion—they have taken a leading role in shaping the city's ongoing revitalization, a role that is clearly bound up with their own ability to profit and to mobilize public policy and funding in their own interests. These interests are not inevitably at odds with the public interest, and Aucella and other promoters of the Tsongas vision insist that such partnerships are, in fact, mutually beneficial. But there are no public regulatory mechanisms within Lowell's revitalization realm now that can really ensure that this is the case. The agencies that might most logically serve as checks and balances to purely economic interests—the city historic board, the local nonprofit development corporation, the national park, many offices of the city government, including the planning department—are tightly linked by association and personnel with the circle of business leaders, developers, and property holders that Paul Tsongas gathered around his vision for the redevelopment plan in the 1980s and 1990s. The kinds of vocal and independent nonprofit organizations that were involved in the early phases of the plan—for example, Patrick Mogan's Human Services Corporation or the Coalition for a Better Acre—are no longer around the table to advocate ideas of less interest or concern to the business community. For a variety of reasons, economic and community development in Lowell have largely gone their separate ways over the past two decades. And so when political winds change—for instance, when federal policy makes it much more profitable to build market-value than low-income housing, a shift that has happened since the tax-credit days in which the Market Mills complex was redeveloped—there are few public ways for low-income advocates to be heard within the tightly integrated redevelopment system that Tsongas did so much to create. His accomplishment—one that the nineteenth-century Boston Associates would have understood and applauded—is no small feat in a city that was for many decades prone to political gridlock and economic stagnation, and many people in Lowell clearly prefer to see some action, however compromised, rather than continuing nonaction.[14] For better or worse, then, Lowell's redevelopment effort, as shaped by Paul Tsongas, is a remarkably top–down, cohesive, and tightly controlled project, with very little room for competing agendas or visions to maneuver. Tsongas himself was aware of these criticisms, but he discounted them. In his programmatic *A Call to Economic Arms* (1991), he described his surprise at

> the feeling by a few non-business people that the [Lowell Development and Financial] Corporation was inappropriate because it would benefit some building owners that they considered unsavory. These people don't deserve to receive financial rewards, they argued, because they are responsible for letting these buildings fall into disarray in the first place. I must admit I felt some sympathy for this righteousness but not enough to change my mind. The corporation was created, and it and its organizational twin, the Lowell Plan, have been very successful. Lowell has become a national model of urban renaissance. Did the "unsavory" people benefit? They sure did. But so did everyone else in a once-depressed mill city with what had seemed a marginal future. So what. (1991:19)

At the end of this chapter, we revisit the obvious question of the extent to which "everybody else" in Lowell has, in fact, benefited from Tsongas's shaping of the redevelopment plans.

Tsongas's strategies were rooted firmly in his neoliberal faith in the ability of free markets to produce prosperity for all. A self-described pro-business liberal, he argued as his protégés continue to argue that only a robust business climate can produce the prosperity necessary to support social programs. In Tsongas's words, " The more we want to solve the great human injustices in our society, the more we are going to need a full throttle economic engine. One cannot exist without the other" (1991:9). Like others from formerly left-of-center political parties (notably Tsongas's successful competitor in the 1992 Democratic nomination campaign, Bill Clinton), Tsongas rejected the leftist critique that social problems and injustices may as often be *caused* by robust markets as be solved by them. This faith—and a misreading of the economic signs pointing to the fundamental restructuring of the American economy around nontangible products like service and knowledge—kept Tsongas from recognizing how inexorable was the logic prompting capital flight and disinvestment in declining industrial places like Lowell. Insisting that that "America should be the pre-eminent manufacturing nation on earth again" (1991:12), he worked energetically to secure new manufacturing jobs for Lowell, primarily by courting Dr. An Wang, then head of one of the most promising companies in the rapidly growing electronics field. In 1978, the same year as the creation of the park, Wang moved his world headquarters and principal manufacturing facility to Lowell, taking advantage of a federal loan to help build three enormous concrete towers on the edge of the city. Lowell saw a spectacular period of economic growth, in which manufacturing jobs in the area increased by 90 percent (10,000 people were employed at Wang alone). By 1988, the city's unemployment rate had dropped to 2.8 percent (Gittell and Flynn 1995). However, intense competition in the glutted personal computer market, along with Wang's failure to keep pace with the rapid innovation in the field, put the company into an abrupt tailspin that ended in a declaration of bankruptcy in August 1992.[15] Hailed in the 1980s as a model of reindustrialization (Butterfield 1982), a "high technology success story" (Flynn 1984), and a town that had been "reborn" (*Newsweek* 1981), Lowell once again came to be viewed as cautionary tale and a symbol of the volatility of capitalist development cycles (see, for example, Ingrassia 1990, Kopkind 1992, Wieffering 1991). In failing to recognize or accept the tectonic changes in the local, regional, and national economies, Tsongas contributed to a striking instance of industrial history's repeating itself.[16] Nevertheless, he continued to be a player in the city's redevelopment until his death, and his many associates continue to follow the course he charted.

The Lowell Historic Preservation Commission

At the crux of Lowell's new experiment in the late 1970s was the question of whether an intentional focus on historic preservation and interpretation could act as the catalyst for the economic and social redevelopment of a depressed and decayed mill city. Although the project itself has encompassed much more than just the national park, the park has always been the central feature of the project. It makes the symbolically important statement that Lowell's industrial past and ethnic cultures are significant within the broad scheme of the nation's history and development, and it has helped to provide an interpretive template for connecting local stories and landscapes to that broader scheme. But the creation of the park also provided a pragmatic set of mechanisms for effecting change in the city. The most important of these was the park's sister agency, the Lowell Historic Preservation Commission.

As Peter Aucella pointed out at the start of his tour, most traditional national parks have been created by the federal government's buying bounded parcels of land that the National Park Service (NPS) then controls and interprets. From the beginning, the Lowell experiment was conceived as something quite different—what one consultant's report called a "new educational/cultural/economic animal" (Ryan 1987:301). Lowell NHP is a dispersed park within an urban area, which was designed not only to preserve and interpret specific properties but also to lead the way in creating a preservation standard and ethos for private property holders within the 137-acre downtown preservation district. Such a role was beyond the capabilities or jurisdiction of the NPS itself, so the 1978 park legislation also created a partner agency, the Preservation Commission, slated to last for ten years and charged with carrying out those functions not deemed appropriate for the national park: preservation and development projects in partnership with private businesses, cultural groups, and other government agencies. The commission successfully bid for a seven-year extension of its life in 1988, and finally closed its doors in 1995. Although the concept of a "partnership park" with a separate commission that would deal with development issues was highly innovative in the 1970s, it has become more common in recent years, as the National Park Service acquires less land outright and plays more of an advisory, planning, or interpretive role within larger preservation or heritage-based redevelopment efforts. Many of these are in urban and/or former industrial places; Lowell has been assiduously studied as a model for planning in these areas.[17]

The Lowell Historic Preservation Commission had fifteen members, of whom ten were appointed locally and five federally, with the entire agency being accountable directly to the Secretary of the Interior.[18] The federal government's initial $40 million commitment to preservation and interpretation activity in Lowell was split about equally between the commission and the national park. Although the Republican era of the 1980s and early 1990s was a time of drastic cuts for many federally funded programs, Lowell managed to retain and even increase its federal support during this period, largely thanks to Massachusetts's extremely well-placed Congressional delegation.[19] This funding paid for the physical development of the park itself—the Visitor Center, the Mogan Cultural Center, a small interpretive area in the Suffolk/Wannalancit Mill, and the enormous Boott Mill project, including the park's share of the Tsongas Industrial History Center. It also supported the multifaceted work of the preservation commission, which included extensive cultural programming, public art projects, and a "carrot and stick" approach to architectural preservation in the downtown area. Unlike the park, the commission was empowered to disperse grant monies—the carrot—to private entities for renovation and redevelopment. Through the close network of association within the redevelopment realm, it could also help building owners and developers negotiate the "red tape" of zoning and permitting processes, and gain access to low-interest loans through the Lowell Development and Finance Corporation and federal programs like the Urban Development Action Grant (UDAG) program (see Kujawa 1998 for a discussion of this program, which ran from 1977 to 1988). The stick—enforcement of the newly created preservation standards for downtown buildings—was wielded through a variety of formal and informal mechanisms ranging from the ability to condemn a noncompliant building to the extreme case of the City Manager's having a building owner's water lines cut as a lesson in the costs of noncooperation. The commission was the driving force behind the creation of the Mogan Cultural Center, Kerouac Park, and Boardinghouse Park, and it was also involved to some extent—often to a very large extent—in the many downtown façade improvements and full-scale renovations in the downtown area. In 1988, when the commission won an additional $13 million in funding and a seven-year extension of its tenure, Peter Aucella was able to point to a ratio of ten private dollars spent for every public dollar invested in the city s redevelopment.

Many of Lowell's impressive accomplishments since 1978 can be traced to the substantial level of federal investment in the city's revitalization project over a period of two decades, a sustained commitment that has generally not been matched in other deindustrialized places. As Peter Aucella put it, "Lowell was created to be a model, you know, for other cities to follow. Of course, as soon as it ran into some costs, the President and Congress said, 'Oh, we can't repeat that—that cost too much money!' And you know what, when the other cities come here and they look at this, they say, 'Yeah, I mean, the level of problem you're solving, takes some money. If you don't put [in] the resources, it ain't gonna happen.'" Paul Marion, the commission's director of cultural affairs from 1984 to 1989, also told me that the money "made a huge difference, I'm convinced. We had a cultural affairs budget in those years that was as large as some states have. . . . We would get like $400,000 a year for arts and humanities in the preservation district alone, you know. It was unbelievable. And it yielded so much good work."

Preservation Commission staff numbered about fifteen at the agency's peak. The first executive director was Fred Faust, formerly a Paul Tsongas aide. Faust left in 1985 to work in real estate management and development, and after a brief interregnum, Peter Aucella, another former Tsongas aide who was then the head of the city's planning and development department, was hired to replace him. Well aware that plum public jobs in Lowell tended to be awarded through patronage, Tsongas made sure that his own influence decided who was hired for such strategically important positions within the planning and development realm, assuring the tight integration that has been a hallmark of Lowell's culture-based project. During its seventeen-year life, thanks to the continued presence of Paul Tsongas in the city and the leadership of two Tsongas loyalists, the Preservation Commission became the point of articulation for many interests and strategies. In particular, it served as a crucial instrument for connecting the economic redevelopment agenda with the preservation and interpretation of history and culture.

Nowhere was this connection clearer than in the conflict over where to situate the national park's main interpretive area. In the 1978 legislation, the park had been charged with acquiring property and establishing exhibits in the Suffolk/Wannalancit Mill, a manufacturing complex slightly outside the central downtown area. The Wannalancit Mill was then occupied by the locally run Lowell Museum and a still-operating textile firm that park planners hoped would function as a "real-life" work exhibit to complement their historical displays. The Preservation Commission, meanwhile, was charged with acquiring and helping to develop the Boott Mill complex, which was closer to downtown and viewed by Tsongas and others as an important site for new residential and commercial office space in the city. They wanted the national park to act as an anchor in the Boott complex to jump-start its overall redevelopment. The impasse continued for some time. As one early park staffer recalled:

> The park staff . . . [was] unanimous in support of . . . the idea of locating at Wannalancit. And the commission staff was unanimous in favor of the Boott. So it was clear that somebody had to break this difference. It wasn't going to happen by itself. And as I recall it, we spent several days or a

week before the meeting preparing for it, because we had our act together. We were going to make *the* case for the Wannalancit. And the meeting took place in [Acting Superintendent Jim] Brown's office. Tsongas walked in with the commission staff and he said to Brown, "I understand you want to locate at the Wannalancit." And Brown said, "Yes, Senator." And before he could finish his sentence, Tsongas said something like, "Well, good luck getting the funding," and turned to walk out. And the conversation lasted another five or ten minutes, and that was that.

The national park shifted its plans to the Boott Mill, where it has fulfilled the role that Tsongas and the commission envisioned for it (and where commercial office space is now the most expensive in Lowell).[20]

The Preservation Commission, then, served as an important bridge between public and private, cultural and economic agendas within Lowell's overall redevelopment project. As Loretta Ryan has pointed out, "In taking on an entrepreneurial role in the city, the Preservation Commission promoted the concept of 'public-private partnership' which represented a departure from the traditional twentieth century hostility between the public and private sectors in Lowell. In a sense, however, the new "partnership" can be seen as a return to the close early nineteenth century relationship between government and industry" (1987:362). Lowell's founders were similarly adept at gaining state support for their industrial and social experiments, in such forms as loosened restrictions on how corporations could operate, public subsidies for privately planned railroads and other infrastructural projects, and favorable tariff policies. Today's support mechanisms are more likely to include zoning regulations, tax breaks, government grants and loans, and—most important for the subject of this study—public funding for the many cultural activities that have become an integral part of postindustrial redevelopment efforts.

At least in theory, those cultural activities—public art, public history, historic preservation efforts, festivals—could stand as counterpractices that might balance or question the more commercially oriented interests of the other components of Lowell's experiment and the coherence of the vision that the experiment promotes. As Deutsche has argued about public art in particular, "Public art must disrupt, rather than secure, the apparent coherence of its new urban sites. . . . Participation in urban design and planning enmeshes public art, unwittingly or not, in spatial politics, but public art can also help appropriate the city, organized to repress contradictions, as a vehicle for illuminating them." (1996:xvi, 78). Exactly the same might be said of public history—particularly the kinds of labor, economic, and social history practiced by public and academic historians associated with Lowell NHP. But when such activities are supported almost entirely by the same funds and agencies that are actively promoting economic redevelopment—when a plan such as Lowell's makes use of what Mary Blewett has termed "public history as venture capital" (1989a:283)—their critical potential is dramatically undercut or altogether lost. This undercutting process is by no means simple or uncontested, as I will show in the final two chapters. But it is highly effective, as I hope my reading of these three tours has shown. The interpretive products of the national park are marked by many of the influences that have helped to shape them, but the most consistent and striking result is that park interpretation is not part of any critical public discussion about the long-term contemporary economic, social, and political processes of which it is a part.

I conclude my discussion of the Lowell Historic Preservation Commission by noting that, when the commission finally closed its doors in 1995, it did not altogether disappear. Commission and park managers were able to enlist support from National Park Service administrators and Congressional sources so that some of its vestigial functions— nominally its oversight of the canal and riverway project plus some smaller undertakings—could be moved under the administrative and financial umbrella of the national park. Commission Director Aucella was made Assistant Superintendent for Development at the park, a position largely independent of the normal Park Service hierarchy. Although in his new role he supervises only a small staff, Aucella retains control over considerable funding and has the ability to continue raising money from outside sources. He also remains an important player in Lowell's broader redevelopment efforts, as demonstrated during the two-year period when he was "loaned" by the park to the city to oversee the construction of the city's stadium and arena. Thus the national park, which initially represented the least local, most potentially independent critical voice within the revitalization experiment, has become even more closely knitted into the economic development agenda that drives the overall effort.

The Costs of Coherence

For Peter Aucella, historic preservation is a very straightforward process. In his words, "Our job is just to bring it back—to bring back [a building's] original character." Aucella is also able to conceive of a project like Lowell's as a set task with a beginning and an end—a coherent, totalizing vision. As he told me,

> Right now what challenges me is seeing whether it is possible to actually finish the revitalization of an area. I mean, is it possible? And of course, it's a career, and you don't see anything done overnight. But I mean, can we really get the rest of the Boott Mills redeveloped. The Mass. Mills. The Lawrence Mills. The Assets buildings. . . . [I]n a few years we're going to have every one of the historic buildings in the master plan done. And that's pretty amazing. Could we ever see any of them done, was the question before. . . . So it's actually a very good time to consider, can we take it the rest of the way?

Like the linear history of the Run of the Mill tour and the unifying ethnicity of the Acre tour, however, this imposed coherence masks many kinds of omissions and exclusions. In Deutsche's words, "The perception of a coherent space cannot be separated from a sense of what threatens that space, of what it would like to exclude" (1996:278). I next examine some of these exclusions, and some of the social costs of pursuing Lowell's impressive and cohesive preservation-based revitalization.

Some of these costs are financial. Like many other municipalities, Lowell has given generous tax credits and other deals to businesses and developers in the hope of sparking new economic activity. Especially in the case of ventures that are supposed to improve the overall "quality of life"—sports facilities, artists' developments, and other cultural or recreational activities—the city has been generous. I have already noted its substantial reduction in rent for the minor-league hockey team; Drew Weber, the owner of its highly profitable minor-league baseball team, the Lowell Spinners, has similarly benefited from the city's largesse, paying an extraordinarily low $25,000 a year to use the city-owned ball park (Campanini 2002). In 2002, Weber opened negotiations to bring another minor-league baseball team to nearby Manchester, New Hampshire, while simultaneously rejecting LDFC proposals to expand the Lowell park, a move harshly criticized by many in Lowell. Especially grating to some critics was the fact that Weber had taken into partnership one of the developers who had bought the former Wang towers for $525,000 in 1994, renovated them with the help of a sizeable tax break and a city-guaranteed $4 million line of credit, then sold them four years later for $100 million (Scott 2002).[21]

The fate of another former Wang property, the downtown education center, illustrates a different kind of financial cost. When Lowell structures built or renovated with the help of public funds have proven unprofitable to their developers, public entities have often stepped in to fill the empty spaces. Thus the downtown Wang building is now home to the state-funded Middlesex Community College. Similarly, the upper floors of the Bon Marché building, formerly a Merrimack Street department store, once housed some of Wang s offices. On his August 2001 tour, Peter Aucella described how the city government itself filled the empty space in the now beautifully renovated building:

> The second floor actually holds . . . the Lowell School Department's administrative offices. . . . [W]hen this development effort came along, the city council said, "Well, the school department's looking for a place to go, we have a building we want to see renovated that's going to need millions of dollars worth of work and it's got to be financeable. So you need tenants." So the city council said, "Let's get the school offices in this building."
>
> The school committee reaction was, "Hey, what do we care about downtown? We're running the schools. It's not our business to be worrying about being in the heart of downtown and renovating buildings." Well, that set the city council off something fierce, and they said, "It is absolutely your business, as a public agency, as an agency of city government, to play a role in the revitalization of the city. We're telling you that we expect you to be here." So they kept working this in the school committee until they had enough votes, and bingo, the school offices are in there. And the school administrators love it. It was never them, it was the politics of the situation, of, "Gee, we've got to pay a real rent per square foot?"

In this case, as in many others, the dissenting voices who objected to "the politics of the situation"—the close links between public and private interests, and the continued channeling of public money into the hands of private developers and businesses—were overridden by the efficiency and determination of Lowell's network of public-private partnerships—a system so effective that it has sometimes been called the Lowell "delivery system."

In addition to the considerable public financial costs involved in supporting Lowell's ongoing redevelopment, there has often been a process of quiet displacement of people and businesses from the areas designated for preservation and redevelopment. This displacement has been much less widespread and violent than the urban renewal projects of the 1950s and 1960s, when virtually the entire French Canadian neighborhood of Little Canada was razed, or when the route of the Lowell Connector, created to link the city with the new Interstate 495, cut a wide swath through another working-class neighborhood. As in most places affected by such draconian strategies, public backlash contributed to the adoption of more humane and measured approaches to urban revitalization. Displacement now occurs in small, sometimes unremarked increments, but it continues to take place nonetheless. To give one example from my fieldwork period, the city expropriated an Acre property owned by one of the area's two remaining independent drugstores as part of a privately financed relandscaping project. Unable to afford the move into the new location offered by the city—in a senior center then being built in the Acre—the pharmacists regretfully sold their profitable business to one of the three large chains that dominate the pharmacy field in Massachusetts (Hughes 2002b).

In another, deeply ironic instance, the city planning department actively courted a small Boston arts organization, the Revolving Museum, by providing economic incentives for it to purchase a building in the center of Lowell's designated arts district. The Revolving Museum opened to great fanfare in the summer of 2002 and was heralded as an exciting new addition to the city's cultural milieu and a stimulus for further arts-related development, including the creation of more artists' lofts in downtown buildings. Shortly afterward, an antiques business whose owner had been extremely active in promoting the work of local artists was evicted from its storefront across the street from the new museum (Hughes 2002c). Many people noted the link between the rising profile of the arts district and the eviction of a business whose lease had been negotiated several years earlier when real estate in the area had not been so valuable. "Frankly," the Lowell *Sun* editorialized, "that's part and parcel of what happens when a real estate market perks up" (Lowell *Sun* 2002c). When an upscale housewares boutique opened in the same storefront early the next year, a reporter for the *Sun* noted, "As the city's arts district begins to gentrify, a creative sprawl is beginning to percolate. With a coffee house, museum and art institute thriving, a modern home decor shop was not far behind. After all, what's the point of living in a loft without cool accoutrements?" (Deely 2003) The irony is that the Revolving Museum, perhaps the biggest spur to the gentrification of the arts district, had itself been displaced from its former home on Boston's once run-down, now gentrifying waterfront, and came to Lowell like many others seeking a comparatively less expensive home in an increasingly expensive region. Moreover, the museum sponsored several exhibits and installations in Boston designed to draw attention to the displacement of artists and others in the postindustrial economy— precisely the kind of counterpractice advocated by Rosalyn Deutsche as a way to disrupt the imposed coherence of redeveloped urban places. Whether the Revolving Museum will find itself able to continue making such statements in its new setting, or whether, like public history, it is already too enmeshed in the mechanisms of economic redevelopment, remains an open question.

Peter Aucella's tour provided evidence of many other such small dislocations and exclusions. In speaking of a building close to the park's headquarters on Kirk Street, Aucella told his audience that:

> In the Commission's plan for downtown, it had targeted this building as a building [that] would tell the story of labor, within the labor history of Lowell and America. As time went by we realized that we had one-third of the space to tell the story and the other two-thirds were run by [a] slumlord who had an outrageous price tag on the building. The other interesting thing is that while our section was unoccupied, there were, no kidding, twenty-three families, southeast Asian families, crowded into the remainder of the building. Now, you realize it's not that big a building, and I've never wanted to do the counting, but I swear that's the number that we were told by the code enforcement people. There were a grand total of three toilets—I use the term "toilet," not bathrooms, in there—they didn't actually have toilet seats, so—it was really, truly a slum.
>
> So we had a dual debate about obviously we wanted to see the building renovated, we wanted to see if national park exhibits could be in there, although that seemed to get more and more secondary all the time, far less important. And then we—the question is, well, you've got poor people living there, do you try to improve it for the poor people, to try to maintain affordable housing, or are we not doing them a service at all?

Are we better off to just say, "Listen, this isn't working?" This number of people—they don't belong there anyway, and certainly that owner wasn't going to do anything about it.

Well, the bank kind of came through and said, "Listen, we want this property," and actually what is in there now is the bank's mortgage department. By the way, this [building next door] is the old elementary school, and it has the bank's data processing operations in it. So it's kind of interesting to see the reuses that you might not suspect from the outside. At any rate, the bank did come in, they bought the one-third from the Preservation Commission, and they paid the price to the slumlord, they emptied out the building, renovated the interior, you know, spent about a million and a half dollars renovating that building. And again, you know, putting the chimneys back on and putting on some of the features that had gone by.

Aucella's account of this transaction avoided both the question of what became of the twenty-three displaced families and the very close relationship of the city's banks to the overall preservation project. Instead, his presentation went on to focus on the architectural details of the building's renovation, drawing on what Deutsche has called "the depoliticized aesthetics instrumental in portraying redevelopment as the preservation of tradition" (1996:xv). In such a portrayal, as Deutsche notes, "Architectural efforts to preserve traditional appearances . . . hide the proof of rupture" (1996:32), and losses and displacements are always secondary to the larger public good. In Aucella's presentation, and in Lowell's heritage redevelopment project generally, that greater good is presented as a rising tide that will eventually float all boats, even those of poor residents or marginal businesses who may suffer in the short term. We are back to Paul Tsongas's confident assertion that, even though the plan created some conflicts of interest and channeled public money to some profiteering developers, such instances are tolerable because of the plan's overall benefit to everyone in the city.

This brings us to the question of whether everyone in Lowell *has* benefited from the city's redevelopment effort. An examination of some demographic facts about the city reveals that this is far from the case. Despite—or rather, because of—Lowell's success at attracting many people from the high end of the new economy, the city's revitalization has exacted a social toll in its contribution to the widening rich–poor split and increased economic volatility so characteristic of postindustrial, service- and knowledge-based economies. Although Lowell can boast of many achievements over the past quarter century, the 2000 census showed that 17 percent of its population still lived below the poverty line—higher than the national average of 12.4 percent and almost double the state average of 9.3 percent. Unemployment, too, remains generally higher in Lowell than in the state as a whole. In January of 2002, unemployment stood at 7.6 percent, while the Massachusetts average was 4.4 percent (Lowell *Sun* 2002a). Workers in Lowell are doubly vulnerable to swings of the economic pendulum. Of the city's jobs, 24.2 percent are still in the manufacturing sector, considerably higher than the rate for the state (12.8 percent) and nation (14.1 percent) (2000 U.S. Census). More than most places in the region and country, then, the city will continue to see job losses as part of the long cycle of economic restructuring that began for Lowell in the 1920s. At the same time, its links with the growing new economy are less robust and far-reaching than, for example, Boston's, leaving it more susceptible to the kind of sudden shifts that sent Wang Laboratories into bankruptcy in the early 1990s. Moreover, much of the new economy throughout Boston's metropolitan area is fueled by federal funding for research and development in the health and human services and defense sectors, funding that is often linked to changing political winds.[22] Such fluctuations are a hazard of the new economy and are reflected in the fact that during the 1980s and 1990s, the entire state of Massachusetts experienced higher economic peaks and lower troughs than the country as a whole (Forrant et al. 2001:7). But the cycle is even steeper in Lowell itself. In 2002, Lowell's employment rate fell by 4.1 percent, as 5,200 jobs disappeared, mostly from the high-technology sector—the fourth highest rate of job loss in the nation for that year (Tutalo 2003b).

Lowell's "rebirth," then, has not solved the problems of poverty, high unemployment, and economic vulnerability that have long plagued the city. It has, however—in concert with the overheated real estate market of postindustrial metropolitan Boston—made Lowell a much more expensive place to live than most comparable small cities in New England. Average housing prices in Lowell have risen steadily since the end of the recession of the early 1990s, making a leap of 25 percent from December 2001 to December 2002 alone (Lowell *Sun* 2003). According to a 2003 study by the National Low Income Housing Coalition, housing in Massachusetts was the least affordable in the nation, with Boston the most expensive urban area in the state and Lowell coming in second. The average fair-market rent for a two-bedroom apartment in the Lowell area in 2002 was $1,065, a price that was "affordable" only to those making more than twenty dollars an hour.[23] Rents are generally higher in the renovated downtown mills and other buildings; Peter Aucella noted, on his August 2001 tour, that a 1,000-square-foot apartment in the Massachusetts Mills rented for about $1,300 a month. He also pointed out proudly that the occupancy rate in the building had been close to 100 percent since the building was renovated. Given Lowell's persistent poverty rates, I was puzzled by this claim until I began meeting new resident after new resident who had come to Lowell to escape Boston's even-higher housing prices. One park visitor on an Acre walking tour, for instance, told me that he found his rent at Massachusetts Mills quite cheap in comparison with the much higher prices along the "Silicon Alley" corridor of Route 128, where he had previously worked and lived. Although affordable housing is a vexed issue in Lowell municipal politics, as in many other places in Massachusetts, it has not been a priority within the Historic Preservation District—just the opposite, in fact. Fred Faust, the first director of the Lowell Historic Preservation Commission and now a real estate developer himself, told me: "I don't think that Lowell has a real commitment at this point to affordable housing. Elements of Lowell, and certain organizations in Lowell, do, but I don't think there's a real housing strategy, and in fact people have seen affordable housing I think in several [municipal] administrations as a sign that you're not successful."

Developers have created affordable housing primarily when it has been to their financial advantage to do so—for example, in the early Market Mills development, when federal tax credits provided a way to raise enough equity to complete a project—or when more high-end alternatives have not been feasible. After telling his audience the story of the property owner who ran afoul of City Manager Joe Tully in the 1980s, Aucella noted that the city had finally taken the building in question and sold it to a non-profit organization that was about to begin renovating it: "It will be housing, it will still be on the affordable side of the spectrum. [The foundation that bought it] actually invited in developers to try to make it condos or something more upscale, and they said, 'Listen, you're right on the sidewalk, it's just not the right atmosphere for it,' even though we thought we had some potential with the nice view.

So that's what it'll be." Of another building close to the Market Mills Visitor Center, Aucella said, "It's 44,000 square feet, great upper-floor space, potential retail space to enliven the street. It was for many years an electrical supply house, which really was not a good mix with the activity here. So we're hoping for more restaurants, arts, stuff like that."

The first choice in the current economic climate, then, is for market-rate housing and other uses that are compatible with the postindustrial image Lowell is working so hard to create, rather than housing that might be affordable for the city's many poor residents or uses that might clash with the officially sanctioned vision of the downtown as a cultural center. Thanks to political skill, aggressive place-marketing, and dogged determination, that vision has been realized to a remarkable extent since the 1970s. Yet success has not rectified, and has in some ways intensified, the imbalances and volatility found in postindustrial places. And Lowell National Historical Park, created to be a catalyst for the broader redevelopment scheme described in this chapter, does little to address or question these new economic realities. In these three chapters, I have implied that this omission is closely related to the fact that the park is a central part of the redevelopment mechanism by which those realities— and the image of the reborn Lowell—are being created. In Part III, I look more closely at the role of professional public historians within that redevelopment project: who they are, how they operate within the social world of Lowell's new experiment, and why their critical questioning has made so few inroads into the subject matter of Lowell's more recent history or the larger trajectory of capitalist development that has always been such a salient factor in shaping this city.

PART III

PUBLIC HISTORY IN LOWELL

FIGURE 12. Students visiting the Tsongas Industrial History Center participate energetically in the "Workers on the Line" workshop, designed to teach them about industrial working conditions. TSONGAS INDUSTRIAL HISTORY CENTER.

CHAPTER 6

Rituals of Reconnection
Work as History and History as Work in
Postindustrial Lowell

Every other Wednesday morning in the winter and spring of 2002, I observed meetings of a team of public historians who were redesigning the final segments of the Boott Cotton Mills Museum exhibit. The meetings were held in a small conference room in what had originally been a circular staircase-tower in the Boott Mills complex. Directly outside the room, the hallway was open to the workshop areas of the Tsongas Industrial History Center, one floor below, and occasionally we would hear large groups of schoolchildren coming and going. Less often, in the late morning, there would be a more surprising sound: a chorus of young voices, energetically shouting, "*Strike! Strike! Strike! Strike!*" The public historians around the table generally acknowledged this with a brief smile before returning to work.

Eventually, I found an explanation for the shouting. The Tsongas Center offers various "hands-on" educational workshops for school groups, focusing on waterpower, immigration, and other themes integral to historic interpretation in Lowell. One of the workshops, "Workers on the Line," puts students through a role-playing exercise in which they serve on an assembly line turning out decorated towels (made, in this case, of paper rather than cloth) (fig. 12). The workshop leader, in the role of overseer, gradually speeds up the pace of production and reduces the number of workers, until the whole operation falls apart in chaos. At that point, the workshop leader becomes a labor organizer who convenes a meeting of the "Teenaged Workers of the World" union to discuss grievances and possible actions to redress them. Often—though not invariably—these meetings lead to noisy calls for a strike for better working conditions.

Once I understood what the "Strike!" calls meant, those occasional noisy moments during the Wednesday morning meetings added a new layer to the situation I was observing. Upstairs, I was watching people at work in the new economy, busy producing ideas, experiences, and information that would be used in various ways by various audiences. These knowledge workers—the public historians at Lowell NHP—were struggling to make statements about work, and about the changing nature of work in the recent past. And I was trying to understand what they were doing *as* work—thinking about why these people had gravitated to these particular kinds of jobs, what their own working conditions were like, and how their labor fit within the broader economic scheme of things in Lowell and beyond. Downstairs, meanwhile, some of the products of that labor were being used to help educate a new generation of workers and citizens, most of whom would never directly experience the kind of labor they were simulating in their role as "workers on the line." And although the work of the Tsongas Industrial History Center is tangential to my overall study, it will become clear in this chapter that the professional educators who populate it—as administrators, workshop leaders, and teachers who bring their classes on field trips—overlap in very significant ways with the public historians at the park and the visitors who come to Lowell.

This chapter is a demographic study of the public historians who work in the interpretive division of Lowell National Historical Park— people who earn a living in the postindustrial economy by interpreting industrial labor and immigration history. First, I explore the professional, socioeconomic, and ethnic backgrounds of these workers, as a prelude to determining how those backgrounds help to shape what they do at the park and their choice of public history as a career. I use my surveys of park visitors to investigate similar aspects of the visitors' backgrounds and their reasons for coming to Lowell NHP, and then combine the data about the two groups—public historians and visitors—in an analysis of the ritual ways in which the park simultaneously helps to create and to bridge various kinds of temporal and socioeconomic differences. Finally, I consider some alternative approaches to this ritual function and their implications for the possibility of a more critical public history in Lowell.

Lowell's Public Historians within the Public History Movement

I have already discussed the genesis of the contemporary public history movement, noting that it was shaped by the twin sources of the academic job crisis of the 1970s and the left-leaning movement toward more engaged scholarship, shared authority, and social history in the 1960s and 1970s. The public history field has continued to develop within a changing postindustrial economy in which culture and knowledge are increasingly important as products, and in which the lines between education, entertainment, and memorialization continue to blur. The careers and value systems of Lowell's public historians demonstrate all these processes. All the people I interviewed were familiar with the term "public history," although they varied in the extent to which they identified themselves with it. I discovered three general categories of identification among my informants. The first category was made up of those who most explicitly saw themselves as part of a field called public history, and who actively participated in that field—for example, by belonging to the National Council on Public History or other related professional organizations, attending the conferences of those groups, reading and/ or contributing to their journals, and so on. Many of them belonged to the first generation of public historians. In general, these people had higher levels of training in the historical discipline than others at the park. Most held master's degrees or Ph.D.'s, and had entered the public history field as a conscious way of finding employment as historians.

The second category contained people with a specific interest in history and the teaching of history, but without advanced (that is, graduate level) training in the discipline. Many of these were former or would-be teachers; several had entered the Lowell public history realm by working as seasonal (school-year) instructors at the Tsongas Industrial History Center, a not uncommon stepping-stone into more regular, secure, and better-paid permanent positions at the national park. Like those in the third group, these workers included several who came to public history as part of a mid-career change. The third category included those who had initially been less interested in history per se than in a particular kind of job—one where they could work directly with people, spend time outdoors, work in a nonprofit or educational setting, or secure a permanent federal government position. The category included some who had entered the National Park Service during the early period of Lowell NHP's development and expansion, as well as some midcareer newcomers. For these people, historical training and education came with their jobs, rather than having been earlier interests. People in this category tended to identify themselves much more strongly with the NPS than with the public history movement; somewhat less diehard Park Service employees often say of such people, "If you cut them, they'll bleed green and gray" (the colors of the Park Service uniform).[1] Although there were differences in specific motivation and training among people in these three categories, I found very broad similarities in their socio-economic and ethnic backgrounds, as well as their general politics and values. In what follows, therefore, I will be treating workers in the inter-pretive division of Lowell NHP as a group, while noting variations where appropriate.

Among those in the first and second categories—that is, people with some level of academic historical training—many had pursued degrees in history out of interest or love, and only encountered the concept of public history after they began looking for ways to earn a living in the historical field. This trajectory was typified by one manager at Lowell NHP, who left the hospitality business in the late 1970s after realizing that his late-night and weekend hours were "not very conducive to fam-ily life":

> So that's when I decided to go back to school and study something I had an interest in. . . . And always with an eye to using the degree—which was my wife's big question, is "What are you going to do with that?" . . . [I thought] of working either in a museum setting or a historic site setting.
>
> *Were you thinking of the term 'public history'? Or would this be before the term was out there?*
> The term was there, though I really probably wasn't all that aware of it or its meaning at that point.
>
> *You just wanted to get a job in history.*
> Right. Exactly. It wasn't until my professors were writing recommenda-tions for grad school that one of them pointed out that "from all my stu-dents, [this one] would be among the top that I would recommend for a career in public history." And public history—of course! That's what it is!

Among the interpretive staff at Lowell NHP, I encountered only one person who was trained as a public historian per se; she had graduated in the 1990s with a master's degree in public history from one of the many credentialing programs that sprang up in the late 1970s and early 1980s. Even this second-generation public historian, though, found it difficult to define the field she had been trained in: "When you say 'public historian'—it's better now, but I remember first starting out not even knowing myself what it really is. And I think it's something that is defined as you work through. . . . My parents will tell me all the time, they'll tell people that I'm a park ranger, and you know, they'll picture me out in Montana on a horse. 'No, it's so much *more* than that!' It's so much deeper." One early manager and interpretive planner at Lowell NHP began graduate school with the assumption that "I had to go through to get a Ph.D. and be a teacher." After studying and teaching at a prestigious university, he became "thoroughly disenchanted" with the academic star system and the use of poorly paid graduate students (who at that time had few expectations of an eventual teaching position of their own) to carry much of the teaching load. He was recruited by the National Park Service to be the staff historian at a small historical park, seized on the creation of Lowell NHP as an exciting interpretive and professional opportunity, and rose quickly through the NPS hierarchy. "I hadn't thought about [working outside the academy]," he told me, "but it seemed like a good idea, you know, work as a historian. And also the job market in academe at that time was just crashing."

Many of the mid- or upper-level public historians I talked to had experienced at firsthand the "jobs crisis" that began for historians in the 1970s. One described how he "was on a Ph.D. track and . . . realized that that wasn't going to happen. You know, my dissertation advisor had a half a dozen students, and he was having trouble placing his top students. And I wasn't his top student. I wasn't his bottom student, I was somewhere in between. And I looked at the whole situation and I said, 'What's going to happen at the end of this?' And I also had no desire to go to some tiny provincial university and spend the rest of my life." This man switched to library school and ultimately entered the public history world as an archivist and collections manager. A younger colleague, who did complete her Ph.D. in history in the mid-1990s, chose to make a career in museums partly because of an interest in working in a public setting but also because, in her words, "You know, in this day and age, none of us think we *can* teach"—that is, the collegiate job market continues to shrink, so remaining in an academic setting is not necessarily an option even for those inclined to pursue it.

Along with the jobs crisis, the leftward, progressivist movement linked with the new social history of the 1960s and 1970s was also clearly reflected in the words of Lowell's public historians. Without exception, all of my informants identified themselves as being left of center on the political spectrum. Most described themselves as moderate leftists, not radicals. Many said that their political preferences had been partially shaped by parents who had been working-class Democratic voters; those who came of age during the 1960s also credited the social movements of that period with having helped to form their views. The specific middle–left position of public historians can perhaps best be measured by their comments about capitalism as an economic system and their own positions within contemporary capitalism. These comments combined (a) varying levels of ambivalence or doubt about capitalism and its human and environmental effects, (b) a desire to have a comfortable life within this system, and (c) some sense that the pursuit of public history as a career could be a way to reconcile the tensions between being critical of capitalism and yet wanting to live prosperously within it. This combination of factors was best illustrated by a woman who said:

> I have a schizophrenic relationship with capitalism. So—I have a materialistic side, I have a strong collective sense of democracy and justice that really is not necessarily compatible with something I might want to buy at the Gap, you know. I feel small in the larger world, as a player. . . . If I feel secure as a worker in the economy, I certainly don't feel confident as someone who's able to change things in a major way. So I'm not really an activist. But I am an activist in the sense that I really see my role as a professional and as a historian to help people reflect upon current conditions. And so there is an activist piece to that. . . . [B]ack to your question—where am I in [global capitalism]? I don't know! I mean, I think I'm finding my way in it like most visitors are.

This woman told me that she did not feel particularly driven to be "more engaged and more thoughtful about that in my own life"—that is, her misgivings about the potential social injustices inherent in capitalism were not strong enough to cause her to alter her own everyday patterns of living, with which she was generally satisfied. Another park employee, a young frontline ranger, exhibited this same combination of being critical of capitalism as a system while seeking a comfortable life within it. He said, "I feel that there's a lot of negative sides to [contemporary capitalism] that aren't really talked about a lot, and that it's sort of . . . it's not little things that I see as being easily solved, it's more the very system itself, which tends to, I don't want to say 'dehumanize,' but it . . . doesn't have a lot of compassion." He added that while he didn't necessarily feel the need for a great deal of money and material possessions, he did recognize that he was becoming more and more enmeshed in the economic system (he had recently bought a house, partly on the strength of having achieved a permanent position in the Park Service) and acknowledged that it would be nice to be able to achieve the level of prosperity that his engineer father had provided:

> It's frustrating, you know, that my yard is smaller [than the house I grew up in] and it backs up to a railroad track.
>
> *It would be nice to have that, a bigger yard.*
> Oh, yeah, I'd love to have that. Absolutely.

Many of the public historians associated with Lowell clearly expressed a desire to avoid the for-profit sector. For some, this was a lifelong choice:

> I have *never* had any interest in being in business, to make money or make a product. I always knew I was going to do something other than that, as far as teaching or some kind of public service. But you know, I'm a child of the sixties. . . . I could never see the point of doing something in order just to make money. I wouldn't mind having a lot of money, but you know, to be a businessman, manufacturing a product, or a service— I suppose you can get into that sort of thing, and I don't mean to say that people are not doing something valuable in the business world, because I know that they are. It's just never something that I ever thought I would want to do.

Others, often having worked in the hospitality or retail trades, had tired of the demands and upheavals of the service economy, and were seeking work that was both more meaningful and more reliable. One man, twice downsized in the highly competitive "big box" store market, "wanted to be in a job where I didn't have to worry about the economics" and where he could pursue a desire to serve the public in some more personally rewarding way. He clearly saw the corporate world as a cut-throat place and drew a revealing parallel between his wife's job at a phone company and the experience of Lowell's earliest mill workers:

> She's like the last generation, when they hired like hordes of women— almost like the mill girl thing, because the phone company did the same thing. They would hire these hordes of women, and they had to have high school diplomas—

Respectable women.
Absolutely. That's right. . . . [I]f you could get in the phone company, you know, it was a good job. It still is. And it's a union job, it's very well protected. And . . . she has seen this thing just change like you wouldn't believe over twenty four years. . . . And now my wife is like the last of that generation, because they only hire professional people . . . where you've got to have something beyond a high school training. . . . And of course they're dying to get rid of these [earlier] people, because . . . they change these jobs to be nonunion.

For this man, as for many of his colleagues, achieving a public history job within the National Park Service was a way to withdraw from that cut-throat arena of corporate capitalism. Although he expressed no direct sense that his new job might be a way to raise these issues in public or to participate in any kind of general debate about social and economic justice, he nonetheless made a clear and critical linkage of current new-economy labor struggles with the history of labor and exploitation as it is interpreted at Lowell. For him, as for many of his colleagues, his choice of career appeared to provide a way to reconcile his search for a secure, rewarding job with his desire to remove himself from some of the more egregious characteristics of the postindustrial labor market, especially its for-profit sector: the weakening of labor organizing, the shrinking middle ground between low-end, de-skilled jobs and those requiring ever higher levels of education and skill, and the volatility that pervades the growth areas of the new economy.

In general, higher-status public historians (those who worked in offices rather than on the "front lines") were more articulate about their relationship to contemporary capitalism. But they, too, revealed a sense of ambivalence and sometimes contradiction when speaking of their place within the economic system they inhabited. One overtly radical and activist public historian, who was responsible for some of the most hard-hitting and Marxist-inflected elements of the Boott Cotton Mills exhibit, was quite explicit about wanting to use his work in public history to foster various kinds of public critiques and discussions. Yet he also acknowledged that there was something of a paradox at the heart of his work as a public historian: "If I'm still philosophically inclined towards anarchism and I'm working for the federal government, a federal bureaucracy, you know, that's a huge contradiction! So there are many contradictions that we all have. I think you just have to accept the fact that that's the case and then move on. . . . But . . . I still think that capitalism as it's played out in this culture is an unfair system. And I would like to see it changed."

When I asked my informants what they thought should be done to counter the inherent unfairness they saw within the capitalist system, most pointed to the state as a necessary counterbalance to the market. In the words of one man,

> I think that what you have to do is harness the force that drives it and shepherd it and keep it moving in a generally constructive direction. . . . [C]apitalist business endeavor constantly evolves and changes, and it develops new forms. And so you have to then look at your regulatory agencies and ask whether or not they have evolved to meet these new challenges. And I do think that the excesses we've seen in the late '90s and whatnot are the sorts of things that are going to cause people to very soberly reassess the need for, continued need for government regulation. And I say government regulation because government is the only force that's large enough. Labor is not, organized labor is largely unheard-from. Organized labor never represented more than 25 percent of the working people of this country . . . even at its height, and it can never stand as a countervailing force.

Even the more centrist of my informants shared this belief that government could and should act to correct the excesses of the free market. Yet most were focused on the idea of regulation; few saw the kinds of state-funded enterprises they were themselves involved in as also a government response to the operation of market forces—in this case, to the kinds of problems caused by deindustrialization, capital flight, and economic restructuring. With the exception of one upper-level manager, who had been instrumental in planning both Lowell NHP and a national heritage corridor in a deindustrialized area of southeast Massachusetts and Rhode Island, none of the public historians I spoke to showed any direct recognition that the state had chosen to invest in their work *as historians* as part of a larger compensatory mechanism that was, at bottom, designed to counterbalance the workings of the market.

This contradictory consciousness manifested itself quite clearly in the meetings of the Boott Mill exhibit redesign team, to which I referred at the beginning of this chapter. This redesign project was the one process at the park where I saw a group of public historians actively seeking to engage in a critical and complex way with the task of interpreting present-day Lowell and its relationship to economic globalization and the new postindustrial U.S. economy. Yet, as with the interpretations of these subjects elsewhere in the park, the planning team's discussions revealed a reluctance to make explicit connections between their own work and the socioeconomic projects of which it was a part. I originally anticipated that I would spend a substantial part of this study analyzing the Boott redesign process, since it was so germane to the questions I was asking. But the project was still at a such an unfinished stage by the time I completed my research—itself a sign of how complex the park's task of interpreting the present is—that a large-scale analysis seemed premature. Instead, I conclude this section with a briefer discussion of the Boott process, focusing on the patterns I have already elaborated on above.

As the main museum facility at the park, the Boott Cotton Mills Museum focuses on the history of textile production in Lowell from the city's beginnings. Because the textile industry and Lowell essentially parted ways in the early twentieth century, ending this exhibit poses a challenge for the park. Pursuing the textile strand further means moving away from the story of Lowell, while telling the story of Lowell today raises many questions about how to represent the city's emerging postindustrial economy, how critical to be of its much-vaunted "rebirth," how to link developments in Lowell with broader socioeconomic trends, and so on. The public historians who initially planned the exhibit in the 1980s intended to focus on the changing nature of work as a unifying theme in the exhibit's final sections. Visitors would be urged to think about their own options for work in the postindustrial economy, and to see Lowell's experience as a microcosm of changes taking place throughout the United States and beyond. However, time and money ran short at the end of the very protracted and expensive Boott Mill project, and

the planners failed to bring this vision to fruition. Instead, park management took over the design of the final part of the Boott exhibit, creating
two rooms that uncritically celebrated Lowell's economic and cultural
renaissance. The weaknesses of this purely celebratory approach were
immediately apparent. Of the eight businesses featured in a series of
bright, corporate-style displays in the "Lowell in the 1990s" section,
four subsequently went out of business or left Lowell; one of its brightest
stars, Wang Laboratories, filed for bankruptcy just two months after the
exhibit opened. The park's public historians had never been happy with
the end of the exhibit, and in 1999 they applied for and received funds to
redesign it.[2] The planning team members included the most highly credentialed and progressive public historians at the park, making the
exhibit redesign process an excellent site at which to observe my primary
informants at work.[3]

The planning, however, proved to be extremely slow and inconclusive, much to the frustration of everyone on the team. Discussions
seemed circular; the project had fallen badly behind schedule; team
members were undecided as to what they could or should say about
ongoing development and exploitation in the global textile industry and
the uneven, complex nature of Lowell's postindustrial recovery. It was
clear that, at bottom, the progressive public historians on the team
wanted the exhibit to reflect their own critical views of capitalism and
were willing to argue for those views against differing opinions. Frus-
trated during one meeting by a team member's concern that too direct
an approach might provoke controversy, one public historian commented
heatedly that American national mythology supported the notion that
the free market was the solution to every problem, "and if anything challenges that, it's 'Oh, who threw the dead cat on the table?' If you're so
afraid of this, why the hell are you in the exhibit business at all?" His
brief outburst seemed to lessen the nearly chronic tension that pervaded
the Boott team meetings, as though he had articulated something that
most team members felt but had hesitated to say so openly. One of his
colleagues responded by saying, "If we believe in this—and we do—then
it behooves us to work the system to make sure that those views are in
there," noting that each successive generation of public historians had its
own "sensitive matters" that it fought to explore in the public sphere.
Despite this acknowledgement, however, the specific matters facing the
Boott team appeared to keep the group in a state of near-paralysis,

unable to resolve recurring questions or to arrive at a lasting consensus on any proposal. The group was well behind its deadline for producing a draft plan by the time I completed my fieldwork in the summer of 2002; at the time this book was drafted (spring 2004), the planning process was still ongoing.

The public historians on the Boott team clearly shared a general ambivalence about capitalism. Despite their stated desire to have visitors see themselves as agents and participants within the postindustrial economy that affected Lowell and other places, however, it was just as obvious that the public historians were not willing to examine too closely their own roles within that economy. At first it was difficult to see this operating directly, although I did note that the group's discussions tended to become most circular, inconclusive, or fractious at points where they felt they needed to make definite statements about the socioeconomic phenomena they were themselves most firmly embedded within. One day, after a particularly frustrating meeting, the curator who was directing the exhibit redesign project asked me whether I had come to any conclusions yet about what was happening within this process. I mentioned my observation that the group seemed reluctant to look too closely at processes they were personally or professionally involved in, particularly the mechanisms by which Lowell's culture-based revitalization was being achieved. She admitted that, of course, team members were a part of these processes, but added immediately and emphatically, "We can't interpret ourselves!" Being an anthropologist, trained in a discipline that has (at least to some extent) accepted the necessity of seeing our own roles in the social settings we interpret, I was struck by her statement. The kind of self-reflexivity I had come to take for granted was clearly not an element of the curator's thought, or that of other public historians on the Boott team. The team's resistance to this approach was made much clearer when the curator went on maternity leave and one of the team's consultants—a historian of cultural processes with a particular interest in the construction and marketing of "tradition"—took over temporarily. The acting curator proposed taking a deconstructive approach to Lowell's recent history, arguing that it would be highly artificial for the exhibit to talk about contemporary Lowell without exploring the workings of the cultural mechanisms that were such a key part of the city's reimaging efforts. She pushed the group to the point of thinking about their own work—as public historians, educators, and participants in the revitalization experiment—in relation to the larger processes playing out in Lowell and beyond, as in the following exchange in which the group tried to come to terms with how to depict the present-day city:

HISTORIAN: If our goal is to say what Lowell is today, then let's go back to [the] outline, which includes three things: it's a service economy, it's historic preservation, and it's the whole issue of reinventing the city's identity.

COLLECTIONS MANAGER: But is that reinvention of a community a *conscious* thing, or does it just happen? That idea of "reinvention" is an intellectual construct—most people don't do it *consciously*. It's more an ethnic group having a festival or a wedding or going to a social club. . . .

ACTING CURATOR: That's the reason it's useful to look historically at these processes. It shows that some stuff is internal, but it's also external people seizing on it and using it. . . .

TSONGAS CENTER DIRECTOR: The packaging aspect is less important to me than the fact that Lowell continues to be an ethnic city, with new ethnic groups adding to the mix all the time.

COLLECTIONS MANAGER: Right. And we should show that this *should* be an unconscious rather than a conscious process—the new groups bring their traditions from their home culture and add to the mix simply by acting out their lives. . . . So could we phrase this as "how the city is reinventing itself" rather than "how it's being reinvented"?

ACTING CURATOR: This is what culture is—it's both. It's an interplay of all these things. It's very messy, and it's very hard to talk about what's authentic and inauthentic in this setting . . . But the real question is, how do you introduce people to the murkiness of cultural processes?

TSONGAS CENTER DIRECTOR: We may not need to do that.

ACTING CURATOR: But it may cause an underlying questioning
                         among visitors, which I'd like to encourage.
                         I've pushed this in previous exhibits that
                         I've done, and I've seen it shake people. And
                         if we don't address it, it will still lurk under-
                         neath in this section of the exhibit.

Team members strongly resisted this reflexive approach, as this
exchange illustrates. The comment of the Tsongas Center director—
"We may not need to do that"—reflected a wider concern, expressed to
me privately and very forcefully by several people on the team, that the
Boott exhibit should be focused on work, not cultural production, and
that blending the two would be confusing and unnecessary. Culture,
some insisted, was already interpreted in the Working People exhibit—it
had no place in a discussion of Lowell's post–textile economy. Ironically,
these cultural workers seemed unable to conceive of culture *as* work, or
to see the production of knowledge and culture as a key and intentional
element of Lowell's new economy and identity. Even the most progressive among the park's public historians, then, shared with their more
center–left colleagues a reluctance to probe too deeply into the underpinnings of their own socioeconomic positions or public history's position within state-sponsored projects related to economic restructuring
and change. As with the Run of the Mill tour, they worked to avoid
direct questions about privilege and positioning within the developing
postindustrial economy or about their own roles in the kinds of cultural
production and consumption that have helped to constitute postindustrial Lowell. The Boott Mill exhibit planning process showed very
clearly the contradictory consciousness by which public historians
attempt to resolve the tension between activism and acquiescence,
between criticizing the economic system in which they live and wanting
to exist prosperously within it—a tension that considerably complicates
their job of interpreting that economic system to the public.

Recent Socioeconomic Mobility among Public Historians

No one familiar with the world of American museums and historical
sites will be surprised at the news that these places are largely staffed and

visited by college-educated, middle-class people of European descent. However, my interviews with interpretive staff in Lowell revealed that, for most public historians as for myself, this middle-class status was something that they or their families had achieved only quite recently. One ranger talked about growing up in a shoe-manufacturing town: "Most of [the] shoe factories had closed down and vacated by the time I was born, but I did grow up across the street from one of the last remaining shoe companies . . . which is a company that's still in production today. . . . So I grew up in the shadow of a factory! I come from a working-class family." For him, as for several other people I interviewed, working in Lowell resonated with their own sense of having working-class and often urban roots. The man who served as Lowell NHP's first interpretive ranger in 1978 reminisced at a 2002 public forum about this resonance: "Now, what did I know, a kid from Gloucester, a fisherman's son, about mills? Nothing. But I always felt at home here in Lowell because I came from a working man's family, an immigrant family, second generation. . . . I felt very comfortable about the story as well, and the meaning and the importance of the story here in Lowell."

Very often, it was the parents of my informants who had made the move into entry-level managerial or professional work, frequently as engineers, teachers, secretaries, shop foremen, or salespeople. In the majority of cases, my informants or their parents had been the first in their families to go to college (or, in some cases, to complete high school). One ranger told me that his family had definitely been working-class, but, "My mother, though, was trying to certainly bring us . . . up to the middle class." Another described how her parents had met while working as a salesgirl and stockboy at a department store in the Maine town where they were born. Both were part of the large French Canadian community in the town, "and she noticed him because he was so well-dressed." His daughter agreed with my speculation that his attention to clothes may have reflected an attempt to claim a higher social status than his working-class family might be assumed to have had. Several people commented to me that it is only in retrospect that they have identified their upbringing as lower middle class or working class: "I think I grew up in, you know, middle-class. We had one family income. And looking back, we probably were—we weren't real well off, but I didn't realize that. I didn't think about it. You know, I didn't think we were poor or anything . . . I think as my parents have aged, they've moved up into the higher middle class as well, but still a very—I think my family's values are still very working-class."

Many felt that their parents expected them to use higher education to improve their own socioeconomic status. One man who did describe his family background as "solidly middle-class" elaborated as follows: "A house, big yard, two cars, family vacation every summer. Expectation that we were going to go to college." Another stated: "[My parents had] an expectation that we would pursue higher education as far as we could go. And I think that had to do with perhaps the mistaken belief, but, you know, a belief that I respect, that I think that they held, which was that hand-work . . . was lower than work of the mind or the intellect." In general, that defining shift—from manual to mental labor, from blue to white collar, from working class to middle class—had occurred within living memory for the great majority of the public historians I spoke to in Lowell. It was often more recent among the frontline and lower-status workers, although this was not invariably the case.[4]

Quite often, the socioeconomic mobility within their own lifetimes seemed to have caused a sense of separation, distance, even loss. One man who was the first in his family to attend college described the tensions that his experiences created with his parents: "I think for a long time they may have felt that I felt I was too good for them or there was something wrong with them because . . . clearly I didn't want to become [what they were]." Working his way through university by way of various unskilled jobs—the kind his parents themselves held—he found, that, "I had to divorce my mind and my self from that work. Otherwise that's what I would have become. . . . It was totally routine, totally dull, totally boring, totally uninteresting. There was nothing stimulating in it, there was no fresh air. It was like being sealed up in the Pharoah's tomb! And the university was sunlight, fresh air, light, intelligence." Another ranger said, "I think . . . both literal[ly] and figuratively, I've moved away from that background. . . . I'm still middle-class, but I think I'm definitely in the upper end of the middle class, and I'm definitely white-collar liberal. So you know, in that sense, I'm definitely the opposite of my parents."

One man, whose grandparents had been farmers and whose father had worked in a factory as a laborer and eventually as a foreman, spoke quite bitterly of his sense of separation from the work his family had done and the skills they had possessed: "*None* of those [farming or hand-labor] skills came down to me. . . . [I]t's so depressing for me that I had no inclination, there was no . . . cultivation, there was no passing down, there was nothing that came down. And part of it was me. I was interested in the fun and games of being American, you know, playing baseball and watching my sports heroes and *I Love Lucy* and Disney and all of that." This man articulated something I sensed in other public historians' comments about the discontinuities in their own backgrounds: that working in public history, and sometimes specifically in Lowell, both accentuated and perhaps offered some chance to reconcile the tensions between where they had come from and where they were now:

> To me, thinking back [coming to work in Lowell] was connecting with the farm-to-factory story, what my family had gone through and what they carried with them from their origins and culture into the town, and how so little of that seems to have gotten passed down as things disbanded from generation to generation, especially with the mass media that's come up. But . . . with education, and the point of education is *not* to work in a factory, *not* to work on a farm, and to work behind a desk and to—I guess, the white-collar professional middle class existence was the goal that I had and my family had. And I lived that dream! [Laughs] The National Park Service—perfect middle-class bureaucrat existence!

Another public historian suggested that her choice to work in public history was linked in some way to the more material kinds of production that had once taken place in the buildings where she worked: "I reside more or less in the world of ideas, but I think why I like public history, and museum work, is because I like the tangible aspect. It's because for me at the end of the day the world of ideas in and of itself is not really satisfying."

Another articulation of this tension—and of the possible choice of a public history career to help bridge the disjunctions that create it—can be found in Martha Norkunas's autobiographical study of monuments and memory in Lowell. Norkunas, a professional folklorist, was for a time the cultural affairs director at the Lowell Historic Preservation Commission, the development arm of the city's redevelopment project. She had family in Lowell, giving her some insider status in the fiercely parochial local political world. But her own parents had moved away geographically and upward socioeconomically, creating a separation that Norkunas was highly aware of, especially after her mother's death: "I was an outsider to [my older female relatives'] telling of the [family]

stories, although they certainly knew that my mother shared those stories with me. Without her, without the transgenerational link between
mother and daughter, I was cut off from all their narratives, and from
the connections embedded in the shared-life stories," (2002:78). Her
training as a folklorist and her subsequent work in the realm of public
history and folklore, however, provided a new set of meanings and uses
for the family material and relationships from which she was half a generation distant: "In graduate school I came to value the stories that Nana
and my mother had told me. I saw them for the first time not only as the
story of my family, but as belonging to the great repertoire of family and
ethnic narratives that folklorists were interpreting. . . . My ethnic and
working-class background, so linked in America, became not identities
to be disavowed, but badges of honor" (2002:26,28).

Barbara Kirshenblatt-Gimblett has described the processes of "transvaluation" by which outmoded places and ways of living are given a second life and a new economic viability as "heritage" (1998:149). Museums
and related cultural institutions play key roles in this transvaluation process, "adding the value of pastness, exhibition, difference, and, where
possible, indigeneity" (1998:150). Kirshenblatt-Gimblett is speaking of
larger social settings, but I see the same process at work here on the
individual level, within practitioners like Norkunas who feel themselves
to be suspended between generations and socioeconomic classes, and
who embark on particular kinds of careers at least partly as a way to span
the gap or resolve the tension it causes. Just as museums and heritage
productions can help to make obsolete places economically viable as historic attractions, education and careers within these institutions may be
one way for individuals to transvalue working-class backgrounds that
have been left behind in the recent move into the middle class, and to
acknowledge a personal sense of connection with working class forebears while escaping the exigencies of working class life and avoiding a
for-profit world that is unappealing to them.

As I have already noted in chapter 2, these people, like myself, have
attained middle-class status in a society where the middle classes are
experiencing new kinds of pressures and patterns. Those of us who produce and consume the products of such fields as public history and public folklore increasingly form part of a distinct social formation, which
John Urry, following Pierre Bourdieu, refers to as "the new petty bourgeoisie" or the new service classes (1990:88–95). As Urry describes

them, people in this category do not possess large amounts of land or financial capital, but they are rich in cultural capital that they have accumulated through education and travel. This gives them access to relatively privileged positions within the new economy, where they are "located within a set of interlocking social institutions which collectively 'service' capital" (Urry 1990:89)—for example, the financial, educational, and cultural organizations that support the creation of places and workers for postindustrial modes of production. Such people are often ambivalent about their middle-class positions, and strive to set themselves apart from the conventional bourgeoisie by rejecting its historical emphasis on acquisition and status-seeking (for example, by choosing health food, microbrewed beer, natural fibers, vernacular architecture, cultural tourism, and so on).

Bourdieu coined the term "new cultural intermediaries" for a particular subset of this new petty bourgeois. He located cultural intermediaries in "all the occupations involving presentation and representation (sales, marketing, advertising, public relations, fashion, decoration and so forth) and in all the institutions providing symbolic goods and services" (1984:359). He appears to have been thinking primarily about media workers, particularly critics and commentators who "mediate" between the producers and consumers of culture. But others (for example, Evans and Foord 2003, Featherstone 1991, Fleming 2004, Negus 2002) have subsequently used the term more broadly, and in ways that encompass the kinds of workers I am talking about in this chapter. In this broader view, cultural intermediaries are those who work in the interstices of the new cultural economy. They are located somewhere between public and private entities, between the producers of cultural materials and their eventual consumers, and between the low and high ends of the new postindustrial service class. (For a fuller discussion of the concept of cultural intermediaries, see Hesmondhalgh 2006).

I am suggesting here that work in the public history niche of this economy is a way for public historians and other cultural intermediaries to locate themselves within the postindustrial present. However, it by no means removes them from the many vicissitudes of postindustrial capitalism. Rather, because public history and similar fields are now so thoroughly embedded in the economic survival strategies of so many places, this kind of work creates new insecurities for the people who pursue it. Museum professionals, like those in many education-related fields, are experiencing pressures to become more professionalized and more accountable to regulating bodies. Moreover, museums, historic sites, and other cultural institutions, especially those created as part of larger redevelopment projects, are expected to contribute substantially to the image-making and place-marketing of their communities. Those that do not or cannot contribute risk losing political and financial support. One early Lowell NHP manager spoke to me about the pressure that he and his colleagues felt to translate their work into hard numbers that could be shown to have a positive economic impact on the city: "[The pressure] was coming from the city. . . . And because it was coming from the city, it was coming from the superintendent. . . . [H]e pressed very hard. He wanted those numbers up. He didn't want to know how we got them up, he just wanted them up!"

Because park staff and others have been successful at portraying Lowell's culture-led revitalization as a long-term process, and because the project's leaders have continued to be exceptionally good at accessing public funds to contribute to the city's many public–private partnerships, Lowell NHP has been viewed as a worthwhile investment even though it has not produced the sizeable and direct tourist revenue that some people first envisioned. In other places with less-well-established funding and political bases, similar projects have struggled. During my 2002 trip to southwestern Pennsylvania's heritage tourist sites, for example, I visited the Altoona Railroaders Memorial Museum, whose costly and extensive permanent exhibit memorializes the Pennsylvania Railroad that was once headquartered in Altoona. Although the museum had opened only four years earlier, it was already in serious financial difficulty, operating with a skeleton staff and selling its gift-shop items at deep discounts. Just as the success of Lowell's original industrial experiment led to emulation, competition, a glutted market, and failure for many places, the very success of the culture-led model pioneered in Lowell seems to have contributed to an ever-more-crowded market for cultural tourism, in which not every venture will survive.

The presence of the National Park Service is some guarantee of stability and sustainability; once created, most national parks have historically remained under federal care. But the Park Service, too, must operate within the unforgiving logic of advanced capitalism, and within a specific neoliberal climate in American politics that sees culture as part of a larger market-oriented calculus. In recent years, national parks have found themselves faced with new federally mandated expenses (including salary increases for staff) which must be paid for from budgets that have not increased, resulting in the need for overall cuts. As a result, in the first five years of the new century, Lowell NHP was slated to lose about a third of its workforce. The Park Service fended off an attempt during the "culture wars" of the mid-1990s to shut down some parks with low visitation rates, but it is now faced with a requirement from the current federal administration to improve its fiscal and operational efficiency by reviewing the possibility of privatizing and outsourcing various staff functions. While I was doing my fieldwork in Lowell, the park's maintenance division was being scrutinized for possible privatization, and I heard occasional resentful comments by maintenance workers about the fact that their division might suffer in order to help the park balance its budget and assure the federally mandated raises of workers in the interpretive division whose jobs were not on the auction block—a deeply ironic situation within a park largely devoted to interpreting labor history. Even within the comparatively safe haven of the National Park Service, then, culture and history-related work is neither secure nor removed from the difficult realities of the postindustrial service sector, in which the gap between highly educated elites and lower-status workers continues to widen and both groups experience the instability of a system increasingly tied to—and based on the workings of—capitalist markets.

Public Historians in the Twilight of Ethnicity

In addition to socioeconomic background and status, I asked my interviewees about their ethnic ancestry, and how active a role ethnicity played in their everyday lives or sense of identity. The great majority were of northern or central European ancestry, particularly German, Dutch, French or French Canadian, English or English Canadian, Irish, or Austrian. Most people's families had been in the United States for at least three generations. Those of primarily English extraction often did not think of themselves in terms of ethnicity at all, reflecting the fact that to be a white Anglo-Saxon Protestant is to belong to a social category not generally marked as ethnic. Of those from other backgrounds, many spoke of having only a vestigial sense of ethnic identity. Almost none of my informants, and few of their parents, grew up speaking a language other than English. One described his ethnic background as "all just white-bread American—all the ethnicity has been washed out a generation or two ago. My mom remembers as a little kid speaking just a word or two in French to her grandparents." Another said that her father, the grandson of Jewish immigrants from eastern Europe, "grew up in a very assimilated world, went to a public high school, did have a bar mitzvah but never really liked his religious upbringing, and had no interest in it at all. Very characteristic of the [19]50s, really washed that out of his life." A man of German Catholic background said that much of his family's sense of themselves as ethnic had been suppressed during the two World Wars against Germany. His mother spoke some German and cooked some German food, "but it didn't really click that much for me, you know, that this was something special." A fourth-generation American man of French Canadian, English Canadian, and Irish background noted: "Our generation was left, you know, with the exception of the kids my age who did have immigrant parents, but the third, fourth generations, which was most of the people during that time . . . got this much [indicating a small amount] [of ethnicity]. And so we didn't, you know, didn't think about that. . . . [P]robably the only kind of ethnic stuff we did, we['d] make a Polish joke. We wouldn't even make a French joke or an Irish joke, I mean, it was just the bare bones of ethnic awareness."

Interestingly enough, this man was a native Lowellian, one of only a handful of local people working in the interpretive division of the national park. In his professional life, he made considerable use of his background and connections within the city's ethnic communities. Yet his comment above makes it clear that he did not grow up with any self-conscious sense of belonging to a particular ethnic community. Like his public history colleagues, he was living in what sociologist Richard Alba has called "the twilight of ethnicity"—an assimilated state where ethnicity has been "washed out" and is not an instrumental part of how people conduct their work or personal lives (Alba 1985). They may have the option of projecting an ethnic identity, adopting what Herbert Gans termed "symbolic ethnicity" (1979), but membership in a particular ethnic community is not socially obligatory or necessary for their economic survival, as it often is for members of the city's newer immigrant groups. Except in the few instances of those who were both locals and professional public historians, ethnicity is not something that my informants found strategically useful or necessary in order to achieve their goals.

(The complex discursive and performative strategies used by Lowell's established "white ethnic" populations are discussed in detail in the following chapter.) In Micaela di Leonardo's terms, these people are "unencumbered" by relationships and obligations arising within specific communities that are identified as ethnic (1998:94). If there is any consciousness of ethnicity in their own family backgrounds, it remains there—in the past. Ethnic assimilation, like socioeconomic mobility, has produced in these public historical workers a sense of separation from what has gone before—and not only a separation, but perhaps even a sense of having evolved from or progressed past the stage of being ethnic.

My Lowell informants would likely disagree with this last statement. That is, they would strenuously deny that they feel in any way superior to those who are more "encumbered" with ethnicity, and would insist that they admire and celebrate the kinds of vibrant ethnic communities that exist in Lowell. Yet this kind of valorization, coming from those who are somehow outside the category of ethnicity, can be distancing at best, patronizing at worst. In his analysis of *The Invention of Ethnicity*, Werner Sollors notes that "any 'ethnic' system [relies] on an opposition to something 'non-ethnic'" (1989:xiv). As with "white privilege," the effects of being nonethnic are usually all but invisible to those at the top end of the scale, while being only too obvious to those farther down. Clues to the hierarchical nature of the difference between ethnics and nonethnics can be gathered from the words of local people who work within Lowell's redevelopment project, like the man who, discussing the insider/outsider division, suggested, "There's probably inevitably a class distinction buried in there"—that is, in the separation of working-class/local/ethnic from professional/outsider/nonethnic. Martha Norkunas, writing of her ambiguous position as an insider/outsider during her tenure with the Lowell Historic Preservation Commission, notes that her purchase of a house in one of Lowell's working-class neighborhoods placed her outside the mainstream practices of the other professional people with whom she worked, perhaps at some cost to her ability to operate in the world of Lowell cultural politics. "Would having a different address, I wondered, have advanced my advocacy of certain projects?" she writes. "I wondered if my access to power and my address were connected" (2002:29).

Another clue can be found in the fact that the only two workers I encountered in the park's interpretive division who *were* immigrants and did speak accented English—that is, who were inescapably "ethnic"—worked in the weave-room of the Boott Cotton Mills exhibit. One, from Puerto Rico, began his Park Service career in Lowell NHP's maintenance division and had learned to be a weaver and then a loom fixer, or mechanic. The other, from Portugal, had come to the park after being laid off after many years as a weaver in one of Lowell's few remaining textile companies. Their presence in the weave room—"The only place in the park where people *really* work," as one of the weave room workers said to me—underscores the association of the ethnic with the working class, and the separation of both from the more intangible products generated by most of the other people in the park's interpretive division. In the professional public history realm, the norm is to be "free" of ethnicity and working-class associations—except, of course, in past generations or carefully framed representations, where they may safely be acknowledged and celebrated. Within Lowell's social taxonomy, professional public historians, who are generally not Lowellians and do not usually live in the city, occupy the nonethnic slot. This places them not only outside the category of ethnicity, but also in some sense above it, or beyond it—farther along on the imagined scale that shows the progression from the traditional to the modern. Like social mobility, ethnic assimilation serves to create a sense of difference and distance between Lowell's public historians and the histories and "others" they are interpreting to the public. And these social patterns appear to produce in public historians, as in many middle-class Euro-Americans, a characteristic and combined sense of autonomy and alienation, of achievement and loss. Speaking of such people among her fellow graduate students, folklorist Martha Norkunas noted that "colleagues who did not have strong ethnic backgrounds began to wonder if they had identities at all" (2002:28). As the author Richard Rodriguez has written,

> At a time when so many children of working-class parents have gone off to college, at a time when so many of us are schooled to become different from our parents, when parents and children no longer share the hope of a future in common, I think it is no coincidence that there has been a middle-class chase for ethnic roots. Such a celebration of community becomes a denial of loss"(1989:6).

Within the kind of postindustrial cultural production so much in evidence in Lowell, such celebrations may also become part of a place's cultural economy, staffed by workers who facilitate the public display of heritage, history, and ethnicity without feeling themselves to be direct participants in what they are celebrating.

"The generation that broke the cycle": Visitors to Lowell

In both of these important areas—recent socioeconomic mobility and a sense of being distant from or beyond the category of ethnicity—the public historians who work in the park's interpretive division are strikingly similar to the people who come to Lowell as tourists.[5] What follows is an analysis of the information I gathered from my surveys and short interviews of visitors to the national park and audience members at the Lowell Folk Festival.[6]

Responses to my questions about visitors' occupations made it very clear that most of the people who come to the national park in Lowell are educated professional workers. Two-thirds worked in management, professional, or related occupations, while another 10 percent were in sales and office jobs. These findings are in contrast with the 2000 U.S. Census figures for the city of Lowell itself, where the majority of workers are much more evenly distributed among management/professional (28%), sales/office (24%), and production/transportation (23%) jobs (see table 1). The largest economic sectors mentioned by park visitors were

TABLE 1:

OCCUPATIONS	PARK VISITORS %	LOWELL RESIDENTS %	MASSACHUSETTS %
MANAGEMENT/PROFESSIONAL	66	28	41
SERVICE	2	16	14
SALES/OFFICE	10	24	26
FARM/FISHING/FORESTRY	3	<1	<1
CONSTRUCTION/MAINTENANCE	3	9	8
PRODUCTION/TRANSPORTATION	3	23	11
OTHER (UNEMPLOYED, HOMEMAKER, ETC.)	13	N/A	N/A

education/health/social services, professional/scientific/management/ administrative, and information. By contrast, the largest economic sectors from the Lowell census figures were manufacturing (still one-quarter of the total), education/health/social services, and retail (see table 2). Park visitors, then, tended to work in jobs that required some college or professional education. Overall, they occupied higher posi-

TABLE 2:

INDUSTRY	PARK VISITORS %	LOWELL RESIDENTS %	MASSACHUSETTS %
FARM/FISHING/ FORESTRY/ MINING	2	<1	<1
CONSTRUCTION	1	5	5
MANUFACTURING	4	24	13
WHOLESALE TRADE	0	3	3
RETAIL TRADE	4	10	11
TRANSPORTATION/UTILITIES	2	4	4
INFORMATION	11	4	4
FINANCE/ INSURANCE/REAL ESTATE	5	5	8
PROFESSIONAL/SCIENTIFIC/ MANAGEMENT/ADMINISTRATIVE	20	10	12
EDUCATION/HEALTH/ SOCIAL SERVICES	29	20	24
ARTS/HOSPITALITY/ RECREATION/FOOD	5	7	7
OTHER SERVICES	2	4	4
PUBLIC ADMINISTRATION	3	4	4
OTHER (UNEMPLOYED, HOMEMAKER, STUDENT, ETC.)	12	N/A	N/A

tions within the new knowledge/service/culture economy than did people in the city of Lowell, where manufacturing continues to play a substantial economic role and where many education, health, and social service jobs are to some extent a reflection of the substantial population of the city's people at or below the poverty level who need publicly funded services. Just as public historians' personal distance from ethnic and working-class life creates a sharp distinction between them and the history and residents of the city they interpret, there is clearly a broad socioeconomic difference between the people who come to the national park as visitors and the people of Lowell itself—a difference that reinforces insider/outsider, present/past, working class/middle class divisions.

However, park visitors' resemblance to public historians goes further than their shared position within the educated, professional middle class. Like public historians, many visitors seemed to have achieved that status comparatively recently. I draw this inference from two types of data in my visitor surveys. First, I was struck by the very large numbers of teachers, nurses, and engineers who visited Lowell NHP. These were the three occupations most commonly mentioned by visitors, making up a third of the total:

Education	17%
Health services (usually nursing)	10%
Engineering	7%

Teaching, nursing, and engineering have all historically tended to be "gateway" professions, accessible to people who may not have tremendous amounts of financial or cultural capital, and offering routes (often highly gendered ones) into the professional world for the sons and daughters of working-class families. In the words of a Lowell man whom I interviewed about his involvement in the early days of the new Lowell experiment: "I think my mother and father, who worked hard and grew up during the Depression and were both children of immigrants, I don't know if they knew any doctors or lawyers, but they knew teachers, and teaching seemed to be a great thing. . . . [N]o one [in my family] had ever gone to college before, and if I could get to college and become a teacher, there was nothing better." After I began to notice this pattern among tourists in Lowell, I came to think of the archetypal Lowell NHP visitors as a white couple in their forties or fifties, a female teacher married to a male engineer. In fact, near the end of my fieldwork, I encountered one such teacher/engineer couple whose parents had been textile-mill workers in a southern cotton mill town, one of many southern communities patterned—and in this case, even named—after Lowell. Like many park visitors and many of my public history informants, these people had entered the middle class at a time when the United States was making its shift from an industrial to a postindustrial economy. Broad economic restructuring, then, added another layer to the changes inherent in class mobility for individuals.

I also asked park visitors whether their personal or family backgrounds intersected in any way with the history of industrialism. Responses were almost evenly split between those who said they had no personal connection (52%) and those, like the couple above, who told me that they or someone in their family had worked in—or, in much rarer cases, owned—a factory (47%). Of the latter group, the connection broke down as:

Grandparents worked in factory	29%
Unspecified family member worked in factory	29%
Parents work/worked in factory	16%
Other kind of connection (owned factory, etc.)	15%
Self/siblings work/worked in factory	7%
Great-grandparents worked in factory	4%

These answers supplied my second clue about to fairly recent socioeconomic mobility among park visitors' families. Of the half who mentioned some connection with industrialism, there was a distinct concentration of factory workers among the grandparents' generation, becoming less with the parents' and with visitors' own generations. These kinds of connections—and visitors' sense that the national park was helping to maintain them—were also evident in selected comments in the Boott Mill visitors' book[7]:

> What a wonderful tribute to the people who gave their lives to make this place successful—my grandmother was a mill girl. She has since died and this has been a wonderful and emotional visit for me. I'll surely be back.

> I learned a lot about what my father and grandparents did for work. What an experience!

> My father was a wool merchant in Boston from the 1930s to the 1970s. . . . [The museum] brings back a lot of memories of him for me and a career, that, even though it came to an end with the changing times, was a very important part of my father's life. Thank you for saving this memory.

> My grandmother had a similar experience in San Diego, California, in the 1920s, working in a . . . canning factory to support her three children, ages 6, 5 and 3, when she was a young widow. These videos of mill-worker interviews brought tears to my eyes.

This progression mirrors the two- to three-generation shift that I saw among public historians from blue-collar to white-collar labor. It is also worth noting that two-thirds of the visitors who cited specific industries in their responses to my survey mentioned either the textile (52%) or garment (15%) trades. These numbers suggest to me that for many of these recently middle-class tourists, there is a highly personal element, even an aspect of pilgrimage, in their visit to Lowell NHP.[8] I expand on this idea in the following section, where I analyze the ritual uses of the national park by its visitors and interpretive staff.

Although half of all visitors mentioned some sense of connection to industrial work, and many of those noted some family connection to the textile industry, the great majority (75%) commented that their own work was very different from industrial work, underscoring the personal sense of separation that most visitors feel from the working-class experiences in their own backgrounds and from the working-class history on display in Lowell. Visitors made a variety of comparisons between their own work lives and those of factory workers. (These are reproduced in the Appendix; I will return to this question of comparison in the last section of this chapter.) It is significant that of the majority who saw difference rather than similarity between their own work and industrial work, 21 percent felt they were utterly different, with comments like "night and day," "a different planet," "a world of difference" or "a totally different world," "miles apart" or "centuries apart," "180 degrees," "it was a horrible time," "theirs was slave labor," and "I'm happy to be living now!" A smaller but very interesting group of responses came from people I came to characterize as "no, buts. . . . " These visitors told me that their own personal or family background definitely did not overlap in any way with industrialism, but then added comments such as, "although my grandfather did work in a shoe factory" or "unless you count the time I worked on an assembly line when I was in college." In somewhat different ways, the "no, buts" and the people who characterized industrial work as "centuries apart" from their own were expressing a shared sense that the industrial labor on display in Lowell was exceedingly distant from their own lives in time, space, and type—a distance created in part by the fact that, in many cases, it was something associated with their own personal pasts.

It was also clear that visitors placed industrial or manual labor on a continuum, where "progress" was achieved through earlier generations' willingness to endure difficult manual labor in order to give their descendants a chance at an easier, more prosperous life. In response to my question "Do you think there is value in preserving the history of the Industrial Revolution?" some visitors wrote comments illustrating their perception that history reveals linear socioeconomic progress over time:

> It's important to preserve that time in history so that future generations can see and hear how our parents and grandparents worked so hard for their children to have a better and easier life than they did.

> It is important to understand how people behaved in another era and the exploitation they endured to insure that our society does not regress from the advances we have made in civil and human rights of our citizens.

> It's important for our youth to know of our history, especially that our nation was once a strong manufacturing center. Afraid our grandchildren will grow up thinking the whole country is employed as consultants—

that no one has to do anything—just talk about it. We hope to bring our grandchildren here.

It's important for future generations to be able to look back on past cultural advances and discouragements.

Helps us to all to understand/appreciate the hardships our ancestors endured in building our prosperous nation.

One park visitor[9] went so far as to comment that "our young people need to realize how far and how much we still need to go to replace the working 'blue collar worker'"—a clear vision of manual labor as an outmoded transitional phase that must ultimately be done away with in the march of progress.

Finally, park visitors also resembled public historians in that they seemed to be living within the "twilight of ethnicity" that I have noted above—and specifically the twilight of European ethnicity. When I asked visitors about their ethnic ancestry, the most frequently named groups were:[10]

Irish	67 times
English	64
German	50
French or French Canadian	39
Other northern Europe	21
Other eastern Europe	20
Italian	19
Scottish	18
Scandinavian	15
Polish	11

As with the interpretive staff I interviewed at the park, the highest concentration was among people with family backgrounds in northern and central Europe. I did not ask specifically how many generations ago visitors' families had come to the United States, but many of my informants mentioned this in the course of answering my other questions: for example, "My great-grandparents came from Quebec to work in the Rhode Island textile mills," or "My grandparents were from Italy." Almost none of the people I surveyed spoke with accents; like the public historians, they were thoroughly assimilated Euro-Americans.

My short interviews with audience members at the Lowell Folk Festival also reflected visitors' sense that they were somehow outside of or beyond ethnicity. This popular festival, held on the last weekend of July each year, is produced jointly by the national park, the city, the Washington-based National Council for the Traditional Arts (NCTA), and the Lowell Folk Festival Foundation, a locally based private organization created as a fiscal and administrative agent for the festival and some other performing arts activities in Lowell. Programming is chosen by the NCTA with substantial input from program committee members from the park and the foundation. The program typically includes Irish and Cajun music, bluegrass, polka, gospel, and blues, suggesting that these Euro-American and African American genres are central to the NCTA's sense of what constitutes the major strands of American folk music tradition. Although most performers are not local, the programmers show some responsiveness to local ethnic politics by regularly including music associated with the city's primary ethnic groups. This is particularly true in the case of the established "white ethnic" groups who were most active in the local folk festivals that preceded and merged with the current festival. Those groups remain somewhat involved as food vendors; dwindling numbers of Irish, Greek, Armenian, and Polish food booths are still to be found alongside the newer Asian, Latino, African, and other booths that are becoming the majority of vendors at the festival.

Given the representation of northern and other European cultures on the program and among the food vendors, then, and the similar concentration of Euro-Americans among the visitors who come to Lowell, one might expect to find the majority of audience members seeing some kind of connections between their own ethnic background and the music, food, or crafts offered at the festival. Yet my interviews at the 2001 and 2002 festivals showed precisely the opposite. The people I talked to clearly associated the festival with ethnicity and ethnic diversity; when I asked them how they would define "folk," or what made this specifically a "folk festival," more than half (54 percent) mentioned ethnic diversity or variety (these responses are marked with an asterisk):

What makes this a "folk festival"? How do you define "folk"?

Ethnic diversity/variety	44%*
Traditional/authentic/indigenous/heritage	15%
Brings people together/like family	8%
Noncommercial	7%
Shows American ethnic diversity	5%*

Transmitted orally/generationally   5%
Participatory/made by ordinary people   4%
Shows local ethnic diversity   3%*
Shows regional ethnic diversity   2%*
Living, evolving tradition   2%
Others (not sure, food, simpler, relaxed)   4%

But when I asked, "Are there any connections in your own ethnic background with any of the different groups that are performing or serving food here?" the majority (61 percent) said no. Another 11 percent said no but revealed that they *did* have some kind of possible connection, as shown below. Like the "no, buts . . . " who did not see their own working-class ancestry as in any way linked with the industrial history on display in Lowell, these people did not seem to connect themselves with the category of "ethnic."

Do you have connections with the ethnic groups on display here?
No   61%

No, but . . . (Greek/Irish from Lowell, family   11%
worked in mills; in-laws worked in mills;
Irish/WASP; Irish;Filipino; French Canadian
from Lowell; Cambodian)

Yes (Irish 7; Filipino 2; Spanish, French   28%
Canadian, West African, Cambodian, Polish,
not specified/other, 4)

The festival was clearly about ethnicity for many of the people who attended it, yet few of these people identified themselves with the specific ethnic communities and traditions being showcased at the festival. Such a disjunction is not surprising—folk events have usually been about displaying modernity's "others" in ways that separate the less-modern groups being represented from the fully modern audiences who are looking at them. But in this case, even some of those who *did* share ethnic backgrounds with the groups on display did not make the connection, suggesting that these audience members did not think of themselves in terms of ethnicity at all—either because they were "beyond" it or (less frequently) because it was not a category that they actively mobilized in their own lives for any reason. Among the people I talked to who said they had no connection with the groups who were performing or cooking, one young man laughed and said, "Not unless there's a white

Anglo-Saxon Protestant band playing." In fact, there were at least three bands on the program that year that could have been described as white, Anglo-Saxon, and Protestant, including a bluegrass group on stage a few hundred feet away at that moment. But WASP is not a category usually marked as ethnic, and this visitor seemed to be seeing neither himself nor the three bands as ethnic in the same sense as, for example, African American gospel or Irish traditional music. Like the public historians at Lowell NHP, these visitors to the city were not only in the twilight of ethnicity, but removed from the category of ethnicity itself.

Also like my public historian informants, many of the visitors I spoke with in Lowell showed some ambivalence about the combined progress and loss inherent in their own social mobility. One stereotypically "new economy" visitor—he had been an attorney, then a real estate developer, then created and sold a high-technology start-up company, and was currently unemployed—took one of the park's walking tours of the Acre as part of his own orientation to the city, having just moved there to escape higher rents in the high-tech corridor outside of Boston. He told me he had no personal connection with the ethnic or immigrant histories that formed the backbone of the tour ("except that I enjoy ethnic food"), but waxed somewhat nostalgic about the city's industrial history. Describing the volatility of the postindustrial economy and his own roller-coaster career within it, he looked at the big red-brick mill building in the shadow of which we were standing as we talked, looked at his hands spread palms up in front of him, and told me, "I've love to build a box— just any kind of product!" His words echoed the comments of one of the public historians at the park, who told me, "I like living in cities where things are made. . . . It makes me feel grounded for some reason. It's like a reality, there's a physicality to the notion that things are being made . . . rather than talked about and analyzed." Neither of these two people would likely have had any tolerance for the reality of actually doing industrial labor, but from the safe distance of their positions in the white-collar world, they found the idea of it appealing.

Other visitors responded in more purely emotional terms to the realization of the distance between themselves and the industrial laborers who had faded into their personal or collective pasts. One wrote in the Boott Mill guest book: "Never thought I'd see Lowell and the work my grandparents, mother, aunts, and uncles did become such a point of interest. It's nice to have them and others and the city honored in this way. From the generation that broke the cycle." A ranger told me a story of encountering a weeping visitor on the second floor of the Boott Cotton Mills Museum. Having passed through the noisy weave room on the second floor, she had had a painful epiphany:

> [She was] talking about her grandmother [who] had worked in a mill and she used to describe it, but you know, as a kid, she kind of listened to it but didn't really, she never really understood what her grandmother went through. She gets up to the second floor of the museum and there's tears coming down her cheeks. And you know, she was in her fifties, and she said, "*Now I know what she meant.* And now she's gone, and I can't ask her."

For these people in "the generation that broke the cycle," Lowell NHP is more than just a place where they can learn more about the Industrial Revolution. It is, rather, a ritual space where they can locate themselves within changing socioeconomic realities and allay some of the anxieties involved in those changes, a process that bears more detailed analysis.

Rituals of Reconnection

My interpretation of the national park as a ritual space emerges from Victor Turner's model of the social drama. Turner developed this model as a way to articulate the connections between individual ritual/performative behaviors and the social structures and historical events that surrounded them. The notion had its origins in older understandings of ritual process, notably that of Arnold van Gennep, the French ethnologist and folklorist who analyzed the three phases in rites of passage: a separation from everyday reality, a liminal or in-between phase, and then a return to the everyday, albeit in a somewhat altered form—as an adult instead of a child, married instead of single, and so on (Gennep 1960[1909]). Turner elaborated on van Gennep's model in much of his own early work, with a particular emphasis on the potentially creative or "anti-structural" qualities of the liminal middle phase. But he also came to see a similar process operating on the larger social level. Significant social events, he felt, followed a pattern that mirrored the separation/transition/return paradigm. First there was some sort of breach or conflict, which, if not resolved, led to a crisis which demanded that society take some kind of redressive action. Such action would result in a resolution, whether that was a healing of the original breach or an ultimate break and a movement toward a new social formation. Turner called this pattern a social drama (1974:23–59, 1982:61–88). The structure of social dramas, he believed, was "not the product of instinct but of models and metaphors carried in the actors' heads" (1974:36), although the liminal character of the redressive phase also had the potential to reshape those models and metaphors. For Turner, the social drama was "the experiential matrix from which the many genres of cultural performance, beginning with redressive ritual and juridical procedures, and eventually including oral and literary narrative, have been generated" (1982:78). Much of the specific content of these performances was drawn from the breach, crisis, and resolution phases of social dramas. The third phase, "redress," was in many ways the most interesting from a theorist's point of view. It was there that human actors struggled to articulate—to perform— their understandings and alternative visions of what was happening around them. Turner's insight into the dialectical relationship between social dramas and ritual or performative behavior is one of the important underpinnings of cultural performance studies. Like much contemporary scholarship that attempts to tease out the linkages between culture and power, his work showed that expressive forms emerged from particular social formations and historical situations, but also had the potential to influence their surroundings in turn. That is, he acknowledged the power of ideas and symbols, but gave us a way to link their operation in concrete ways to a more materialist analysis of the kind that I am attempting here for public historians in Lowell. Equally important is the fact that Turner's model can be used to examine many different types of societies and many kinds of performative forms—legal cases, television shows, tourist productions, religious rituals, museum exhibits, educational workshops, protest marches—in relation to one another and within the same overarching social framework. The notion of the social drama is particularly useful when examining diffuse, complex cultural settings such as the one within which Lowell NHP functions.

The social drama playing itself out in contemporary Lowell was precipitated by deindustrialization and the movement of capital away from the city. This breach—Christine Boyer's first "erasure"—separated the city's landscape and people alike from long-standing patterns shaped by the textile industry, and led to a crisis as leaders and citizens struggled to understand what had happened to their community and how they might repair the damage and make the city more viable within a changing set of economic realities. This crisis phase corresponds with John Urry's view of the large-scale social "disorganization" involved in making the shift into postindustrialism. Established patterns on many levels—political, economic, spatial—are shaken and reordered, a disruptive process that various social groupings approach in different ways, with differing rates of success (1995:112–25). Lowell's search for redress eventually culminated in the broadly supported decision to use the city's history as a basis for revitalization.

This process included the kind of prolific generation of performative and expressive forms that Turner saw as characteristic of the redressive stage of social dramas. Tours, historical markers and designations, oral history collections, museum and art exhibits, festivals and plays, educational workshops, Congressional hearings—all signaled a sharp increase in Lowell of the kind of collective self-examination that Turner viewed as "necessary if crisis is to be rendered meaningful" (1982:76). Although few if any of these activities were literally framed as rituals, all served a key ritual function in helping to express and reorder the culturally significant materials that were in play. The creation of the national park in 1978 was both a coalescing of these myriad expressive forms and a springboard for the creation of many new ones—continuing landscape and architectural renovation, new layers of administrative and legal oversight, additional performing arts activities and museum exhibits, a large-scale annual folk festival, the industrial history center, and so on. The redressive phase of postindustrial culture-led development involves a kind of creative destruction, a double process of cultural production and displacement. This is Boyer's "second erasure," or what Kirshenblatt-Grimblett has termed "the reciprocity of disappearance and exhibition" (1998:56).

The resolution of Lowell's breach and crisis is by no means complete or monolithic. Lowell's increased prosperity does not reach everyone equally, and it is unclear how durable the culture-based experiment will be in the long term. But the project is so solidly entrenched in the city— and has been received with such widespread praise outside it—that it seems fair to say that Lowell's social drama has entered a final stage in the minds of most of the people who participate in it. That final stage is the movement into a postindustrial society, representing a largely successful reintegration into the regional, national, and global economies. And because Lowell has made this successful transition, at least symbolically, it is able to serve as a ritual site for the kinds of people who are seeking to locate themselves within the wider postindustrial social drama taking place in the United States and other Western nations. These people, public historians and their primary visitors, have generally experienced a less abrupt breach and crisis than that of Lowell's painful deindustrialization. But they are nonetheless afloat between classes and economies, often mourning lost connections and kinds of knowledge while trying to maintain a certain level of prosperity within the shifting conditions of postindustrial capitalism. The breaches or separations experienced by my informants in Lowell have been caused by the recent socioeconomic changes in their own families and in the larger U.S. movement toward a postindustrial economy. Although this has produced a degree of prosperity—often a high degree—it also creates a sense of dislocation, loss, and uncertainty. Prosperity itself is often tenuous in this new economy, as we see in the shorter and shorter boom-and-bust cycles of high technology (like the Wang renaissance that "revived" Lowell for little more than a decade) and the phenomenon of widespread white-collar job loss within new sectors of the economy. And many who benefit from it perceive it to be morally tenuous as well. Despite the grandiose promises of neoliberal development policies, the distance between rich and poor continues to widen on local, national, and global levels, leading many liberals to the conclusion that our own comfortable standards of living are often maintained at the expense of misery and poverty elsewhere. Yet it is difficult to give up affluence and status once they are attained. What is a well-meaning white-collar liberal to do with such uncomfortable knowledge, such convoluted interweavings of progress and poverty, past and present?

Ritual offers one solution to those seeking to mend or come to terms with this personal and collective rupture. In the liminal, performative space of the national park in Lowell—set aside from everyday life and constructed of symbolically rich materials made available for reflection and rearrangement—postindustrial citizens can imaginatively participate in a narrative that makes sense of the trajectories of their own lives and the changing society around them. There are many possible ways to arrange the available materials, and as we have seen, Lowell NHP arranges them more critically than many industrial history sites. But the questioning, leftist rhetoric of much of the park's interpretation does not seem to make significant inroads on the "models and metaphors" that visitors bring with them to the park. Most people appear to absorb or confirm the message that economic and social change in the modern world has consisted of a linear, three-part, evolutionary progress from agricultural to industrial to postindustrial, with each successive phase producing a higher standard of living than the previous one. This is the cycle that has been enacted within the past handful of generations in visitors' and public historians' own Euro-American backgrounds, and which has manifested itself quite recently in their own move into white-collar professional work and status. Visitors' personal narratives thus echo Lowell's larger social drama, in which the phase of industry or manual labor has now been replaced by a brighter postindustrial present and future. In this linear, teleological narrative, industry is "centuries away" or on "a different planet." Visitors see little or no connection between industrial labor and their own, and blue collar work is an undesirable holdover from an earlier time. The goal now is to "break the cycle" and move into a more advanced and comfortable plane of existence.

That plane, of course, is the one that visitors already occupy. These are the very people that Lowell NHP and the city of Lowell seek to attract, as visitors, residents, entrepreneurs, and investors. Tony Bennett has argued that museums have always located their target audiences at the peak of whatever series they display (1995:82), in this case, in the postindustrial phase. The experience provided by Lowell NHP, the ritual reconnection with lost or absent working-class, ethnic, or immigrant forebears—serves to locate these particular postindustrial subjects firmly at the leading edge of economic change. It confirms that they are the end result of a progression that is moving, with a few bumps here and there, in a generally positive direction. Visitors can return to their everyday lives reassured that society is advancing as it should, and that their forebears' sacrifices and hard work were not in vain. Those sacrifices produced our present prosperity, and they are now suitably memorialized and valorized at a national park. As participants in "rituals of reconnection" spawned by Lowell's own transformative social drama, visitors can return to their everyday lives feeling more secure in their position within postindustrial society, because they have a clearer sense of where they themselves fit within an overall coherent pattern or sequence.

MacCannell, following Marx, locates the need for this kind of ritual within the industrial cycle itself, noting that as a solution to the problem of culture, industrial work is a failure. It repulses the individual, sending him away to search for his identity or soul in off-the-job activities: in music, sports, church, political scandal and other collective diversions. Among these diversions is found a cultural production of a curious and special kind marking the death of industrial society and the beginning of [post]modernity: a museumization of work and work relations, a cultural production I call a *work display*. (1999:36)

In MacCannell's Marxist formulation, work was once a means by which individuals could forge a connection with their cultures. But industrial work alienated workers from their labor, giving rise to leisure-time activities through which people sought a clearer sense of collective or individual identity. As capitalism has evolved, these leisure-time pursuits have assumed greater and greater social and economic importance, to the point that they have now become industries and commodities in themselves. And so in postindustrial societies, a curious elaboration has developed. People now visit industrial work sites themselves as a touristic or educational activity—a ritual designed to span some of the many discontinuities created by the restructuring of postindustrial societies. This is precisely what is happening in Lowell. By making an imaginative connection with what is lost, past, or unknown in their own histories, visitors are more fully able to determine where they fit in the present. Far from being blank slates on which the park's public historians can inscribe new knowledge, they are eager participants in a ritual for which their own histories have prepared them well.

Where do Lowell's public historians fit within this process? The park is not a liminal space for them; it is their everyday reality, their workplace. But they are, nonetheless, crucial to the park's ritual functioning as facilitators and active participants. Here it will be useful to differentiate between the upper-level public historians at the park—those most involved in planning exhibits and determining which overall directions the park's interpretation will take—and the rangers who most often interact with visitors. As I have already noted, the higher-status workers are likely to have studied history at the graduate level and to be somewhat more open about their critical or ambivalent stance on contemporary capitalism. Thus, they are both professionally and personally predisposed to ask questions that challenge the socioeconomic status quo and the kind of linear narrative that forms the basis of the park's rituals of reconnection. Indeed, it is largely the presence of such public historians that accounts for the most progressive elements of Lowell NHP's existing interpretation. By virtue of their higher status, however, such workers are also the farthest removed from the front lines where the rituals I have described are taking place. Moreover, the past/present, local/outsider division of labor that I will explore in the following chapter means that their work has tended to focus more on the distant than the recent past. As we have already seen in the Run of the Mill tours, this has had the effect of limiting the park's more critical statements to the most distant past, weakening their potential connections with visitors' own lives in the present. The various layers of social and temporal distance—between visitors and the most critical public historians, between the interpretation of past and present, between blue collar/low status and white-collar/higher status workers on many levels—limit the extent to which the public historians' questions and critiques can disrupt visitors' expectations and the teleological narratives they bring with them and refine through their experiences at the park.

The frontline rangers are much more direct participants in the park's rituals of reconnection. These rituals enable visitors to reconnect with what is lost, absent, or past by supplying various kinds of stand-ins for immigrants or mill workers: voices or images in the museum exhibits, weavers in the weave room, or the rangers who lead tours and answer visitors' questions. Of these, only the rangers are fully accessible to visitors. Although many people comment on the powerful effect of the videotaped textile workers talking about their memories of working in the mill, the people on the videotape are not physically present for visitors to engage with. The weavers *are* present, but there are many barriers to direct interaction with them: the overwhelming noise of the looms, the necessity for the workers to be tending the machines constantly, the fact that the weavers are not, strictly speaking, there to talk, but rather to make cloth (fig. 13). This leaves the rangers, whose primary work *is* to talk and interact with visitors, and whose personal backgrounds are so strikingly similar to those of the people who visit Lowell.

Rangers' jobs, like those of other frontline public history interpreters, are becoming increasingly standardized and professionalized.[11] Much of this professionalization involves rationalizing and managing the visitor/ interpreter encounter so that visitors consistently feel a sense of personal and authentic connection with the site, the interpreter, or—ideally—both. Within the field, this process is seen as important primarily

FIGURE 13. Lowell National Historical Park's exhibits include this re-creation of a 1920s weave room, with working power looms tended by park-employed weavers. CATHY STANTON.

because it helps visitors to feel more closely connected with the past, with the nation, or with the specific site that is being presented to them. An essay written by a senior manager at Lowell NHP and included in the resource materials for the National Park Service's Interpretive Development Program spells out this philosophy: "There is no one INTERPRETATION, no single perfect way, but rather multiple techniques and relationships, linking visitors with the real, the tangible, resource and its immeasurable intangible and universal meanings to forge a lifetime bond" (Kryston 1996:2). And Freeman Tilden, in *Interpreting Our Heritage* (long the bible of the interpreter's craft at many American historical institutions) states that, the "vulnerable spot that most people share in common . . . [is] the longing for community, whether it be . . . of their own human family or race, or of the subtler kind that relates the puzzled human to the physical world he sees around him" (1977:91). Tilden makes it clear that the creation of this bond or community depends upon direct encounters among specific people—tourists and interpreters: "What interpreters can do is to communicate, from their own conviction, *by indirection but with warmth*, [an] appeal to an always receptive human heart" (1977:114, italics in original). This is a striving for what

MacCannell has called "the fragile solidarity of modernity" (1999:83)—the fostering of a sense of connection or community by means of the very social forces and institutions that helped to create our alienation in the first place: the separation of work from leisure, past from present, one generation from another. These rationales are ripe with the language of what Turner termed *communitas*, the powerful bond that the ritual process creates between individuals and the collectivity, whether that be a cohort of fellow initiates or a larger social grouping, or both.

A more materialist reading of the professionalized interpreter/visitor encounter is found in Handler and Gable's study of Colonial Williamsburg, where this encounter is analyzed in some depth. The authors conclude that the goal of interpreter training at Williamsburg is to create what they call "good vibes," a positive and friendly experience that is one of the institution's most marketable products. Ultimately, Handler and Gable trace the marketing of this product to the corporate agenda that they see driving the institution, arguing that "good vibes becomes a corporate goal, and employees for the most part become willing participants in achieving it," to the detriment of the more critical approaches to history promoted by Williamsburg's public historians (1997:196). Handler and Gable do acknowledge the creation of a certain communitas at the site (without using this terminology), but they see it as part of the mystification inherent in Williamsburg's central goal of reinforcing the social and economic order that it both depicts and helps to create.

My overall conclusion differs little from Handler and Gable's. I have already argued that the national park is shaped and driven primarily by the need to reinvent the city's economy within changing regional, national, and global realities, and that on many levels, this agenda deeply limits both what Lowell's public historians say about present-day economic conditions and the kinds of audiences to whom they speak at all. Within this setting, specific kinds of visitors ritually reassure themselves about their places within the new socioeconomic order. This ritual is facilitated by professional public historians—keepers of a postindustrial shrine—who resemble those visitors in many significant ways. I see dangers, however, in the more purely materialist route that Handler and Gable take to understanding the interpretive encounter. It is easy, in this approach, to lose sight of individual agency and motivation, something I am trying to read back into the visitor/interpreter relationship by blending a materialist approach with Turner's more symbolic analysis. My reading does not change the overall picture but renders it more complex, and perhaps ultimately lets us identify possible avenues and strategies for change. In particular, I take a different view of the interpreter's role from the one delineated in Handler and Gable's study. They suggest that interpreters at Williamsburg *"become* willing participants" (1997:196; italics added) in the mystified encounters at the site, presumably by virtue of working there and being initiated into its values and practices. In contrast, I argue that public historians in Lowell are already willing, even eager, to participate in the national park's rituals of reconnection, because this activity responds to so many of their own desires and circumstances. They are drawn to this kind of work precisely because they, too, are seeking a secure and satisfying place in the new economy, and because they share the specific sense of discontinuity, loss, and status anxiety of many of the park's middle-class visitors.

Furthermore, these particular workers have specifically rejected the kinds of jobs that alienate people from their work and send them away to find meaningful identities in their leisure time. Their choice to take jobs in public history is a comment—sometimes direct, sometimes more veiled—on their frustration with the kinds of human interactions and experiences that many have experienced in other areas of the postindustrial economy. Their solution to this dilemma has been to find work in the public history field, where they feel they are doing socially valuable work and experiencing genuine encounters with other human beings. Many of the frontline rangers at Lowell NHP talked to me about the excitement and satisfaction of feeling they had "clicked" or created a "spark" with visitors:

> I feel like I need that as an outlet. . . . It's almost a real sense of need. I will find myself, some days like, "I've just got to get out there and get a program. I've got to go out there and do—you know, talk to visitors, I've got to—" And like yesterday, I had a conversation with this couple who were just visiting, and it was one of those situations where their questions and my answers, and my questions and their answers, just jelled so well that it was like forty minutes went by and I finally caught myself, I said, "I'm sorry, I didn't mean to have taken your time." And they're like, "No, no, we were—you weren't, trust me." I'm always conscious, I don't want to be talking someone to death. And there's just times when that feels so good, to have that spark of intellect with someone else. And I think that's—I think everybody needs that, and we find it in different ways. And for me,

I can find that through doing tours or giving programs or training or whatever. And so I start to feel really stagnant if I don't have that. . . . So I think I give as much as I get. And I get as much as I give.

Another ranger specifically linked that sense of connection with visitors and the experience of *re*connecting with working-class forebears:

The satisfaction [of the job] is that it's interacting with people—I thrive on that. Helping folks discover why this place is important, and seeing that realization in them, when they make that connection between this site and their own—you know, a lot of times, I'll say to people, "How many of us have factory workers one or two generations back?" And a lot of people will say, "Oh, yeah!" You know, maybe it was just a summer job, but, "I understand what that's like, working in a factory." And so it's nice, to hear people's stories. On the second floor of the Boott, in the museum, the types of stories that people want to tell me, because of something they see or one of the oral history videos they watch, you get great reactions. And it's great for people to be able to talk about that stuff.

Especially for frontline interpreters, these interactions provide a sense of genuine human connection, something that they have found to be missing in other kinds of postindustrial workplaces.

I have been differentiating somewhat between the ways in which frontline and upper-level public historians approach and experience the rituals of reconnection enacted at the national park. I will now bring the two groups back together again by noting that, in a general sense, all of the workers in the interpretive division are able to participate whole-heartedly in the park's ritual function whether they are behind the scenes in offices or on the front lines interacting with visitors. As dwellers in the twilight of ethnicity and as recent migrants into the middle class who now constitute part of an emerging and unsettled service class, they share the need for the reassurance that those rituals can provide, and they find in their work an answer to many of the dilemmas presented by the contemporary economy. Lowell NHP's rituals of reconnection create a feeling of communitas between participants and the larger society they are a part of by reaffirming their place in the linear narrative of assimilation and progress—the social drama taking place on an individual and a societal level and echoing Lowell's transition into postindustrialism. The rituals produce a more immediate kind of communitas between park visitors and rangers, but all of the park's interpretive workers share in the more generalized communitas that the park provides. All are able to valorize the work and lives of industrial workers and immigrants because they themselves occupy similar positions within the postindustrial social drama, which is being enacted on many levels from the individual to the global. Most of Lowell's public historians have working-class and immigrant forebears of their own. All find themselves maneuvering to find a secure foothold in the shifting territory of the postindustrial symbolic economy. Because of such shared experiences and memories, these public historians—especially, but not exclusively, the frontline rangers—can empathize readily with a visitor who is weeping in sudden recognition of what a lost grandparent suffered, or delight in the "spark of intellect" with other postindustrial citizens who are using the story of the Industrial Revolution to try to understand and symbolically solidify their own place in the world. Like the visitors, they are making use of the personal materials they bring with them and the historical materials provided by the national park in ways that ultimately serve to locate themselves and their work more firmly in the present day.

Conclusion

The history on display at Lowell NHP is unusually critical and progressive, raising questions of exploitation, inequality, and agency within industrial capitalism. Yet one of the park's primary functions is to turn those difficult questions into a system of positive reinforcement for people who have already managed to free themselves—however tenuously—from the most damaging effects of working within a system dedicated ultimately to profit. Lowell NHP endows blue-collar work and life with an aura of "pastness" so that the city, its white-collar visitors, and its new professional class of cultural producers can move more confidently into the future. Bella Dicks sees this in itself as valuable, as it offers a way for individuals to situate themselves within larger historical processes: "In bringing biography and culture together, heritage displays offer a space for the intertwining of public, exhibitionary space and private, biographical space. . . . In this perspective, heritage is not so much sight-seeing (the public display of the other) as cultural biography (the public recognition of the self and its stories)" (2003:126). Although this recognition may be "public," it still takes place on a very limited scale, seemingly unconnected to active participation in the everyday world. I did see, however, some isolated moments in the visitor–interpreter encounter that suggested there was potential to explore in more critical ways the many questions raised by Lowell's history and to create openings for more politicized and perhaps active connections with real-life questions connected to that history. I conclude this chapter with a look at some of those moments and consideration of why they remained so unconnected to overall interpretive agendas.

I have already written of one such instance—the sudden folding in of past and present during a "Run of the Mill" tour in the summer of 2001. I have given considerable attention to this example because it was so unusual. In my two years of attending park programs and events, I never heard another frontline interpreter make so vivid and pointed a comment on the human costs of present-day prosperity or the repetitive nature of the economic and social cycles that have been playing themselves out in Lowell. A significant minority of park visitors, though, did seem to make these kinds of connections for themselves. Some of these can be found in comments from the Boott Cotton Mills Museum visitor book:

> The slide show confirmed my thinking that we are dealing, 100 years later, with many of the same issues.

> It made me feel real sad to be reminded how the power of money chooses to exploit humanity.

> The price of liberty is eternal vigilance! Returning to pre-union times is a disaster. Strike breaking and weakening of the unions has become a national pastime since Ronald Reagan set the example with the air traffic controllers. God forbid we should return to such a disastrous way of non-life.

> Nothing has changed. Individuals are still the slaves of industry and greed. It's interesting how little has changed as far as worker welfare and contentment. Money is power. Liberty is a dream.

I heard some similar comments from the minority of visitors in my survey who saw similarities between their own work and the kind of labor done in factories. A few of these visitors actually worked on assembly lines (mostly in the high-technology industry) but most were white-collar workers who drew various comparisons between their work lives and those of factory workers. Several remarked that working hours were becoming longer again, reversing the historical trend over the past century and a half. Others noted similarities between the effects of past and present technological innovation on workers, commenting that their own work was still dependent on machines. A few commented on labor–management relationships, saying they felt lower-level workers were still not adequately respected or compensated, and that corporations' overriding focus on profit had remained the same over time.

I was struck by the fact that the more critical labor-oriented comments often came from women working in traditionally female jobs like teaching and nursing—two thoroughly unionized and highly politicized areas of the service sector in which issues of gender, power, and unequal access to resources are regularly acted out. These visitors clearly saw their own working lives as part of a continuum that included the stories told at Lowell, and they were very ready to engage with what they saw at the national park in critical and presentist ways. One such visitor, a friend who came to see me and tour the park while I lived in Lowell, commented that the mill girls' labor struggles of the 1830s and 1840s reminded her vividly of the issues and obstacles she herself had faced as a labor organizer working with female clerical workers in the 1970s. As I was talking with a ranger outside the Boott Mill theatre one afternoon, a pair of women visitors came out after viewing the slide show. One noted approvingly that the show had dealt with the income disparities between workers and owners in the past, but suggested that the script should be updated to reflect the fact that these gaps had widened greatly in recent decades. As the visitors moved off through the exhibit, the ranger—herself a former teacher—said to me, "She's a really interesting woman—a teacher. We were talking a lot earlier." I was starting to describe my developing thesis that teachers were among the more radical users of Lowell's messages when, as if on cue, the woman came back to say, "You know, I was just wondering—do *you* people have a union?" The ranger admitted that Lowell's rangers, as with most rangers at national parks, were not unionized, and that, in fact, some park staff had recently been asking themselves what kind of leverage they might be able to exert to save certain health benefits likely to be cut in the tightened budget of the next fiscal year.

These and other small incidents and exchanges suggest to me that there is some potential at Lowell NHP to use the park in the kind of political, activist way that progressive public historians have envisioned. Yet these individual moments existed only in isolation, in visitors' conversations or occasional informal encounters with a ranger rather than in concert with any wider discussions or interpretive offerings. The atypical scene around the working loom in the Run of the Mill tour seemed to reveal the perception of danger that hovers around such explicitly presentist readings of Lowell's history. The seasonal ranger who led that tour—himself a teacher during the rest of the year—hedged his comments with gentle qualifications to mute the impact of an essentially radical statement ("It's just something to think about") and was reluctant to talk with me after the tour about his decision to make the statement at all, as though he had broken a taboo by pushing visitors to the point of seeing how their own lives intersected with those who are less privileged in the global economy.

In a way, his action *did* break a taboo, which is why such moments so seldom occur despite the park's official interpretive policy of encouraging visitors to make these kinds of intellectual connections. Unofficially but powerfully, the site's main function is precisely to *mask* these connections, by placing visitors within a linear progression where manual labor is framed as past and as less evolved. Because too direct an encounter with actual blue-collar workers or work might disrupt the rituals of reconnection that are so central to the functioning of the park, many safeguards have been unconsciously created against such encounters. Actual working-class people might destabilize the ritual by promoting an unexpected agenda, underscoring the privileged and affluent position of the tourists, or undercutting the need for the interpreters' mediating presence. And so these people are absent from the park's official interpretive realm except in the weave room, where their voices are effectively—and ironically—drowned by the noise of the looms. The occasional moments when someone does break through the silence or the noise—a weaver who is willing to shut down the machines to speak at length with visitors, or a visitor who pierces the park's invisible mediating surface to ask whether park employees themselves are unionized—are exceptions, often noted with interest by park staff, but never pursued by them in any consequential way. The park's rituals of reconnection are designed to bridge personal distances—between visitors' and public historians' own family pasts and personal presents—while denying the social distances between these postindustrial workers and people less fortunately situated in the present day. This ritual function connects visitors to their own individual pasts, which are experienced as earlier phases of the postindustrial social drama. But it also masks their connections to present-day disparities, with the result that the critical or activist potential of Lowell NHP goes largely unrealized. Rosalyn Deutsche laments the cooptation of public art into the postindustrial cultural economy, arguing that "the real social function of the new public art [is] to present as natural the conditions of the late-capitalist city into which it hopes to integrate us" (1996:66). Public history in Lowell fulfills the same naturalizing function, despite the fact that many of the professional public historians at the park have been trained to question exactly such teleological narratives.

Let me end this chapter where I began, with the "*Strike!*" calls drifting periodically upstairs from the Tsongas Industrial History Center in the Boott Mill. As one of the national park's most important partnerships, the Tsongas Center is actively helping to educate the workforce of the future—the people who will populate the economy and society that has been developing in the United States over the past two generations. Students who come to the "Workers on the Line" program learn about worker struggles and labor activism, but only as something linked with a kind of labor that most of them will never perform. The people charged with educating these students—their own teachers, the workshop educators at the Tsongas Center, the interpretive staff of the park, hard at work upstairs designing the park's newest exhibits—are themselves seeking a secure foothold in this emerging economy. Jobs within the interpretive division of the national park provide one such foothold, from which Lowell's public historians hesitate to look too critically at the postindustrial economy and their position within it.

Moments of critical connection do occur in the Tsongas Center as elsewhere around the park. For example, during one "Workers on the Line" workshop I heard a young workshop leader (a University of Massachusetts employee, not a park ranger) ask, "Is this [strikes and labor activism] something that only happened in the nineteenth century?" The students knew it wasn't, but none, when pressed, could think of anyone they knew who was in a union. Their teacher said pointedly, "*I'm* in a union!" One puzzled student asked which union, and she replied, "The *teachers'* union!" The workshop leader went on to describe a recent national United Parcel Service workers strike, which had used the strategy of halting deliveries just before Christmas, as an example of successful labor organizing. More typically, though, the "Workers on the Line" program places students within the same linear progression that adult visitors to the park use for understanding their own experiences. At one workshop, I spoke with a chaperone who turned out to be both a parent of a student in the group and the principal of the school from which the class had come. When I asked him how he thought the workshop had gone, he replied, "Well, I think they got the message." I asked what message he meant, and he said, "Just what things were really like back then. I don't think any of these kids have any idea what this kind of work was like. I worked in a shoe factory when I was a teenager, so I know firsthand how bad it could be. It wasn't nearly as bad as the conditions in those old mills, but it was bad enough." And he concluded, "That's what prompted *me* to get an education, I can tell you!" Now safely ensconced in the professional classes via the standard mechanism for socioeconomic mobility, a college education, this man could join unquestioningly with Lowell's interpreters and educators to help his own young charges similarly locate themselves securely at the privileged edge of the story and the hierarchy. Pastness, once it has been created by the interpretive efforts of the park and its partners, is constantly reinforced through the redressive rituals taking place around the park. When I first asked a Tsongas Center employee—one who worked for the park, not the university—about "Workers on the Line," she outlined the program for me, describing the assembly-line scenario and the different ways that students reacted to the demands placed on them. When she told me about the "union meeting" and the frequent "*Strike!*" calls, I said it sounded as though they were training a new generation of labor activists. "Oh, no," she reassured me. "We're just trying to show them how it used to be."

Meanwhile, in the upstairs meeting room at the Boott Mill, the team of park and Tsongas Center staff continued their frustrating work on the plan to redesign the final sections of the Boott Mill exhibit, which brings the story of Lowell into the postindustrial present. One day, at the end of a particularly contentious meeting, the discussion stalled at the question of what the exhibit should say about the choices facing new workers—for example, the local students among the Tsongas Center's visitors—who were entering the economy of postindustrial Lowell. "You live here, you have these skills, what do you do?" mused the director of the Tsongas Center. He paused, then finally answered his own question: "You get a job at the national park." None of the people around the table responded to his comment.

CHAPTER 7

Feasting on Lowell
Authority and Accommodation in Lowell's New Cultural Economy

In May of 2002, the Patrick J. Mogan Cultural Center held a public forum and open house to announce to the public that it was back in business. The Mogan Center was one of the proudest achievements of the Lowell Historic Preservation Commission, which renovated a much-altered Boott Mill boardinghouse into a building that combined exhibit and archive space with meeting rooms. It opened in 1989, with the goal of providing a space where local people could actively participate in the study, exhibition, and ongoing creation of Lowell's history and local culture within the city's new public historical spaces. Named for the Lowell educator who had been the most prominent early advocate of a culture- and heritage-based revitalization plan,[1] the Mogan Center hosted a series of community-generated exhibits and some university continuing-education classes and other activities in the early 1990s.[2] But when the Preservation Commission closed its doors in 1995, activity dwindled. Moreover, the general consensus among people involved with the center was that it had never fully lived up to its original mission. In the words of Paul Marion, cultural affairs director at the Preservation Commission when the center opened and still an active cultural leader in Lowell, "What didn't work out was somehow having the community *drive* this building. . . . It didn't take on the character of a community cultural center with the community in the lead."

Shortly before I began my fieldwork in Lowell, there was a concerted effort to change that state of affairs. Stepping into the vacuum left after the closing of the Preservation Commission, managers at Lowell National Historical Park took the lead in renegotiating a partnership with the university and reconstituting a Mogan Center advisory committee that included representatives from the park, the university, and the community at large. This committee and a half-time coordinator hired by the park were charged with planning a program of community-oriented events and collaborations that would rejuvenate the Mogan Center and bring it closer to accomplishing its original goals. The official reinauguration in May 2002 featured the presentation of a draft long-range plan, guided tours of the building, an open rehearsal by a Cambodian dance troupe that had recently taken up residence on the top floor, and finally a "food performance" in which two southeast Asian cooks demonstrated salad-making techniques with the aid of a Cambodian translator and two folklorists hired by the center. It is the food demonstration, one of a three-part series called "Feasting on Lowell," that I use as a starting point for a discussion of localness, authority, and accommodation within Lowell's culture-led redevelopment project.

The food demonstration was not a particularly remarkable production, nor were the Mogan Center committee or the participants especially enthusiastic about it. It came about through a clumsy process with which everyone concerned expressed frustration. Park management and the advisory committee wanted an event that would make a striking statement about the rebirth of the Mogan Center and the complex cultural life of the city it was supposed to represent; the Cambodian translator saw it as an opportunity for the empowerment of refugees who felt marginal to the larger Lowell community; the folklorists were trying to foster greater reflexivity about cultural processes among participants and audience members alike; everyone involved hoped to encourage some genuine cross-cultural exchange. No one seemed to feel that the food demonstration accomplished these aims to any noteworthy extent, although no one apparently felt strongly enough about it to insist that things be handled otherwise. It was a pleasant enough gathering, and most of us who attended it enjoyed tasting the southeast Asian salads and socializing casually with people we knew (fig. 14). In that sense, it was very like most of the public history and cultural events I attended within Lowell's public historical spaces: polite, predictable, safe. This one attracted a somewhat more ethnically diverse audience owing to the presence of representatives

FIGURE 14. The May 2002 "Feasting on Lowell" event featured southeast Asian food at the Patrick J. Mogan Cultural Center. CATHY STANTON

of various cultural organizations who had been invited to the open house. But, as with the park's tours of the Acre, it did nothing to challenge either the feel-good celebration of multiculturalism or the conventional model of colorful ethnic others performing their culture for an audience composed primarily of middle-class people of European descent. At first glance, it was not an event that would seem to offer much scope for new analysis, since it merely reproduced patterns that I have already discussed in some detail. Nor did it contain any obvious drama or tension. Despite the low-level frustration expressed by those involved in planning and staging it, there was no real discord or contestation. None of the social relationships within Lowell's heritage realm were changed because of it.

Yet those very qualities make it worthy of attention, precisely because it was so typical of the events that that I saw in and around the national park in Lowell and that are to be found throughout similar culture-based revitalization efforts. When I began my fieldwork, I expected that I would find more overt discussions and disagreements about the multiple meanings of Lowell's past and present. My expectations were shaped by an awareness that such exchanges had colored the early years of the Lowell's redevelopment project (Ryan's 1987 dissertation provides copious evidence of this), and by my academic grounding in several literatures—including cultural performance scholarship—that have tended to emphasize the marginal and subaltern, the transgressive and oppositional, and questions of agency and resistance. My awareness of Lowell NHP's reputation as an uncommonly critical interpreter of early industrial capitalism and my sense of public history as a left-leaning field also played a role, as did my personal politics. How, I thought, could a site focused on labor, gender, capitalism, immigration, ethnicity, and technology possibly fail to touch on at least some sensitive contemporary nerves? As my counterreadings of three park tours have demonstrated, it seemed obvious to me from the outset that the basic subject matter for Lowell's cultural experiment contains many volatile and urgent questions. I wanted to see how those questions were being represented and negotiated in the public historical spaces of the national park. From a methodological standpoint, I admit that I had hoped to see instances of active contention, so that I would have a way of observing and assessing the currents of debate swirling around the local and park interpretation of Lowell's industrial past and postindustrial present. Instead, what I saw, over and over again, were events like the Mogan Center foodways program—congenial, controlled, unchallenging. It became plain that, even if there had once been more direct dialogue about the meanings of the past and the uses to which it was being put, those dialogues were no longer a salient aspect of the city's public historical realm. Furthermore, if I wanted to grasp how that realm really worked, I would have to learn to look beneath the surface of such apparently unmemorable events as the one I have described above.

Cultural performance theory provides some useful insights for understanding such events. Performance scholars have generally tended to concentrate on the dynamic and "subjunctive" or "betwixt and between" qualities of cultural performances—their potential for change, innovation, and opposition (see, for example, Bakhtin 1965, Goldstein 1997, Grimes 1982, Manning 1983, Poole 1990, Schechner 1985 and 1993, Turner 1982 and 1986). However, this body of theory also recognizes that cultural performance is sometimes about maintenance rather than change, and that there may be as much social activity going on in a seemingly static performance as in a dramatic or confrontational one.[3] In Victor Turner's words,

> Even when . . . conflict may appear to be muted or deflected or rendered as a playful or joyous struggle, it is not hard to detect threads of connec-

tion between elements of the play and sources of conflict in sociocultural milieus. The very mufflings and evasions of scenes of discord in some theatrical and natural traditions speak eloquently to their real presence in society, and may perhaps be regarded as a cultural defense-mechanism against conflict rather than a metacommentary upon it. (1982:105–6)

Robert Lavenda has analyzed community festivals in Minnesota from this perspective, and agrees with Turner insofar as he discovers disparate segments of small-town societies agreeing to let the dominant middle classes run festivals largely as a way of avoiding social divisions that would be harmful to the community as a whole. But Lavenda, like most scholars who have written about cultural performance, remains optimistic about the possibility of finding the polyphonic and the carnivalesque at the heart of performance, noting that festivals "may speak with and to more than one voice at the same time and . . . this loophole is the dialogic potential at the heart of public culture" (1992:101).

Dialogic potential was what I was looking for when I began my fieldwork in Lowell, but after two years I saw almost no evidence that it operated to any notable extent in the heritage realm that I was observing. Lowell challenged my optimism about public history's potential as a critical practice and forced me to rethink how cultural performances actually work. As a theoretical framework for analyzing the Mogan Center foodways program, I have found it helpful to adopt the view of Kirk Fuoss (1998), who proposes shifting the question away from whether specific performances are contestatory and dialogic or not. For Fuoss, as for Turner, *all* performance is inherently agonistic. Something is always being negotiated whenever human beings make public representations, and performance situations are dynamic and generative even if there is little evidence of those qualities on the surface. The question, in Fuoss's mind, is, "What precisely is being generated?"

As so many scholars have demonstrated, cultural performances can commandeer, generate, or change the meaning of symbols, and so on. But equally—and importantly, for my study of Lowell—performance situations may actively *prevent* things from happening, often in ways that are like small twitches of the reins, invisible to observers. The task, then, is to tease those hidden mechanisms into view. As Fuoss states, "It is no longer enough for performance scholars to maintain that all performances are shaped by and shape social contexts. Instead, we need to engage in microanalyses geared toward uncovering specific modalities through which the culture–performance dialectic operates in specific performances" (1998:115). In this chapter I attempt such a microanalysis, looking beneath the surface of an apparently unexceptional event to unpack the layers of participation and negotiation that contributed to it in both an immediate and a longer-term sense. I begin by discussing two poles of discourse about the past in Lowell, one organized around localness and the other around outsiderhood. I describe how these two poles have formed over the past twenty-five years and how they have operated in the creation of exhibits and activities at the Mogan Cultural Center, including the spring 2002 food demonstration.

Locals, Blow-ins, and Outsiders

So significant is the distinction between locals and outsiders in Lowell that many local people use a specific term for those who live in the city but were not born there: such a person is a "blow-in," a term that appears to have originated as a description by Irish natives of colonial administrators and other English people of the professional classes in Ireland. Given the significant Irish American presence in Lowell's political and social arenas and the arrival of increasing numbers of outsider professionals in the planning and development areas beginning earlier in the twentieth century, it seems reasonable that the term was adapted for use in Lowell.[4] People who work in the city but do not live in the immediate area are not even granted blow-in status; they are outsiders, plain and simple. These distinctions make themselves felt in many ways, some subtle, some direct, throughout and beyond Lowell's redevelopment sphere. Martha Norkunas, cultural affairs director for the Historic Preservation Commission from 1989 to 1994, has written that

> Lowell is a place where one is known, and one's family is known. I have attended many meetings that began with people introducing themselves by stating their names and professional titles, and then describing their ethnic backgrounds and how their families came to America and to Lowell. People here earn their authority to advocate ideas through loyalty to the city, longevity, and ethnic associations. (2002:30)

Those without these attributes are made to feel their lack of them. Even though Norkunas had family connections among Lowell's white ethnic groups, she felt additional pressure to buy property in the city upon taking her job with the Preservation Commission: "Buying a house in the city, declaring that my roots were deep, was an unofficial requirement of my position" (2002:28). The park curator, who lived near Boston, told me that she might consider moving to Lowell for its own sake because she felt drawn to the city as a place, but

> another reason to live in Lowell is, quite frankly, the peer pressure. . . . I sit on the Mogan Committee, I work with colleagues in and out of the park . . . to some of whom it makes a huge difference who lives in Lowell and who does not. And I'm on one side of the divide. And I know it, I feel it, and I'm treated that way. . . . [I]t's about authority, and so I believe that the things that I do bring to Lowell, to this park, and to this city, that don't have to do with where I live, are dismissed, tend to be dismissed, can often be dismissed, not by everybody, and . . . some particular people care more than others. But out of hand, just quite frankly, because I'm not from here. Now that of course raises the issue that if I lived here, would I be *from* here? I still wouldn't be from here. So it's kind of—I don't know how you actually win the game. You know, I don't know if it's a game you *can* win. But I think it's a game you can play in a more participatory way than in others.

The park's first ranger, returning to Lowell in 2002 for a public forum to which he had been invited to share his reminiscences about the park's early days, began his speech by expressing his deference to localness and local memory:

> I do feel as though, as a blow-in, and that's a term that I learned when I first got here, because I was reminded that I was a blow-in from Gloucester, it's sort of strange being a blow-in to come back to remember Lowell. In fact . . . I really feel as though the people that lived here, that have lived here for all that time, the people that were born and bred here, schooled and stayed here, who lived in Lowell, who lived Lowell's story, bad and good, the survivors, are the ones that can best tell Lowell's story or remember it.

The half-time Mogan Center coordinator, a native Lowellian who had been hired by the national park largely because of his varied and useful contacts among many of the city's ethnic communities, spoke very plainly about the strategic uses of localness. Having lived for a time in Hawaii, he recognized the politics of insiderhood at work there:

No matter how smart a comment was from a *haole* [a nonnative Hawaiian], they were always an outsider, and . . . you could never be right all the time outside of your homeland. So in other words, you can *never* be wrong when you're at home.

You have sort of the moral authority—
To always whip out the blow-in card. "Your comment doesn't make sense because you're not from here, and you cannot tell us what to do."

His comment was half-joking, and he amended it later in our interview to note that this authority was far from absolute:

It's not so much the authority to speak, but always to have the card in the back pocket, to say, it's not that you're always going to be right on your home turf, because certainly locals disagree all the time, but . . . it's being at ease to know you're the insider and not the outsider. . . . [And I'm] always mindful . . . if I go back to Hawaii or I go to Colorado, or wherever, that . . . *I'm* the blow-in. And I have to be incredibly careful on saying, you know, "You're wrong, and this is the way it should be." So I think it's a humbling, leveling effect on people to understand localness.

These two characteristics, localness and outsiderhood, to a large extent organize what happens within Lowell's symbolic economy. Although, as I show, the distinctions between the two poles are by no means as clear as one would sometimes gather from the way they are used, their ideal versions can be roughly plotted as follows:

LOCALNESS	OUTSIDERHOOD
born in Lowell	born elsewhere
live in Lowell or immediate suburbs	live outside Greater Lowell
associated with ethnic/immigrant culture	not marked as ethnic
festival/folklife	exhibits/tours/books
culture/heritage	history
focused on present/recent past	focused on more distant past
subjective/based on memory	objective/based on written history
rooted in place/permanent	transitory
associated with amateurism	associated with professionalism
associated with blue-collar background	associated with white-collar background
most often celebratory	more often critical
focused on unity	more interested in looking at conflict

In Chapter 4, I showed how the local pole was largely constructed during the 1970s through the efforts of Patrick Mogan and his cohort, who focused on a unifying discourse about ethnicity and culture as a starting point for Lowell's social and economic revitalization. More critical, professional, historical perspectives were present during the early days of the new Lowell experiment, largely through the contributions of public and academic historians such as Mary Blewett, Thomas Dublin, Patrick Malone, and others who insisted that the national park should have a critical as well as a celebratory component. But the critical/outsider pole was not really institutionalized until the creation of the national park in 1978. At that point, responsibility for interpreting and representing Lowell was largely given over to a group of people who were, from the local standpoint, unknown and unaccountable to local conventions and social networks. The largest concentration of such outsiders—the professional public historians who are the central subject of this study—continues to be found within the interpretive division of Lowell NHP.

These outsiders have multiple allegiances and their sources of authority are found in disciplines and structures that extend far beyond Lowell. The most important of these, the National Park Service, is a large federal bureaucracy with its own well-established hierarchy and standard operating procedures. Its employees—particularly its knowledge workers and/or those who are ambitious about professional advancement—tend to be geographically quite mobile; traditionally it has been difficult to climb too far up the promotional ladder while remaining at a single park or even within a single geographical region. Professional historians are a decided minority within the Park Service, and their authority stems not only from the agency itself but also from their association with academe, whose approbation the Park Service likes to have if possible. However, Park Service historians, too, feel pressure to ascend in the hierarchy rather than remaining in one place for a whole career. Other public historical and cultural institutions in Lowell are similarly linked with nonlocal professional hierarchies and structures of authority—for example, the museum or folklore fields—whose practices and hierarchies potentially conflict with the local construction of heritage discourse.

My interviews with public historians at Lowell NHP revealed that, although many of them had been at the park for longer than is typical in the Park Service, their commitment to the park as a workplace and to the stories told by the park did not extend as far living in the city itself. Almost none actually lived in Lowell. Many had done so briefly before moving to more suburban or rural places in the region, reflecting their own socioeconomic backgrounds and preferences. As one ranger told me

> It was good for me to move to Lowell and have the urban experience. ... But that last year, I just couldn't handle the drive-down-the-road-and-wail-on-your-horn to tell the person that you're there to come pick them up. Which is a way of the city. . . . So that—it was a good experience, but I was fed up with having neighbors so close, and neighbors arguing. I grew up in a family that if my parents just *discussed* something, it's like, "Don't fight! Don't fight!" . . . So I had kind of got acclimated to urban life, moved to the city, dealt with it, it was fine. But I really wanted space. I was used to having 65 acres to play on, and I don't even know how big that little postage-sized house [in Lowell] was.

Another ranger who had grown up in a very small town rented "the most beautiful place" when she first moved to Lowell, but moved out of the city after a year and a half of having to negotiate one of Lowell's poorest neighborhoods and most bottle-necked bridge crossings to get home:

> I'd walk to work every day. And coming down the hill you could see the factories. It was awe-inspiring. Except living there, I'd have to—where it was frustrating, I'd work until 4:30 in the afternoon, and it gets so dark here in New England, because of the neighborhoods I had to walk through on the way home, I had to drive. And in the winter, I hated it. It took me longer to drive than it did to walk home, trying to cross the bridge.

Others who were more at home in urban settings tended to commute from communities closer to Boston. As I showed in the preceding chapter, many of these public historians appear to be drawn to Lowell precisely because of its working-class history and its "awe-inspiring" industrial landscape. But for them, the city is primarily a workplace, not a home. In this, they are similar to other new-economy workers in Lowell, many of whom are not deeply rooted (or rooted at all) in the place itself. The most striking example of this distance I encountered during my time in Lowell was a young man who worked for the university helping to incubate business start-ups in the city. We fell into conversation at a southeast Asian restaurant in the Acre one day, as we were mutually curious about each other's work. Although he was enthusiastic about this particular restaurant and often took clients to lunch there because he felt it was a highly authentic place, he himself lived in Boston, and was amazed to discover that I was then living in Lowell. "You actually *live* here?" he said. "What's it like?"

Such people often bring skills and knowledge that are valuable for local purposes, and their presence has contributed a good deal to Lowell's slow transition from the industrial to the postindustrial. From a local point of view, however, these outsiders are not to be trusted too far to plan for the city's future or to represent its past and present. This distrust was pointed up by a conversation I had one day with a "blow-in" who had long been active in the city's heritage field. I had commented that the park's frontline interpreters often seemed to struggle when they were called on to make statements about Lowell's recent history. "I'll tell you why it is," the woman said immediately. "It's because—" she lowered her voice and became more forceful. "*They don't love this place.* . . . None of the rangers live in Lowell. They don't want to live here. They have a—well, disdain might be too strong a word for it." She tried unsuccessfully to find a more accurate word. I asked whether it was more a sense of separation from the city and its stories, but she replied, "No, it's closer to disdain than that!" Such outsiders, whose lack of personal commitment to the city is read as something that is not quite but almost disdain, pose a lasting challenge to the local pole of authority within the heritage project.

That project encompasses many things, including the economic agendas discussed in Chapter 5. But one important element from the beginning of the city's culture-led redevelopment efforts has been the local insistence that people who live in Lowell should participate in and help shape the representations of the city's past and present. This view was clearly articulated for me by Paul Marion, who in many ways has taken up Patrick Mogan's banner within Lowell's cultural realm:

> The living culture is essentially what this whole experiment is about. And preservation is key, and tradition and remembrance is key, but if you stop the process, you've killed it. And Pat's admonition about, you know, "Beware of becoming spectators of your own culture" just kind of rings more true the more Lowell becomes kind of a full-blown tourist center, tourist destination. You know, the tension is going to get more and more strong. And there's going to be this tension between being a platform for people to gather round so that they can consume cultural experiences, and actually creating, preserving, and presenting culture that's distinc-

tive of this place. . . . [U]ltimately, if we stop creating an original culture here, I think it'll be the death of the whole proposition. . . . I think one of the challenges is that, as Lowell has moved into a kind of institutional culture phase, can the institutions absorb the local in a way that helps these institutions develop a kind of authentic personality that sets them apart, that makes them something that people want to participate in.

How, then, can local cultural leaders ensure that outsiders are somewhat accountable to this vision? Their key strategy has been the bifurcation of Lowell's heritage realm into the twin poles I have delineated above, which creates a separate but balanced authority for insiders and outsiders. To counter the weight of the professional outsiders who now represent and interpret Lowell for a living, local cultural activists assert an influence based, as Norkunas has said, on loyalty, permanence, and ethnicity.

To better understand how that influence is used, it is important first to ask who is using it. The group I have labeled as "local cultural activists" is made up of quite a small number of people, the majority of whom are associated with the fields of education and culture. Just as the economic wing of the heritage redevelopment project is dominated by a limited, highly cohesive group of men, the same faces and names turn up everywhere throughout the cultural side of the project, to the extent that they have often formed a series of interlocking directorates that would have made the early nineteenth-century "Boston Associates" proud. Some older cultural activists in Lowell have been involved in the culture-led redevelopment project since it was first proposed within the Model Cities program of the late 1960s. Many of these people and others were a part of the Human Services Corporation, the organization that Mogan founded largely to carry forward the ideas that had come out of the Model Cities initiatives.

Membership in the Model Cities and Human Services networks has overlapped significantly with other cultural and historical organizations such as the Greater Lowell Regatta Committee and its successor, the Lowell Festival Foundation, the Lowell Historical Society, the city's cultural affairs office and historic board, and—most significantly for the purposes of this discussion—the Lowell Historic Preservation Commission and the community advisory board that the commission convened to help oversee activity at the Mogan Cultural Center. One woman who had been active in the heritage project since its beginning talked of sitting at a board meeting with several close friends and colleagues, and joking that they could not remember even which group they were meeting as that evening. "I had to remember which hat I was wearing," she told me. "They always used to kid me about having a beanie—well, what hat am I wearing?" Another member of this circle said, "There's a kind of an activist tribe that know each other and seem to show up again and again and again." Loretta Ryan's study of the genesis of the national park in Lowell suggests that this has long been the case; she speaks of a "a conscious effort to create an image of public participation" (1987:292) at early park-planning events, which actually only involved a relatively small and homogeneous group. People from this group still constitute much of the "public" at the national park's public forums (for example, those held to solicit public commentary about new exhibit plans) and its locally oriented presentations. Although its most vocal and visible proponents, like Patrick Mogan, have tended to be male, much of the energy of this "tribe" comes from the many women who are active within it, reflecting a somewhat gendered split between economic and cultural activity in the city. Most people in this group have family connections among Lowell's major Euro-American ethnic groups: Irish, Greek, French Canadian, Polish, and Portuguese. An important exception is Mogan himself, who, although Irish American, comes not from Lowell but from Norwood, a town south of Boston. Mogan's connection by marriage to a prominent Lowell family and his own eminence in the postindustrial city, however, appear to endow him with honorary local status.

The local pole of Lowell heritage discourse gains its power from the implication that as local people with ethnic backgrounds rooted in a working-class industrial city, these activists are able to speak authoritatively about what it means to be part of Lowell's ethnic, working-class culture. Even though they themselves are not immigrants or blue-collar workers, they are connected by descent, memory, and geography with the histories and cultures represented at the national park and its partner programs. They are closely affiliated with ethnicity and the city's "folk." They make use of this form of cultural capital to balance the authority of the professional outsiders who, as we saw in the preceding chapter, are not identified as ethnic or working-class. However, an examination of the backgrounds of the Lowell cultural activists with whom I became acquainted during my fieldwork revealed some intriguing patterns in this group's connection with ethnic and working-class culture. In terms of class identity, the local activists either occupied the same recently middle-class status as my public historian informants, or—more commonly—came from families that had long had at least one foot solidly in the mercantile or professional classes. Paul Marion, whose ancestors came to Lowell from Quebec in the 1880s, noted that his family story "wasn't a sort of classic millworker story, for example my grandfather ran markets, you know, that kind of thing," and that his parents' and his own generation had experienced "a typically upwardly mobile family development, the next generation has it a little bit better." The Polish immigrant grandparents of another woman had run an inn, a lumberyard, and a grocery store. A third was descended from a long line of Lowell Irish politicians and public figures; many in previous generations of her family had also gravitated toward teaching and nursing. Far from being the sons and daughters of blue-collar textile workers, then, these people came from relatively high-status backgrounds within the working-class city. Although they shared in the general indignity of Lowell's abysmal reputation during its low point in the 1960s and 1970s, they were not among those who personally felt the harshest effects of the city's decline. Yet the general aura of the working-class city, revalorized by the new Lowell experiment, lends a great deal of weight to the cultural activists' dealings with the professional outsiders who interpret the city for Lowell's new publics.

The insiders' association with ethnicity and local ethnic communities and culture carries similar weight. But here, too, the relationship is more symbolic than actual. Like the public historians and visitors I surveyed in the preceding chapter, most of Lowell's cultural activists clearly exist in the twilight of ethnicity. Paul Marion, a poet as well as an activist, has captured this beautifully in a poem called "Parlez-Vous?," in which a distant Canadian radio station transmits broken bits of French that Marion recognizes but cannot fully understand across the distance in space and time:

> I'm picking up key words, leaning towards
> the Panasonic Solid-State portable
>
> ·
>
> Bouchard and his callers talk football, hockey;
> a commercial praises lovely Montreal,
> Paris of North America, cosmopolitan hive.
> They wish each other "Joyeux Noel,"
> voices blinking slowly like fancy tree lights. (Marion 1989:27)

In Marion's family, he told me, fluency in French "pretty much ends with my mother and father . . . . I never, other than a few words, talked to my grandparents in French." Although "there were some elements to what we did and how we lived that had a French Canadian tinge," he added, "my mother and father weren't sort of, you know, ethnic conservators. They didn't go out of the way to maintain some kind of Franco-American identity. They just sort of went with the flow, you know."

When I asked another of Lowell's cultural activists about the role her ethnicity played in her everyday life, she replied, "That's an interesting question. I think about that. I *have* been to Poland, and I never felt more American than when I was in Poland! And . . . my Polish-ness, I don't think, you know, defines my every waking moment as maybe Dr. Mogan would think at some point that our ethnicity would define—but . . . I think it's part and parcel of who I am." She acknowledged that as an active element of her own and her Polish family and friends' identity, "it definitely is going away, I think," but added, "certainly there's some identification I think in the community of me as Polish. . . . I'm sort of like a Polish resource person!"

That role has been defined by this woman's active participation in the Lowell redevelopment project for almost thirty years. For her, as for many of Lowell's cultural activists, a conscious ethnic identity appears to be something that has largely resulted from the revitalization experiment, rather than predating it. Another woman pointed to Patrick Mogan's impact on her own thinking about her Irish background, which had not previously been a conscious element of how people in her family identified themselves:

> My mother's generation . . . kept in touch with the family over there, but it was a family thing rather than a heritage thing. We really got very much into the heritage thing in the late '60s and early '70s. My brother's done a lot of research, I've done some. But the whole idea of the *history* then became much more [important]. . . . [I]t was that whole thing going on with [Pat Mogan] in the city, having, getting a better handle on what my own heritage was.

Shaped by Mogan's strategic public emphasis on ethnicity, and by the many social currents of the 1960s and 1970s that contributed to a celebratory search for roots among assimilated Euro-Americans, this woman and others have used their involvement in the city's many festivals, exhibits, and educational programs to shape institutional networks and modes of presentation that have supported the tight linkage of Lowell—of localness—with ethnicity. Although many of my public historian informants shared with the local activists a two- or three-generation distance from ethnic or immigrant ancestors, the public historians could not or did not claim authority based on ethnicity. In the separate-but-equal balance between the local and outsider poles, that claim is reserved solely for locals (see figure below).

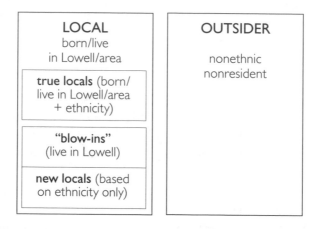

Within the local pole itself, there is a discernible division (shown above) between the "true locals" who can claim both ethnicity and longevity in the city and those who can claim only one of these attributes. This division inevitably privileges the long-established Euro-American groups—notably the Irish, Greeks, and French Canadians—whose members were most active in the early days of the revitalization experiment and who have long dominated local politics. The second category within the local pole contains two kinds of people. First there are blow-ins who have lived in the city long enough to have demonstrated their loyalty to it but who are not identified as ethnic for the purposes of their work in the heritage realm. They include planners, artists, scholars, educators, and other professionals who have chosen to make Lowell their home, whether they arrived before the inception of the culture-led redevelopment experiment and participated in its creation, were drawn to the city by new professional opportunities within the redevelopment project, or have found the resulting postindustrial city a congenial place to settle.

This category contains many of the people associated with Paul Tsongas, like Lowell NHP Assistant Superintendent Peter Aucella, who has lived in Lowell for many years. Aucella is Italian American, the grandson of an immigrant laborer, but he makes no active use of his ethnicity in his work or social life in the city. It is true that there were very few Italian immigrants to Lowell, but even in the case of blow-ins whose ancestors came from an ethnic group that *did* settle in the city, the distinction between localness and outsiderhood is still maintained. The national park superintendent frequently alluded to his own Irish American background in public statements about cultural conservation and celebration, but it seemed to be clearly understood by all that he was using this to show solidarity, not to claim the specific kind of authority wielded by true locals. Some outsiders may occasionally claim ethnicity as a source of local credibility, like the historian at the University of Massachusetts Lowell who had been involved in Lowell's public history realm for many years and who described his ethnic background to me as English, Irish, Scotsh, and Dutch, "but I'm also French Canadian—I can pull that if I want! It trumps most." The fact that he lived in one of the well-to-do suburban towns near Lowell, rather than in the city itself, however, lowered the value of his ethnicity card, as did the fact that he did not have family ties within Lowell's Franco-American community. The great majority of blow-ins whom I met lived in Belvidere, the city's most elite and expensive neighborhood.

Although blow-ins, like outsiders, bring valued expertise and energy to Lowell's redevelopment project, their socioeconomic parity with the true locals also makes them a force that the true locals feel the need to counterbalance. They do so by frequent small reminders designed to assert the "humbling, leveling effect" of localness. For example, the 2001 Lowell Folk Festival featured a panel discussion on public–private partnerships in the city's historic preservation efforts, at which Paul Marion, former Historic Preservation Commission directors Peter Aucella and Fred Faust, and the head of the Lowell Historic Board spoke about how Lowell had become, in the moderator's words, "the poster child for preservation." Two older local men, who had participated animatedly the previous day in an audience discussion following a panel on preservation techniques, paused briefly next to the chair where I was seated just before the panel started, but declined the panelists' invitations to sit down. One muttered to the other that he wasn't interested in hearing these panelists talk about preservation. "Aucella and Fred Faust should get down on their knees and give thanks for the city of Lowell," he added. "It's what's made them their money." This was the sound of true localness telling the blow-ins—*sotto voce*—who came first. At one point during the panel discussion, Faust handed the microphone to Paul Marion, "the only native from Lowell sitting here today." The head of the Historic Board protested that he had also been born in Lowell but was reminded that, because he had moved away for many years and then come back, he could not claim to be a true local. Such comments, sometimes gentle, sometimes more barbed, serve to maintain the balance between true locals and blow-ins in the local discursive pole.

In the case of the second subcategory of localness, the balancing act is more complex. This second category contains recent nonwhite or non-English-speaking migrants to the city—those who are automatically identified as ethnic. I never heard anyone refer to Lowell's Cambodians, Brazilians, or Africans as blow-ins. Rather, people in this category seem to be granted a kind of provisional localness, which will presumably be confirmed once they have enacted enough of the rest of the story— climbing the ladder and proving their worth to the groups ahead of them—to demonstrate a lasting commitment to and presence within the city. These people uphold true localness by virtue of their participation in the narrative cycle that gives true localness its claim to authority within the Lowell experiment—the story of immigration, settlement within ethnic enclaves in Lowell, struggles with poverty and prejudice, and eventual adjustment to life in the city and in America. Blow-ins who come from assimilated Euro-American backgrounds similar to those of true locals *challenge* the authority vested in that narrative by showing that it is not unique to Lowell. Their presence is in some sense a reminder of the objection raised by Park Service officials when the proposal for a national park in Lowell was first made—that "after 1860," as one early manager put it, "it's just another mill town." As we saw in Chapter 4, local cultural activists worked diligently to counter that argument, insisting that the national park should interpret a broader narrative about Lowell's industrial history that included immigrants and their cultures as well as the early "golden age" of mill girls and technological innovation. Lowell's new ethnic locals do double duty in reinforcing that insistence. First, they represent a continuation of the broader narrative about Lowell, underscoring its importance as an enduring aspect of the city. And they do so in ways that are linked to specific Lowell places and neighborhoods—the Acre, the Lower Highlands, Middlesex Village—and unique characteristics (for example, the fact that Lowell is home to the second-largest concentration of Cambodians in the United States). The new locals inhabit narratives and places that are important in the discursive foundations for the reimaged Lowell, and hence they are a deeply valued element of the local pole of heritage discourse.

But while they are valued as performers, bearers of ethnic traditions, and living continuations of some of the city's key narratives about itself, the newcomers represent other dangers to the redevelopment experiment. The tendency of ethnic discourse to be particularist and oppositional poses a threat to the unifying rhetoric agreed upon in the 1970s by civic leaders from Lowell's established Euro-American groups. Those groups, of course, could afford to relinquish more narrowly specific ethnic agendas, because they had long since established their own political and social bases of power in the city. Their "twilight of ethnicity" was very different from the high noon in which the newer groups negotiate many pressing questions of bicultural identity, economic survival, civic presence and power. Cultural performances about culture and ethnicity in such a setting almost inevitably involve political maneuvering among different factions and groups, whose machinations and frequent instabilities run directly counter to the rhetoric of cooperation and unity that forms the conceptual and organizational basis for the culture-led experiment. During my fieldwork period in Lowell, for example, the city's largest Cambodian organization, the Cambodian Mutual Assistance Association (CMAA), assumed the management of many important Cambodian cultural performances, including the New Year's celebration and the popular Southeast Asian Water Festival. The CMAA's central role in these events, as well as its apparent close connections with the regime of Cambodian Prime Minister Hun Sen, whom many Cambodians consider an illegitimate and repressive ruler, sparked considerable resentment among some southeast Asians in the city. Running the ambitious events also overextended the CMAA, contributing to its eventual financial and administrative collapse and the virtual eclipse of what had been a thriving and vital cultural, educational, and social service organization.

Moreover, the concerns that recent immigrants negotiate through their cultural performances are often extremely different from those that true locals see as significant or worthy of public performance. For instance, many Cambodians and Cambodian Americans are deeply troubled by generational ruptures between adults and youth. Such schisms threaten many of the social-support mechanisms on which they rely for emotional and economic survival in the often-inhospitable setting of America's advanced capitalist society. Many Cambodians are willing to go to great lengths to mend generational breaches and integrate younger people as fully as possible into a sense of Cambodian American community. I attended several Cambodian social and cultural events that included hip-hop and rap performances along with other kinds of Cambodian singing and dancing. The angry posturing and explicitly sexual gestures of the young performers were clearly distasteful to many of the adults present, who seemed suspicious of the lyrics and dismayed by the volume level, but still were willing to endure both rather than exclude their children from their gatherings. In turn, some younger performers actively and skillfully use popular music to bridge these same gaps. Tony Roun, founder and leader of a hip-hop group called Seásia, uses provocative rap lyrics and performances as a way of attracting attention from a young audience, which he then attempts to turn sometimes directly, sometimes in more long-term ways toward more community-oriented issues. His is a tenuous and sometimes contradictory balancing act that depends largely on the charisma of his bad-boy rapper persona to redirect his young fans' attention to such matters as the dire poverty of contemporary Cambodia or the importance of showing respect for elders.

Such approaches, however, are at odds with the conventions of Lowell's heritage mainstream, which favors cultural forms framed as "folk" or "traditional" and prefers that its heritage productions be imbued with an aura of pastness and noncommercialism. Kirshenblatt-Gimblett has written that such preferences create performances and festivals in which "respectability and decorum, values of the dominant cultural institutions that stage the event, tend to diffuse the oppositional potential so essential to festivals. For this and other reasons, these festivals have a tendency to reinforce the status quo even as enlightened organizers and performers struggle to use them to voice oppositional values. Carnival represented is carnival tamed" (1998:77). It is no coincidence that the only Cambodian group officially affiliated with the national park is the Angkor Dance Troupe, which took up residence in the Mogan Cultural Center in 2001 and which teaches royal court dance and classically choreographed folk dances to its young members. The troupe gives a nod to the attractions of hip-hop in one number, in which young men portraying monkeys suddenly begin to break-dance halfway through the performance, but this carefully stage-managed representation of youthful rebellion is very different from the more presentist and carnivalesque performances of Tony Roun and Seásia. The conventional approach maintains and exoticizes otherness rather than allowing it to enter and possibly transform the dominant cultural sphere. This approach was clearly operating during the Mogan Center advisory committee's early meetings (discussed later in this chapter). Some committee members argued that offering English classes would quickly accomplish the group's stated goal of attracting people from the city s new immigrant populations. Others, however, questioned whether English classes were "cultural" enough, and hence in keeping with the center s mission. Instead, they decided to offer classes in Khmer (later adding Portuguese and Spanish). These, of course, were not of interest to the great majority of recent immigrants. Rather, they tended to draw people from the same class of new-economy workers and assimilated Euro-American ethnic backgrounds that already inhabited Lowell's heritage spaces.

Lowell's new locals, then, pose a threat to the city's heritage establishment because they are negotiating particularist present-day ethnic business through their cultural performances rather than allowing those concerns to be subsumed in a general unifying discourse about ethnicity. The multiple loyalties of many immigrant cultural leaders also make them less than fully accountable to Lowell's own cultural networks. Several of the most active young Cambodian American leaders I met in Lowell were strongly drawn to work in Cambodia, whose battered infrastructure remains greatly in need of educational and other resources. And, finally, not all of Lowell's new immigrant groups necessarily reinforce the dominant narrative of immigration, adaptation, and progress, nor do their stories always reflect the image of Lowell as a desirable destination or America as a conscious and preferred choice among immigrants. The presence of large numbers of Latinos and southeast Asians in Lowell, as in other American places, is in many ways a result of often-questionable economic and military intervention by the United States in other nations. Their experiences of immigration do not fit the classic Euro-American paradigm around which the coalition that developed Lowell's new experiment gathered in the 1970s.[5]

Thus the new locals are welcomed—selectively—as cultural performers, and the true locals who populate the boards of directors of the city's
cultural and historical institutions frequently comment that they would
like to see more representation by newer groups around those board
tables. But, as the final section of this chapter illustrates, actual over-
tures from these institutions have been extremely tentative, with the
result that there are almost no new locals in decision-making positions
within the city's heritage realm. This exclusion is a product not of discrimination or even of simple turf-consciousness, but rather of a high
degree of vigilance on the part of those who carry the institutional
memories of the culture-based experiment. For true locals who remember Lowell at its most depressed and despised, the accomplishments of
the past thirty years—and the image-making mechanisms that have
been key to achieving them—are to be closely guarded. Although new
locals and blow-ins are welcomed into the local discursive pole, they still
remain to some extent outsiders who have not yet demonstrated long-
term loyalty and are not to be fully trusted with the management of
those mechanisms.

The Working People Exhibit

This balance between locals and outsiders was not achieved without some
struggle. To understand how this cultural division of labor and the twin
poles of heritage and historical discourse have developed over time, it will
be helpful to examine the evolution of the Mogan Cultural Center, particularly the Working People exhibit that it houses. The Mogan Center
was a pet project of the Lowell Historic Preservation Commission, the
development partner of the national park. In Chapter 5, I discussed the
commission's role as a bridge between the economic and cultural aspects
of the revitalization plan. Both philosophically and in terms of personnel,
the commission represented a blending of the Mogan-inspired celebratory ethnicity and Tsongas-led economic development program that had
emerged, sometimes clashed, and ultimately joined forces in the decade
before the park and commission were created. Mogan himself was among
the first commissioners; two former Tsongas aides served as executive
directors for most of the commission's seventeen-year tenure. However,
the commission was also a crucial mechanism for negotiating the relationship between locals and outsiders, including local people with a

long-standing involvement in the culture-led experiment and national park staff who came on the scene after the park's creation in 1978. Although the division was, once again, far from absolute—some local people worked at the national park and some outsiders were among the commission members and staff—in general the commission claimed the local voice, while park staff spoke from a more distanced, outside perspective (see Norkunas 2002:37–38 for a discussion of this division). This difference manifested itself in many aspects of the collaboration between the sister institutions, but perhaps most clearly in the creation of the Working People exhibit in the Mogan Center.

In the flurry of development during the early phase of the national park's life in Lowell, many different plans were mooted for exhibits and other public historical spaces. Some of these—for example, the park Visitor Center in the Market Mills complex—were achieved almost as envisioned. Others changed greatly between plan and execution or disappeared altogether, in response to shifting relationships and agendas. Thus the national park's main museum exhibit at the Boott Mill represents a marked change from the original plan to base the park's interpretive efforts at the Wannalancit/Suffolk Mill complex. (The somewhat orphaned waterpower exhibit that remains at the Suffolk Mill is an artifact of the debate between the park and the Preservation Commission over the choice between the two locations.) Similarly, the building known as both "the boardinghouse" and the Mogan Center was the focus of various plans and goals. The building as it exists today is very much a reflection of the relationships among the organizations promoting those ideas.

As concrete plans for the redevelopment project took shape in the mid-1970s, leading up to the 1977 publication of the key planning document known as the Brown Book, planners united around the idea of finding a way to show the close spatial and architectural relationships between work and living space in early Lowell—that is, between the textile mill buildings and the corporation boardinghouses. One of the few places where this configuration could be made clear was at the Boott Mill, where a single four-story boardinghouse block—greatly altered and in use by a paper goods company in the 1970s—remained next to the mill complex (see fig. 10). This block was named in the 1978 legislation as one of the few properties to be bought outright by the federal government.[6] In the Brown Book, it was proposed that the boardinghouse block house should primarily house a national park exhibit about

FIGURE 15. This former textile corporation boardinghouse was owned by a paper company before being restored to its original appearance. Re-christened as the Patrick J. Mogan Cultural Center in 1989, it forms part of the central node of cultural activity in postindustrial Lowell, along with the adjacent Boardinghouse Park and the Boott Cotton Mills Museum. JIM HIGGINS

the mill girls (Lowell Historic Canal District Commission 1977:40). Staff at the Historic Preservation Commission, however, had very different ideas about the building and the area that surrounded it (fig. 15). In its 1980 Preservation Plan, the document that guided its work over the busy first decade of development, the commission proposed that two-thirds of the boardinghouse be given over to a restaurant that would combine dining with interpretation by "utilizing historic menus and an interpretive backdrop exhibiting the influential role the boarding house played in the lives of the 'mill girls.'" Restored boardinghouse rooms would overlook the dining areas. The remaining third of the building would be a community cultural center "designed to both celebrate and sustain Lowell's sense of its own heritage." In it, residents and visitors alike would be able to conduct research in a facility run by the University of Massachusetts/Lowell, buy Lowell-related materials and memorabilia, and create and view temporary exhibits about Lowell's history and culture. The center would also provide rehearsal and performance space, classrooms, and a backstage area for the outdoor performing arts

stage that the commission hoped to build on the lot next to the boardinghouse building (Lowell Historic Preservation Commission 1980:44–
45). This plan reflected both the cultural and economic agendas of the
Historic Preservation Commission. The idea of a community cultural
center was very much an extension of Patrick Mogan's early vision for
the urban park as a place for community learning and expression.[7] At the
same time, the commission's plan was designed to support its goal of
drawing activity and energy into the downtown area, the primary focus
of its economic redevelopment efforts. The boardinghouse/cultural center and the adjacent performing arts park—eventually known as Boardinghouse Park—were seen as one way to combine these functions. The
commission took the lead in developing the boardinghouse and the outdoor performing-arts space, an extensive and expensive undertaking.[8]

In the meantime, a third component had been added to the mix of elements that would occupy the boardinghouse block: labor. The inclusion of
labor history in the national park's proposed interpretation had been an
important early selling point to Lowellians who were skeptical that the
park would simply glorify capitalist achievements and benefit already
wealthy property owners in the city (Ryan 1987:357–58). The Greater
Lowell Central Labor Council, an AFL–CIO affiliate that acted as an umbrella for a wide range of union locals, had been involved in the culture-
led redevelopment project from the beginning, participating in the Lowell
Regattas that prefigured later festivals and ethnic celebrations, and taking
an active part in the lobbying efforts leading to the establishment of the
national park. The federal legislation creating the Preservation Commission had provided a seat for organized labor on the commission, formal-
izing the existing relationship between working unions and Lowell's new
experiment. Labor history was also an important point of convergence
with the work of the new social historians, who in the 1970s and 1980s
were enthusiastically investigating the development of a working-class
culture and consciousness in the United States and elsewhere. Thus there
was considerable impetus to create park exhibits that would focus on labor
as well as technology, production, waterpower, and capital.

Originally, park and commission plans proposed a building dedicated
entirely to labor, where national park exhibits could share space with the
Labor Council. The Preservation Commission's 1980 plan called for the
commission to buy a building on Kirk Street, next to the national park's
administrative headquarters. The commission was to renovate this struc-

ture cooperatively with the Labor Council, whose members were to provide free construction labor in exchange for a low-cost lease that would
give them office space and meeting rooms for union gatherings and public educational programs. The commission promoted this latter idea as a
way of "reviving the historical Chatauqua conference" and the tradition
of popular adult education (Lowell Historic Preservation Commission
1980:43). It was also a reflection of the goal of community participation
and continuing education that had been held by community educators
like Pat Mogan from the earliest stages of the revitalization project. However, the commission's plan for the Kirk Street building was never
realized. As Peter Aucella described in his August 2001 tour of the
downtown, the building in question was owned in part by a landlord
who was taking advantage of the influx of southeast Asian refugees in
the early 1980s by crowding as many people as possible into his rented
rooms. The commission was unwilling to enter directly into the politics
of affordable housing or to pay the landlord's exorbitant selling price.
It was also gun-shy from a previous battle with a property owner who
instigated a lengthy legal battle over an overpriced building that the
commission attempted to take by eminent domain. The eventual solution to the Kirk Street dilemma was that a downtown bank closely allied
with the redevelopment network agreed to pay the landlord's price and
acquired the building to house its mortgage division.

The idea of a labor exhibit and a partnership with the Central Labor
Council then became part of the commission's plans for the new cultural
center being created in the boardinghouse building. The original notion
of a restaurant did not take hold; instead, the plan shifted to a three-
way partnership around the theme of "the working people of Lowell."
The commission would physically develop the building and oversee the
creation of an active community cultural center as well as an exhibit
about Lowell's immigrants; the national park would create an exhibit
about mill girls; and the Central Labor Council would have offices, a
meeting room, and some exhibit space in the building. In addition, the
university would house its special local collection, the Center for Lowell
History, in the newly built section of the old boardinghouse block. The
unions' presence in the heart of the redevelopment project would have
rendered the boundary between performance and everyday life particularly porous, allowing for a flow of symbolic and political materials back
and forth across the line that separates display from lived reality. Over

time, however, the partnership with the Central Labor Council weakened and finally dissolved, for reasons I was unable to determine fully. None of the people I interviewed could recall exactly what went wrong. Paul Marion thought that "it was a bit of an overlay on the whole process that maybe hadn't been thought through carefully." A public historian on the park staff attributed the failure of the relationship to the fact that, as he put it, "the Labor Council was never in the business of doing public history or public history interpretation or museum development. So it was all new to them, and I don't know if they were uncomfortable with the process or they didn't understand it or what. But it was never developed well." My efforts to locate the former leader of the Central Labor Council during my fieldwork period were unsuccessful, and I was left with a vague impression that a general incompatibility in goals and methods had caused the dissolution of a once-active partnership.

This left the park and the commission to work together on what would become known as the Working People exhibit. Although it has a single title and was designed and fabricated by the same contractor, the project was actually envisioned as two linked exhibits, with the national park and the Preservation Commission overseeing and paying for the mill girl and immigrant sections, respectively.[9] The exhibit occupies about half the floor space on two stories of the original boardinghouse structure. It begins on the ground floor with a recreated boardinghouse dining room and housekeeper's room, designed to show what daily life in a corporation boardinghouse was like in Lowell's earliest days. A popular wall display illustrates the kind of food typically provided by the boardinghouses, and the dining room tables are set for a meal. This downstairs section was intended to reflect worker life "as mill owners and their agents intended it to be." Upstairs, a recreated worker bedroom and wall display focus on "aspects of the nineteenth-century world which the mill girls themselves actively helped create while living in Lowell" (Center for History Now 1984:4, 9)—the cultural and consumer activities, periodicals and other writings, and labor-oriented debate through which Lowell's earliest workforce helped to shape the new city.

The mill girl section faithfully reflects the historiographical approach of the new social historians who helped shape Lowell NHP's interpretation, which emphasized the agency of workers and the periodic conflicts between them and mill owners and managers. However, these themes—and, to a large extent, the very notion of work itself—abruptly vanish at the end of the mill girls section of the exhibit. A mezzanine deck between the two segments of the exhibit was meant as a transitional area, but is in fact more of what one reviewer called "a wide seam" straining to hold together two very different conceptions of what the exhibit should be (Laurie 1989:876). The immigrant section begins with a catchall time line of facts about Lowell, including information about the arrival of the city's major immigrant groups up to the start of the southeast Asian migration of the early 1980s (the time line ends in 1986). The mezzanine deck looks out on a room lined with national flags, photo montages, signs and other artifacts from ethnic organizations and businesses in Lowell. Three large and crowded display cases in the center of the room focus on a variety of themes relating to immigrant life—ethnic enclaves, Americanization, and so on. There is a small case devoted to Lowell's Franco-American Jack Kerouac, a seating area where visitors can watch two short videos about Lowell's past and present immigrants, and a small temporary exhibit space. Paul Marion, cultural affairs director at the Preservation Commission during the period when the Working People exhibit was created, told me, "I used to say that the Immigrants section required that we present/ interpret in some way the experience of people from more than 50 ethnic groups over a period of about 150 years." As a result, the immigrant exhibit is like a scrapbook or a photo album whose creators wanted to make sure that no family member or bit of information was left out. Typically, visitors do not pause to try to make sense of this collection of objects and artifacts. From the convenient vantage point of the mezzanine above the immigrant exhibit, I watched many visitors who had spent considerable time in the mill girls section simply walk through the later part of the exhibit with just a glance or two at the display cases.

Labor historian Bruce Laurie, who reviewed the exhibit for the *Journal of American History*, commented critically on the disjunction between its two halves. Laurie noted that "the planning and development of 'The Working People' reflects the disparate perspectives of its creators, the Lowell National Historical Park and the Lowell Historic Preservation Commission" (1989:875). Park planners agreed; as one member of the park exhibit planning team told me:

> I think the balance was maybe a little out of whack, as if the mill girls were somehow a different species than what came after them. . . . I think on the mill workers, the immigrants' side, that it's a little mushy. That

it sort of becomes—it's not clear whether we're trying to tell a serious social history story or just celebrate with flags and bunting. . . . And that, I think, reflects the dichotomy between the park folks who really wanted to focus on the story, and the commission folks who were there to sort of help the community celebrate their history. I think that exhibit, more than any other thing in the park, kind of reflects that inability to quite bring these things together into a common vision.

There were several points of contention between park and commission staff during the planning process for the Working People exhibit. One of these concerned a proposal to depict a conversation among a family of immigrant workers at their kitchen table. This became, in Paul Marion's words, "a flashpoint that forced the contractors, the government, and community to work through a serious conflict." In the recreated bedroom of the mill girls section of the exhibit, visitors hear an audio recording of several women's voices discussing working and living conditions in early Lowell. Attempting to create a visually and thematically unified exhibit that would link the very different approaches of the park and the commission, the exhibit designers at the Center for History Now put forward a plan for a second audio segment in which an immigrant family would discuss life and work around their kitchen table in a somewhat later Lowell. Paul Marion, as the Preservation Commission's project manager for the immigrant section of the exhibit, strongly objected to the proposal. He felt it duplicated not only the dining area on the first floor of the mill girls section, but also a tenement kitchen that had been a feature of the Lowell Museum, the locally developed museum that had acted as a forerunner of the national park exhibits until its closing in 1982 (see Ryan 1987:255–88 on the Lowell Museum). But Marion's objections were philosophical as well. In his words:

> I was convinced that the Immigrants section of the Working People Exhibit should stress the larger world of the ethnic peoples—making a tenement kitchen the focus of that section seemed to be to be the wrong focus and too narrow as a presentation of the overall experience—these were people who won elections and ran businesses and built churches, and who made an impact on the city at large. (I saw the tenement kitchen as a kind of ethnic cliché that stressed the domestic life rather than the public life of the people who made Lowell what it is today.)[10]

Both sides invoked strategic considerations in the debate over the kitchen proposal. For the park planners and exhibit designers, the kitchen scene was a way to personalize and humanize a complex story of immigration and labor in a way that would allow park visitors—who were likely to be socioeconomically distanced from this working-class, ethnic world—to feel a sense of connection to it. Kitchens, one planner told me, "just capture people. People love kitchens! And they can just get into it." In proposing the kitchen scene, then, park planners were hoping to facilitate rituals of reconnection for people who already had a foot in the new economy. Marion, on the other hand, was supporting the underlying local purpose of the culture-led experiment of helping Lowell reinvent itself within that economy. He was pursuing the strategic course set by Patrick Mogan, who had hit upon the tactic of celebratory ethnicity as a way to create common ground among people from the older white ethnic groups in the tenuous early stages of Lowell's redevelopment. For Marion, as for Mogan, maintaining the strength and solidarity of local networks created during this formative period was more important than the internal or intellectual coherence of any single museum exhibit, especially at a time when the rapid influx of new immigrants was creating new ethnic and political tensions in the city and threatening the fragile gains already made in enhancing the city's image. Marion's opposition to the kitchen plan was a way of asserting the strength of the local voice and of refusing to let the multiple histories of Lowell's immigrants be subsumed by a single, thematically unified "story" told by outsiders.

Debate over the kitchen proposal was contentious, and "could be excruciating sometimes," according to one park planner. Eventually, Marion whipped out the blow-in card: "[I] pulled rank as a Lowell native and someone whose family had been in Lowell since 1880. I did not refrain from making my objection personal in that I said the Immigrants exhibit was about my family, and that I believed that the exhibit should emphasize the larger lives of the ethnic peoples in the community rather than putting undue emphasis on home life in what little space was allocated for this story." "Paul was adamant on it," another member of the park planning team told me. "And he had the weight of the commission." That weight, backing up Marion's own claim of local authority, was enough to veto the kitchen plan and to help ensure that the public historians' more critical, thematic approach would not penetrate the immigrant section of the exhibit. Ironically, the proposed kitchen scene could have shown at least as much—and probably more—political and civic involvement and agency on the part of the immigrant workers as is conveyed by the scrapbook-style exhibit that was ultimately installed. Although Marion objected to the domestic setting, it seems likely, given the kinds of themes treated in the earlier mill girl section of the exhibit and the intellectual interests of the public historians and designers involved in the planning process, that the kitchen-table vignette would have focused on labor, working-class culture, and class and ethnic relations rather than purely on "home life." As it stands, work all but disappears as a theme in the final part of the Working People exhibit, which makes no cohesive statements about the immigrants as workers or as members of a working class. Just as ironically, because the immigrant section of the exhibit makes no clear statements at all, it leaves the door open for another kind of totalizing narrative: the unidirectional "American dream" story that we have seen operating in the Acre tours and that most park visitors bring with them as part of their personal understanding of cultural change and socioeconomic progress.

Marion's objections make more sense, however, if they are seen less as arguments over content and more as reflections of a process of social negotiation between people from the local and outsider poles of Lowell's new heritage field. The kitchen controversy revealed how Lowell's cultural activists have confronted the predicament that often bedevils "natives" who turn to heritage-based economic survival strategies—the danger that they may be pushed into what Dean MacCannell has termed a "forced traditionalism" (1999:178; many scholars have studied this phenomenon, including Batteau 1990, Bruner and Kirshenblatt-Gimblett 1994, Chambers 2000, Desmond 1999, Evans-Pritchard 1987, Olwig 1999, Whisnant 1983). These activists have constructed an authoritative voice for themselves, one largely based on their association (however distant) with ethnicity and industrial labor. But although much of their authority within the heritage realm is based on their implied association with ethnic and working-class life, too close an association with those things can be risky—in the same way that the Acre is a source of roots and authenticity but also a place of danger and shame for many middle-class Lowellians. The cultural activists who speak on behalf of the community within the culture-led experiment fear that they themselves may be stereotyped or discounted by the critical outsiders who have come to the city to tell "the story" of Lowell. They have no wish to find themselves symbolically or literally located in a kitchen but never in a boardroom. This dilemma is perhaps particularly acute for the local cultural activists whose own forebears were more likely to have been civic, religious, and business leaders than industrial laborers, and who themselves have been so active in shaping the city's new cultural economy. It is precisely because they are deeply embedded in the structures of the city's revitalization efforts that they have been able to leverage institutional support for their own assertions of authority, as the case of the kitchen controversy in the Working People exhibit demonstrates. The risk of "forced traditionalism" inherent in the construction of the local pole of heritage discourse is countered by a close network of social and institutional connections that reaches deeply into the central workings of the city's redevelopment project.

Public historians, not yet securely embedded within that project, were in this case unable to leverage their own authority to the point of being able to insist on some linkage of the earlier, more critical themes of the mill girl exhibit with the later immigrant section. An exchange between Lowell NHP historian Robert Weible and reviewer Bruce Laurie in the pages of the *Journal of American History* (1990) revealed how the public historians were caught between the social demands of their situation in Lowell and the intellectual demands of their scholarly discipline. Laurie deplored the effects of the strong local voice on the planning team, stating that the direct intervention of "new players with more discordant voices and perhaps political clout and economic influence" (1989:874) ultimately posed a threat to public historians' ability to create coherent and intellectually sound exhibits. Noting that this was doubly serious because of Lowell NHP's pioneering role in the public history movement, Laurie concluded, "If, as is likely, the Lowell model . . . is adopted at other historical parks, we can expect continuing conflict and confusion (1989:879)." In response, Weible defended the public history model that was being pioneered in Lowell. Although he himself had been among the park staff members strongly advocating a more critical and unified interpretation in the Working People exhibit, he nonetheless argued in print that the possible drawbacks of local or amateur involvement were more than offset by the benefits of fostering a collaborative approach to presenting history in public. Historians' own "self-serving and hierarchical notions of academic superiority," he maintained, had "brought the profession to a sorry junction in its own history—a junction at which we historians may have learned to speak to each other with what we regard as growing authority, but at which our determination to pursue a path of what might be termed 'pure professionalism' will surely lead us to what the rest of the world will consider a dead end of irrelevance" (1990:384). Weible saw the Working People exhibit planning process as a brave attempt to reach the goal of "democratically expanding the ways in which all of us understand past and present" (1990:384)—a clear statement of the central goal of progressive public history. In a counter-response, Laurie insisted that that goal could not be reached unless public and academic historians made peace and found ways to foster public dialogues in which historical voices—that is, those informed by the critical, scholarly approach of the profession—were equal partners.

Weible and Laurie were essentially in agreement about this goal, yet neither addressed the social and political realities of how it might be possible to bring it about. Weible defended the existing forum in which Paul Marion's blow-in card had trumped the public historians' proposal and produced an exhibit that reflected collegiality and coexistence but not true collaboration or dialogue. Unlike Weible, Laurie made a direct case for the value of what a more critical or historical perspective might have brought to the exhibit, yet he did so in a way that denied the performative, "up for grabs" quality of historical inquiry and illustrated all too clearly why historians' claims to authority have often been resented by their various publics. Laurie's complaint that "The voice of the people often violates established themes of immigrant history" reflected academic historians' impatience with the views of those who had no particular allegiance to or respect for the disciplinary forum in which those themes had been established. At the same time, his declaration that "context. . . . is the stuff of history; history without context makes flawed history and flawed exhibitions" (1990:385) ignored the reality that, as Shannon Jackson has written, "Acts of contextualization—whether in the montage effects of museum exhibition or historical writing—are inseparably linked to questions of politics and partiality" (1998:269). The context provided by public and academic historians was no more inherently "correct" than Paul Marion's context for understanding Lowell's immigrant history. Both were equally constructed, but in different social and political settings. Historians would argue—and I would agree—that their own perspective does bring something of value to the public discussion of the past. But Laurie's and Weible's statements reveal the difficulty that historians have had in balancing that value with other kinds of authority operating in particular social forums. Laurie's words revealed a lack of deference to those other authorities; Weible and his colleagues perhaps ultimately erred on the side of too much deference, or perhaps they were simply unable to mobilize their own authority effectively at that early stage of the city's revitalization. In any case, the local pole in the Working People exhibit planning process proved to be the stronger, resulting in an exhibit in which the critical views of public historians end abruptly at the mid-nineteenth-century point when they encounter the ancestors of present-day Lowell's cultural activists. This division has persisted throughout the national park's interpretation, making itself felt whenever the topics of immigration, culture, or ethnicity arise. We saw it at work in the walking tours of the Acre in Chapter 4; now we will see it operating during the park's recent attempt to rejuvenate the Mogan Center.

Reviving the Mogan Center

Many of the ingredients of the kitchen controversy were strikingly replicated in the May 2002 food program described at the beginning of this chapter. In both cases, people from the local and outsider poles of Lowell's heritage discourse were working together on a cultural production at the Mogan Center. The task involved representing the people of the city, including its ethnic populations, within public historical space. In addition to local cultural activists and public historians (including some of the same people who had been involved in creating the Working People exhibit), the project made use of contracted professionals from outside Lowell. Like the exhibit-design team whose suggestion for the kitchen vignette sparked such contention, the folklorists responsible for the "Feasting on Lowell" program represented in many ways the most critical and intellectual perspective on the material they were proposing to display. And in both cases, the displays themselves revolved around food, kitchens, and ethnicity. Yet these very similar ingredients produced a very different outcome, reflecting the changed relationships between locals and outsiders and the changed demography of the city itself. Now that we have seen how the categories of localness and outsiderhood were constructed and how they have been maneuvered into balance with one another over time, we can return to the "Feasting on Lowell" food demonstration with a better understanding of the subtle but powerful social dynamics operating just under its apparently unre-markable surface.

With the end of the Lowell Historic Preservation Commission in 1995, community-related activities at the Mogan Community Cultural Center all but came to a standstill. When I began my fieldwork in 2000, the park had just recently convened a public forum focusing on its rela-tionship to the city's diverse populations. Forum attendees included many from the small tribe of local cultural activists, but also some newer faces, including some from the "new local" groups. People at this gath-ering urged the park to make better use of the Mogan Center as a meet-ing place between the park and the city, a notion that resonated with a larger management concern among National Park Service leaders. Wholly dependent on public support and tax dollars, the Park Service is justifiably uneasy about the preponderance of Euro-Americans among the staff, visitors, and histories at its sites, given shifting demographic patterns that predict Euro-Americans will be a minority in the United States within the next few decades (Murdock 1995).[11] For both philo-sophical and pragmatic reasons, the Park Service increasingly feels the need to court new constituencies and establish working relationships beyond its traditional base of support. At the same time, true locals who had been active in the culture-led experiment over its lifetime were beginning to turn their attention to similar questions of support and succession. "I'm getting tired," one local cultural activist confessed to me. "A cause of great distress for me is that, well, I'm not old, but I can't do the things I used to do, I don't have the energy, I don't even have the ability to focus on these things as much as I used to. And I don't see anybody coming—I'm distressed about that." Paul Marion was among those promoting the idea of using the Mogan Center as a place where the city's culture-led redevelopment efforts could be revitalized by new people and new energies. In one interview with me, he spoke hopefully of the center's advisory committee as "kind of a leadership mill . . . where people who haven't been involved with some of these organiza-tions and agencies and processes and projects are getting exposed to it and getting their chance to come in now and take a leadership role." With a quarter-century of achievement behind them and a continually changing city all around them, both the locals and the outsiders in the cultural realm felt the time was ripe to revisit the question of how the national park and the city related to one another.

In partnership with the University of Massachusetts Lowell, park management made a commitment in the spring of 2001 to fund activities at the Mogan Center and appointed a Patrick J. Mogan Cultural Center Community Committee to advise the park on new programming. The committee met for the first time in September 2001 and began working quickly toward the goal of planning that year's schedule, which they hoped would include a substantial, professionally produced exhibit as part of an official reinaugural event in the spring of 2002. Their chosen theme, "The People of Lowell: Past and Present," was intended to produce a project that would "reflect the city's social mosaic in a way that contributes to positive cross-cultural exchanges among residents" and "present the personality of the city and its people in a creative way." The call for proposals was not distributed until late November; applicants had just six weeks to craft and submit their proposals before the mid-January deadline. Because of the short turnaround time, the committee received just a handful of proposals, only one of which, from a pair of Boston-area folklorists who had previously done contract work on various folklife projects in Lowell, met the committee's key criterion of promoting cross-cultural exchange. Their proposal, "Feasting on Lowell," used food as a starting point for talking about the city's people. The project would include an exhibit on the city's ethnic food markets, a small-scale scholarly conference, and a series of cooking demonstrations by people from Lowell's various ethnic communities.

As with the kitchen vignette in the Working People exhibit, then, the folklorists were proposing to link ethnicity and immigrants with food and cooking—the same combination that had roused Paul Marion to vocal opposition a decade and a half earlier. Marion, in fact, was once again part of the planning team for this exhibit; he held one of three seats on the Mogan Center committee reserved for representatives of the university.[12] These three along with three public historians from the national park (the historian, curator, and volunteer/outreach coordinator), three at-large community representatives, and the part-time Mogan Center coordinator recently hired by the park, proceeded to debate the merits of the proposal. The main arguments raised against it were that the plan too closely resembled other projects already carried out in the city; that the conference would attract primarily professionals and not a wide cross section of the community; that food was not a substantial enough topic for the center's reopening exhibit; that the exhibit itself would emphasize artifacts and signs rather than people, the intended focus of the project; and that the folklorists themselves were "hired guns" who were not from Lowell—that is, as outsiders, they should not be entrusted with the representation of Lowell's people and cultures. Countering these points, one of the public historians echoed the folklorists' own rationale by insisting that food could, in fact, be very a useful lens for observing people. Other supporters of the plan found it the most appealing and lively of the proposals, with a serious critical and historical component and the potential to foster exactly the kind of cultural exchange and encounter that the committee hoped to see. The folklorists themselves argued that, while they were indisputably outsiders, as one of them put it to me, "there is a purpose to be served by this anthropological role. There are things that we can do as outsiders, that we can *see* as outsiders, that we can kind of oversee, that you can't do when you're on the inside"—for example, to provide a critical perspective that could have value for everyone involved.

At committee meetings to discuss the proposals, it was clear that the park and university representatives felt both external and internal pressure to reach a prompt decision. There was a sense that the committee needed to produce something quickly in order to show park management and the public that there was new activity at the center. But the internal pressure for agreement within the committee was also a powerful force. "It would be nice to get off the ground with some consensus on our first big exhibit," Paul Marion said at one point, and others echoed his comment that compromise was preferable to division. Although there was disagreement over the proposals the committee had received, and different people obviously liked or disliked the various ideas under consideration, the arguments tended to lose themselves in these calls for consensus and action, rather than turning into more extensive debates over the ramifications of representing Lowell's people in one way or another. Some committee members noted to me that the rushed pace of the whole process left little time for such in-depth discussions, but my sense was that, even with more time, the outcome still might have been very similar. No one seemed to want to take a definite stand if it might provoke a direct confrontation with others in the group, and so the many minor sticking points of the discussion were quite quickly smoothed

over. Despite my very close observation of the final committee vote on
the proposals, I was unable to tell who had voted for what, or even who
was voting at all. Paul Marion, normally acute and articulate, was unable
to clarify this for me afterward; when I asked about the process, he
replied, "I didn't have a vote—I don't think I voted, maybe I voted, I
don't know. I don't think I voted. But—I think I didn't vote." When it
came time to make a decision, strong opinions were set aside in favor of
group solidarity, the hallmark of the new Lowell experiment.

The committee made a counterproposal to the folklorists to drop the
conference and the exhibit components of their plan, and simply hold
three ethnic-cooking demonstrations, the first of which would coincide
with the Mogan Center's public reinaugural event in May. This was the
plan that was eventually implemented, resulting in an event that showed
two southeast Asian women—an older Cambodian refugee and a younger
Laotian American—preparing chicken and papaya salads for an audience
of park staff, committee members, and invited guests. A Cambodian
American man who frequently acted as a bridge between Cambodians and
Euro-Americans in Lowell translated for the Cambodian woman, who
did not speak English fluently, while the folklorists provided occasional
comments and served as hosts, displaying the completed dishes and urging the audience to sample them. The event was steeped in an unques-
tioned exoticism, focused on introducing unfamiliar foods and cooking techniques to people from the dominant culture. Questions from the
audience were undemanding—"Why do you boil the chicken instead of
roasting it?"—and were more often answered by the folklorists than the
performers themselves. The atmosphere was friendly and casual, but the
southeast Asians remained on one side of the table, the audience of West-
erners on the other, with the mediating professionals in between. The
scenario against which Paul Marion had argued so vigorously in the mid-
1980s—ethnic people and immigrants located firmly in the kitchen, associated with food and domesticity rather than politics or power—unfolded
serenely during the reinaugural open house, despite Marion's presence on
the planning committee and his continued lack of enthusiasm for the idea
("So we're now the Mogan Food Center," he said pointedly, after the committee had voted to accept the scaled-down proposal).

Three different kinds of potentially critical perspectives—that is,
points of view that might have posed questions or challenges—existed
within the Mogan Center committee during the course of the process I

have described above. First, there were the true locals, with their tendency to resist outside representational authority and to insist that cultural productions in Lowell—especially those dealing with the contemporary city—should be meaningful and accountable to people from the city itself. Second, were the outside professionals—the public historians and, in this case, public folklorists as well—whose training and politics generally prompted them to argue that cultural productions should include acts of contextualization and linkages to broader and often critical patterns of interpretation. And finally, the otherness and the particularist agendas of the new locals had the potential to challenge and provide alternatives to dominant practices of cultural representation. The Cambodian translator commented obliquely on this possibility in an interview with me, agreeing with my remark that it was usually only ethnic others, not members of the dominant culture, who were expected to perform their culture in ways framed as folkloric or traditional. "I think learning shouldn't be like just one way," he told me. "Whenever you do creative programs you should think of ways you can teach the other and the other teaches you."

Yet none of these three types of critical potential was operating within the May 2002 Mogan Center event. The true locals and long-settled blow-ins on the committee still cast themselves in a somewhat oppositional role—"We still never let [the Park Service] totally off the hook," one local cultural activist told me—but deference now clearly went both ways, with the established local voices often ceding ground to the park without a struggle. As Paul Marion told me, "There's such a long, layered, complex set of relationships that I think, in the end, you know, people look to work it out." Contention over specific issues, he noted, was now "like a family dispute," in which everyone was ultimately on the same side. Similarly, the outsider public historians who worked at the park had accepted the structural authority of the local pole, and in the Mogan Center process appeared to align themselves with it in opposition to the even-less-local folklorists. Although the folklorists and the public historians shared a preference for a foodways event that would have explored the relationship between food and culture more analytically, the public historians appeared unwilling to advocate such an approach if it meant a direct confrontation with localness. For their part, the folklorists were philosophical about this lack of support and the scaled-down, uncritical event that resulted from it. Resigned to having little institutionalized authority and wholly dependent, like many cultural workers in the "creative economy," on short-term contracts, they had no platform or incentive for making a successful defense of their original proposal. Although no one was deeply enthusiastic about the May 2002 event, in one sense all of these actors gained something from it: the kind of continuing amity and unbroken accord on which the overall Lowell experiment—and the network of cultural production that supports their own work—seems to depend.

And what of the new locals, those whose presence in the city to a large extent prompted the park's renewed support of the Mogan Center, and whose otherness constitutes a potential challenge to the balance and conventions that have been created over the past three decades in Lowell's cultural realm? People from this category were present on the reconstituted Mogan Center committee as they had not been during the planning for the Working People exhibit in the 1980s. Indeed, the three at-large community seats on the committee were all occupied by people of color and/or immigrants. Despite the assertions of others on the committee that these members were not chosen to fill specific ethnic or racial slots, it seemed clear that "the community" with which the park was trying to connect was defined as the southeast Asians, Latinos, Brazilians, African Americans, and other racial and ethnic minorities who currently make up a majority of Lowell's population. Their presence on the committee was somewhat tentative, however, revealing the delicate balancing act between established and new ethnic groups within the city's cultural realm. Almost all of the park's first community appointees dropped out after attending one or no meetings, and in the meetings that I observed in late 2001 and early 2002, their successors attended much less regularly than did the park and university people.

One significant barrier to their participation was the fact that the committee met during working hours. This was a conscious strategy reflecting the belief that, as Paul Marion put it, "Lowell is a mature enough sort of community now, with a multiplicity of agencies and organizations and institutions, that I'm convinced we can find people who are a diverse group but that can participate in this as part of their professional life." In practice, this meant tapping people closely associated with mainstream cultural institutions, like the university, who are long-term supporters of the redevelopment project. Members from this pool of people were often already overextended; in addition, they did not necessarily bring notably new perspectives to the table. The preference for reinforcing the close integration of people and organizations within Lowell's cultural realm, then, along with the professionalization of cultural production in the city, worked against the inclusion of a wider range of community voices. More disparate voices might have challenged the stereotypical linking of food and immigrants on the same grounds that Marion had used years earlier: that this association marginalized and domesticated immigrant groups, denying the full range of their experiences and public participation. But although the older white ethnic groups have been present in both kitchens *and* boardrooms since the 1960s—running food booths at folk festivals but also sitting as directors of the Lowell Festival Foundation, for example—the newer groups are simply not at the table within most of the decision-making forums where they might raise challenges. Only one community representative on the Mogan Center committee—the one least personally connected with the city's new immigrant groups—was present when the committee's decision on the food demonstration was made. Nor do the new locals occupy positions of power within the city's political, social, and economic realms. The platform from which they might raise challenges to the status quo is much less solid than was Paul Marion's in the case of the kitchen controversy. In the specific case of the Cambodians, moreover, many people within this most visible and numerous of Lowell's new local groups prefer to avoid direct confrontation at all costs. Their tendency to accommodate rather than challenge authority can sometimes be an oppositional tactic,[13] but even then, it is one that dovetails remarkably well with the preference for accommodation within Lowell's cultural realm. This may be one reason there has been considerable support for Cambodian cultural performance from the city's heritage establishment, while other groups have been less successful in gaining a foothold there.

I have suggested above that, in the earlier kitchen controversy, the direct competition between two different forms of authority—the local and the outsider/public historical—resulted in a bipolar exhibit rather than a collaborative statement about working people. Bruce Laurie predicted that this foreshadowed "continuing conflict and confusion" in public historical projects embedded in culture-led redevelopment projects constructed on the Lowell model. By extension, it might seem logical that once the two forms of authority were more in balance with one another, more collaborative, dialogic productions would become possible. The two types of critical voices—the one resisting imposed stories, the other insisting on the importance of placing local experience into wider and more explicitly political contexts—might have drawn strength from each other, producing a nuanced view responsive to both local constituencies and the principles of the progressive element of the public history movement. But the food demonstration at the Mogan Center suggests that precisely the opposite has happened in Lowell. Instead of strengthening both, the closer relationship and greater balance between the two poles of authority appear to have curbed the critical potential of both. Further, it seems to have limited the potential for challenging or alternative voices to come from either outside professionals or new locals at the margins of the park's cultural productions.

Within those productions, as within Lowell's redevelopment project generally, solidarity trumps conflict. As progressive public historians have become deeply woven into the city's new cultural economy, their insistence that historical interpretation must acknowledge conflict has ironically been muted by a lower tolerance for direct conflicts with localness in their own work lives, a development that has muted their critical potential over time. As I noted at the outset, "heritage" projects—the kind that combine local celebration and economic redevelopment with professional interpretation—contain many tensions and contradictions that make them, in Kirk Fuoss's terms, "essentially contestatory" (1998:115). Yet the example of Lowell shows this inherent contestation has been channeled, over time, into a quiet, ongoing accommodation among a small and closely connected group of people. The tension between "heritage" and "history," which could serve as an opening for continuing discussions about the meanings and uses of Lowell's past, appears to have been ironed out over time. Why has this happened? And because it is happening in Lowell, does that mean it is typical of culture-led redevelopment efforts generally?

I see two related reasons for this is accomodation in Lowell. First, the very success of the city's efforts to become a postindustrial place has foreshortened the kinds of broader and more public discussions about meanings, equality, exclusions, class relationships, and so on that took place in the earlier phases of the culture-led experiment. In those formative days, much more was "up for grabs." With the growing accomplishment of many of the major goals of the new Lowell experiment, much of the existing conceptual open space has been grabbed—that is, the interpretation of history and culture in Lowell has become institutionalized and codified in a new status quo that is not entirely closed to new ideas but that patrols the boundaries of its considerable achievements with great vigilance. Those within the pale are now engaged in consolidating gains rather than engaging in new or renewed discussions about inclusion and exclusion. The potential for such debates is still there, of course—performative moments are always at least potentially available for different kinds of people to seize and use in sometimes unexpected ways. The border between cultural performance and real-life politics is never entirely closed. But it may be very heavily guarded, as it currently is in Lowell's cultural economy. Although to some extent this is a natural progression for any institutionalized form of expression, it is also a reflection of the historical relationships among the groups and people who have, with great effort, helped to create postindustrial Lowell over the past four decades.

The second factor concerns the specific positioning of those people and groups within the postindustrial economy. Although people at the local and outsider poles of cultural discourse in Lowell have often been at odds with one another over their relative authority within the city's redevelopment project, they also structurally occupy extremely similar socioeconomic positions within the wider society that is emerging in the wake of economic restructuring in the United States. They are all "cultural intermediaries" who stand at the intersection of culture and economics, the local and the global. These people help to create that society through their work and patterns of consumption. They are its beneficiaries; their jobs, their status and authority, and many of the satisfactions of their lives are derived from the particular set of economic and cultural conditions that characterize postindustrial places. Many, as we have seen, are also among its critics, but their ambivalence toward some of the effects of the new economy does not alter their basic relationship to it. And it is that shared relationship that accounts for the blurring of the lines between history and heritage, between interpreters and visitors, between locals and outsiders. It would be too strong to say that there is any class consciousness or any overt mobilization of shared class interests occurring within these shifting sands of postindustrial social realignments. But the structural similarity among knowledge and culture workers in the postindustrial economy does negate much of the potential that their work and the institutions they inhabit can serve as truly critical voices in the public sphere that they are helping to produce. Lowell's experiences do not determine what will happen elsewhere, of course, and perhaps this muting of critical potential will play out differently in other places, or even in Lowell, as the postindustrial society continues to change. But at present, Lowell is perhaps the best site we have for observing the effects of culture-led redevelopment over a span of decades. And what Lowell teaches us in this case is that truly critical perspectives increasingly struggle to make headway against the layered social and economic forces—within the globalizing economy, local redevelopment efforts, and individuals' own lives and worksites—that serve on so many levels to dampen them.

Epilogue

In May 2005, as I was completing the revision of this book, I made a final brief fieldwork foray. There is always a temptation to do this with an ethnographic project that is close to home, especially after there has been a stretch of time to write about and reflect on the data gathered in the original fieldwork phase. One last interview or a quick look at one additional site, we think, will surely provide the final piece of the puzzle.

In this case, there were two more things I wanted to accomplish. As I have already noted, I spent considerable time during my initial fieldwork period observing the planning process for the renovated Boott Cotton Mills Museum exhibit. This project had allowed me to watch my primary informants—Lowell's progressive public historians—grappling with the creation of an exhibit that would carry the park's interpretation of Lowell, labor, and textiles into the present day, a task that was particularly pertinent to my own central inquiry. Considerably overdue when I left Lowell in the summer of 2002, the exhibit plans were finally almost ready, and it seemed important for me to review them. Throughout this book I have made a case that the park's interpretation shies away from making too direct a connection between past and present. In many subtle ways and for a variety of reasons, as I have shown, its sharply critical statements about early capitalist development in Lowell are not fully allowed to inform questions about how capitalism is developing in contemporary Lowell and around the world. The plans for the revised ending of the Boott Mill exhibit would let me see whether the park's public historians had come any closer to the kind of critical discussion that, I have argued, public history in Lowell has the potential to foster among visitors and others who partake of its productions. My second goal on that May day was to interview an informant I had not previously been able to locate: the union official who headed the Greater Lowell Central Labor Council in the final phases of its involvement with the culture-led redevelopment project. None of my Lowell informants had remained in touch with him after he had moved away from the city some years earlier, and my own efforts to find him during my fieldwork had been unsuccessful. Finally, though, I had tracked him down through a Boston union of which he was now a member, and I hoped to speak with him about an unanswered question that seemed important to resolve if I could: What had gone wrong with the relationship between the labor unions and the park? This partnership had seemed so much in keeping with the original vision of the park as a place where a critical knowledge of the past could connect with active, present-day discussions about work and culture in the changing economy and society of Lowell and beyond. Why had the collaboration foundered?

The two pieces of data that I added as a result of this last fieldwork trip appeared, at first glance, to belong to completely different puzzles. First, the plans for the revised Boott Mill exhibit deeply unsettled the conclusions I had reached about the unwillingness of Lowell's public historians to confront the connections between industrial production in Lowell's past and in the present in other places in the world, or between cultural production and the new postindustrial economy. In fact, the proposed exhibit renovation will encourage audiences to make these connections in a remarkably clear and critical way. In considering contemporary textile production, the exhibit addresses economic globalization and both the opportunities and the dangers that have been claimed for it. The "new Lowell mill girls" in recently industrializing countries are portrayed in images and words, and the parallels with Lowell are made explicit. The exhibit touches on the ongoing shift from agrarian to industrial economies around the world, the opportunities for new industrial workers to make cash wages, but also the reality of worker exploitation in many places, and the increasing mobility of capital and its search for ever-cheaper labor. A "hands-on" component of the exhibit uses everyday articles of clothing—pants, T-shirts—to pose tough questions about costs, profitability, and consumer choices. The isolated moment around the working loom in the 2001 Run of the Mill tour is firmly encoded into the museum's performance here, effectively breaking the frame between the exhibit and its audiences' lives and socioeconomic positioning.

Further, the exhibit comes very close to breaching the more sacrosanct frame between its own producers and what it depicts. Replacing the simplistic boosterism of the old "Lowell Today" room, the renovated displays will show how people in Lowell mobilized historic preservation and cultural production as a foundation for the city's ongoing economic and social revitalization. The question of what constitutes a "postindustrial society" is posed directly, again challenging viewers to consider their own places within the story of capitalist development. If this part of the exhibit is less hard-hitting than the most demanding observer might wish—it stops short, for example, of raising questions about gentrification, displacement, the widening rich–poor gap, the marketing of cultural experiences themselves as a new kind of product, and so on—it nevertheless opens the way for visitors to consider many connections that have long been masked by Lowell NHP's presentations. When it is installed, the new ending of the Boott Cotton Mills Museum exhibit will supply a crucial piece that has been missing for many years in the public historical treatment of Lowell's story, and it should add to the park's deserved reputation as one of the most significant and thought-provoking of all industrial sites. The Boott Mills exhibit renovation, then, turned out to be almost everything I had hoped for but had not expected to see. This radically undermined my critique of the park's interpretation and made me wonder whether I had taken a very wrong turn somewhere along the way. Such are the dangers of returning to a fieldwork site *after* having written it up!

My interview with the former Greater Lowell Central Labor Council president seemed to complicate my thinking further. It was useful to have, for the first time, a perspective from the union side of the abortive partnership between organized labor and Lowell's redevelopment project. It became clear that there had been considerable enthusiasm among union members for the prospect of participating in ongoing cultural performances of labor history. The idea of a building on Kirk Street entirely dedicated to labor may have fallen through, but the salvaged plan that would have placed the Labor Council in the renovated board-inghouse block offered the same set of tangible and intangible benefits. Instead of meeting in a rented downtown hall and conducting business from scattered offices in various buildings and officials' homes through-out the area, the unions would be able to consolidate their operations in a single central location.

> And you would have a working union hall at night, with the charters, you know, the union charters, hung all around the wall, because every local has their own charter, you know.
>
> *Would that have been on display during the day?*
> Oh, sure. Oh yeah, you would have seen them all, you could come in ... walk around, smell the cigar smoke, wipe the blood off the chairs ... [laughs]. It was going to be really a living, working place.

In addition to the pragmatic value of office and meeting space, there had been excitement among many union members about the connec-tion with the new national park and the chance to be a part of the story of labor told there. "I think there was a feeling that we were important to something," the former union leader told me. "You know what I mean? That somebody was saying something right." It was, he added, "very much the spirit of Lowell, which was upbeat at the time. . . . [The city] was trying to come back." The unions, then, had seemed support-ive of the vision of the national park as a place where there was a highly porous boundary between exhibitry and the everyday business of labor organizing, where both could ultimately contribute to a renewed and more flourishing Lowell.

Then what had gone wrong? My informant had no definite answers to my main question about precisely why the relationship between the Labor Council and the redevelopment project fell apart in the late 1980s. It was clear that a number of factors had contributed: changes in person-nel within the various organizations involved, personality clashes, ten-sions over money, and an ironic 1988 incident that I had heard men-tioned from other sources. The boardinghouse block, later christened the Mogan Cultural Center, was at that time being renovated as a home for the labor offices and meeting hall along with the park's Working People exhibit and the university's local archive. Due to an oversight by a contractor and some trading of favors typical of Lowell's cronyish insider network, the masons hired to lay the brick on the exterior of the building turned out to be nonunion laborers. A local reporter seized on the story and publicized it, making it difficult for the Labor Council to defend its continued involvement in the project. In one of the more ironic twists in the story of the new Lowell experiment, a dispute over brick—that quintessential symbol of industrial cities—dealt a final blow to the disintegrating partnership between organized labor and public history.

Yet my conversation with the former union leader did not fully explain why the bedrock commitment to that collaboration had not been strong enough to survive these setbacks. Throughout Lowell's redevelopment, well-placed players have made heroic efforts on behalf of certain projects deemed essential to the success of the overall venture. Personality clashes, money woes, and other similar problems have arisen and been surmounted in these instances. Why was the relationship with organized labor not among them? It seemed apparent that the partnership was simply not a high enough priority for those in powerful positions to fight for its continuance, and that the kinds of personal and structural interconnections that might have supported it—such as existed in the financing, real estate, education, and public history areas of the project—were not in place in this case. The former Labor Council leader speculated that labor's presence may not have been fully supported by all those on the Historic Preservation Commission: "I don't know that. But it was vastly deemphasized." Beyond that, however, he would not go. Like the other people I spoke to in Lowell about this subject, he was vague in his recollections about the dissolution of the partnership. At the end of our interview, I was left with the same sense of things not being said, and of a promising vision that had not been realized for reasons that no one could or would point to with real certainty.

How can we reconcile these two final pieces of data? The renovated Boott Mill exhibit appears to point in one direction, toward a public historical voice able to pose important questions about the kind of society that is emerging as capitalism continues to develop and expand its reach. The fragmented recollections of a severed partnership, on the other hand, seemed to say something very different about public history. It was evidence of another small but significant displacement, of the loss of social connection with another set of active voices speaking in concrete, instrumental terms about questions that the park's exhibits were representing in more symbolic form. Which of these two is the accurate picture?

The answer, of course, is that they both are. They coexist, unreconciled, within the kinds of postindustrial and public historical developments that have become so common throughout the United States and in other places. They appear to point in opposing directions because they exist in very different relationships to the gap—Boyer's "double erasure," Turner's breach in the social drama, Jackson's "necessity for ruins"—caused by economic and social change taking place on many levels. The truncated relationship with organized labor represents one of many incomplete attempts in Lowell to carry relationships and instrumental activities across the gap—that is, to insist that history-making should play an active role in the everyday struggles of a wide range of people to comprehend and operate in their world. The "wide range" is the key notion here. Places like Lowell NHP *do* provide tools for people to understand their world, but the people in question represent only a small and very specific segment of contemporary U.S. society. And they are using these public historical spaces primarily in ways that are atomized, individual, and largely inward-looking.[1] The new Boott Mill exhibit, excellent though it is, approaches the gap from the far side. It creates documentary and conceptual connections between past and present but it does so in isolation from people outside of that same strikingly homogeneous class of cultural producers and consumers. The exhibit is a way of looking back at the gap, not a tool for getting across it or struggling with what is happening within it, as the partnership with labor might very well have been.

Lowell's new experiment has been blessed over time with a concentration of unusually critical public historians, and so the distance between past and present, performance and politics at Lowell NHP is narrower than it is at many other historical and heritage sites. But the gap remains deep and, within the logic of culture-led redevelopment, perhaps inevitable. It is a crucial component of the decline-and-redemption narrative that drives such projects, and so its edges are carefully guarded in many direct and indirect ways. It is essential to what MacCannell has called the "fragile solidarity" (1999:83) that postindustrial people and places crave and create for themselves in the face of the continual uncertainty and change of capitalist societies. It ensures that revitalization efforts like Lowell's are buffered from voices that might too sharply challenge the underlying assumptions about growth and progress on which the overall efforts are built. These kinds of challenges can and have appeared within Lowell's cultural experiment—the new ending for the Boott Mill exhibit is just one of these challenges—but they are not permitted to be raised in ways that would directly confront the mechanisms of power by which growth is encouraged and "progress" supported.

This buffering takes place in complex ways that are difficult to trace directly. It makes itself felt through the self-selection of public history as a profession by certain kinds of people, and of industrial history sites as a destination by certain other, very similar kinds of people. It is reinforced by the fact that many of the most critical and questioning voices in the public history world are to be found either at the edge of the field that overlaps most closely with the academy or in the higher echelons of public history organizations. These are the people who are most heavily invested in the prestige and politics of their institutions. And they are also the farthest removed both from the "front lines" of public history, where its characteristic rituals take place, and from the real-life struggles of people outside the "creative classes" to which they themselves belong and to whom their work speaks most directly.[2] Another reflection of the buffering mechanism can be seen in the fact that while redevelopment projects like Lowell's are being conceived on ever-larger scales throughout the United States, they appear to be used in more and more fragmented and less truly public ways. While culture-led revitalization is expanding exponentially as a social and economic tool, then, the spaces within it for collective discourse—particularly of the kind that might result in critical action—are dwindling. And the buffering process is reinforced by losses and truncations—like the failed relationship with organized labor—all of which have their own explanations and rationales, but add up over time to a weakening of the potential for public historical spaces to support that kind of critical collective conversation. The logic of culture-led redevelopment projects dictates that certain relationships and cultural productions will be nurtured while others—those that somehow violate or defy the underlying economic purposes of the project—will not receive the kind of long-term support that they need in order to survive.

Meanwhile, the postindustrial economy continues to become more entrenched and elaborated. This point was driven home to me by a third piece of data I collected on my final fieldwork day: the editorial in that day's Lowell *Sun*. Entitled "Renaissance City," it noted that the city's revitalization was proceeding apace with two new projects. First, the ribbon had just been cut on 5 new units of affordable housing in the Acre. And in the same week, a plan to create 170 luxury condominiums in one of the remaining empty mills in Lowell, the Lawrence Mills, was approved for federal loan assistance. The editorial noted that officials at the U.S. Department of Housing and Urban Development had originally objected to the use of federal funds for the project, but that the efforts of the city's politicians—the ever-effective Lowell "delivery system"—eventually won the day:

> The project is considered one of the most exciting in Lowell and is expected to add to the city's reputation as an affordable alternative for professionals and families who can't, or don't want to, pay exorbitant Boston real-estate prices. . . . The Lawrence Mills plans is yet another example of how the public and private sectors work together in Lowell to improve the city and the lives of its residents (2005:7)

The striking ratio of 5 affordable to 170 market-rate housing units in this account is typical of what is happening in postindustrial places like Lowell. The newspaper, an active backer of the culture-led redevelopment for many years, is not likely to raise its voice in criticism of this ratio. Nor are the developers, planners, and promoters who are most involved in Lowell's ongoing economic "renaissance." But what would it take to envision a public historical practice that might do so? Despite the many structural and personal reasons that militate against it, is it possible for public history to be a more active participant in public debates about the kinds of new places and conditions—including the new exclusions and imbalances, like the handful of affordable housing units to the mill full of luxury condominiums—that are being widely produced in the postindustrial climate? Is it realistic to ask the field to fulfill this function? Can we envision it ever doing so?

There are no doubt many public historians who would dispute my contention that they should concern themselves deeply with these questions. And throughout this book, I have argued that, even for those who might wish to do so, there are inherent obstacles that make such an approach problematic, maybe impractical, particularly within the kind of redevelopment projects we are now seeing built on the Lowell model. Yet I want to believe that it is both possible and crucial for public history to reconnect with the more radical energies that have historically been a significant element of its character. The task is daunting in the contemporary economic and cultural climate, but that only makes it all the more important to search for ways to struggle in this direction. And simply *because* culture-led redevelopment is so ubiquitous, it offers countless small opportunities for a reradicalized public history to chip away at the layers of distance that separate us from the stark political implications of histories like Lowell's, and to seek closer connections with people who are already questioning—in individual or collective ways—the powerful imperatives of capitalist growth and the kind of society we are becoming in the early twenty-first century.

A starting point for this venture, it seems to me, is clarifying what we think that society looks like and how it has been and is being achieved. This is one goal I have been pursuing toward in this book, and in part, it represents my own answer to the dilemma of how to be a critical intellectual voice within the knowledge and culture economy that simultaneously dismays and feeds me. It is also a task that public historians are well-equipped to tackle, as the new Boott Mill exhibit ending amply demonstrates. At present, though, even such impressive accomplishments still perform their knowledge in relative isolation, speaking only to the converted and not connecting to more public discussions to which they might relate. There is no cigar smoke lingering in these public historical spaces from union meetings of the night before, and this points to the social level of work that must be done to achieve a real renewal of public history's progressive energies and the greater fulfillment of the promise of places like Lowell National Historical Park. That renewal will ultimately depend not on exhibitry or documentation, but on new social projects and alignments. It will require the will and ingenuity of people working within cultural projects to shake up and politicize the emerging solidarity of the new creative classes, to take careful note of their own positions within the cultural economy, and to reach beyond the kind of relationships that presently endure in public historical spaces. Currently, these relationships are devoted to one primary task: the overall effort of remaking places and citizens to conform to the demands of the postindustrial world in which we now live. The public history I would hope to see in Lowell and places like it is one that could foster relationships with a wider, more encompassing set of people and thus a broader vision about what that world might become.

APPENDIX
Visitor Survey Summary, Lowell National Historical Park,
Summer 2001 and 2002

Survey Statistics

Total number of surveys completed		162	
Total number of visitors included in surveys		357	
COMPOSITION[1]	Adults	301	(84%)
	Female	173	(57%)
	Male	128	(43%)
	Children	56	(16%)
GROUP SIZE	1 visitor	44 surveys	(27%)
	2 visitors	69	(43%)
	3 visitors	25	(15%)
	4 visitors	22	(9%)
	more than four	12	(7%)[2]

---

1. I chose visitors at random, based on their apparent availability and willingness to speak with me (for example, if their body language indicated they were in a hurry, I did not approach them). Nonetheless, I attempted to speak with what appeared to be a cross section of the park's typical visitors. Although I did not note visitors' race, I did attempt to speak with as many of the park's few nonwhite visitors as possible, so these are probably slightly *over* represented in the survey.

2. The average size of these 12 groups was 4.75. It quickly became clear that it was difficult to conduct this survey with groups of more than three people. Gathering information about occupations, ethnicity, etc. was very cumbersome and time-consuming, which decreased people's willingness to continue speaking with me. Conversely, in the cases where visitors were happy to provide the information, it was difficult to record it all and to clarify whose information was whose, since I kept a single record sheet for each group I spoke with. Therefore I concentrated on smaller groups, who seemed to constitute, in any case, the majority of park visitors.

GROUP COMPOSITION	34 groups (21%) included at least one child.[3]
	34% of adults (102 people/51 couples) surveyed were part of a male–female couple.
	10% of adults were women visiting the park on their own (as compared with 4% men).

PLACE OF ORIGIN[4]		
	Lowell	14
	Greater Lowell[5]	16
	Greater Boston[6]	30
	Other Massachusetts	21
	Other New England	32
	New Hampshire	17
	Connecticut	8
	Maine	3
	Rhode Island	3
	Vermont	1
	Other U.S.	56
	New York	12
	California	5
	New Jersey	5
	Virginia	5
	Wisconsin	5
	Colorado	3
	Illinois	3
	Pennsylvania	3
	Oregon	2
	Utah	2
	Alaska, Arizona, Florida, Georgia, Indiana, Iowa, Maryland, Michigan, Minnesota, Missouri, Ohio, Texas, Washington	1

3. Groups with children are probably underrepresented in this survey. I found that people with young children were generally less willing to take time to speak with me, since they were often focused on the children's needs (especially at the end of a canal or museum tour). On the other hand, some people I surveyed did have children who were in the bathrooms, playing in the children's area of the Visitor Center, etc. I counted only children who were actually present while I was conducting the survey. With very few exceptions, responses are entirely from the adults. I did not address questions directly to children, although a few parents redirected my questions and the children would answer them.

4. The number of places of origin mentioned does not correspond to the number of visitors or surveys, because I did not always make an exact count of how many visitors in a group were from which place of origin mentioned. For example, in a group of four people from two different places, I would count each place name once, rather than taking the time to determine precisely which visitors were from each place. Visitors mentioned a total of 174 different places of origin.

5. To define the Greater Lowell region, I used the Lowell Labor Market Area list of Lowell plus eight neighboring towns: Billerica, Chelmsford, Dracut, Dunstable, Groton, Tewksbury, Tyngsborough, and Westford.

6. I included any towns within the Route 495 circle as Greater Boston.

Canada	1
Outside North America	12
United Kingdom	5
Germany	3
China, Colombia, France, Israel	1

PREVIOUS VISITS TO LOWELL NHP

90 of the groups surveyed (56%) had never been to Lowell NHP before.

47 (29%) had been to the park before. This included 8 groups who said they had visited the park "many years [15–20 years] ago" and had been curious to come back and see what it was like now.

21 groups (13%) included some people who had visited the park and some who hadn't.

4 groups (2%) had been to the city for other reasons but never to the park.

REASONS FOR VISITING LOWELL NHP

Wanted to return to park/bring others to see park	36
On vacation in area/looking for something to do	33
Interested in history/industrial history/mills/museums	20
included specific interest in	
textiles	6
NPS sites	5
engineering	1
mills	1
turbines	1
Learned of park through promotion	18
sources mentioned	
newspaper	7
guide book	4
AAA guide	3
Internet	1
Yankee magazine	1
travel magazine	1
sign on Rt. 495	1
Curious about/interested in Lowell specifically	17
Quilt Museum/quilt festival	11
Wanted to take a canal tour	9
Came for concert	7
specifically children's concert	4
Heard about park by word of mouth	6
Visiting family in Lowell	5
In area on other business	5
Came for Canal Heritage Day	
(esp. free admission, costumed interpretation	4
Nice weather, looking for something to do outdoors	3
Interested in Kerouac	3

Wanted to learn something	3
Working on school/college project/paper	3
Recently moved to city, wanted to learn more about it	3
Visit related to teaching work	3
Looking for children's activities	3
Came for conference	2
Child at Tsongas Center program	2
Came with tour group	2
Planned another activity which was cancelled, came here instead	2
"Lyddie" fan	1
Lowellian who drops by Visitor Center on walk home	1
In Lowell for Folk Festival	1
Came to see Visitor Center film	1
To use Visitor Center bathrooms	1

ACTIVITIES AT PARK

This question was designed to give me a *general* idea of which activities and offerings in the park and the city visitors were most likely to be drawn to. They do not give a systematic view of visitor activity, because I spoke to people at different points in their visits (those who were near the end of the visit could tell me more specifically what they had done than those who had just arrived and were still planning their day). As well, the location where I did the surveys influenced the responses I got (for example, most of my 2001 surveys were conducted at the Boott Cotton Mills Museum, so I was obviously speaking only to the visitors who chose to come to the Boott, while missing the many who only went to the Visitor Center, did a canal tour, etc.).

I have listed each activity mentioned by visitors, and the number of times it was mentioned. The percentages total much more than 100% because most visitors mentioned more than one activity.

Visitor Center mentioned 110 times		68%
Boott Cotton Mills Museum	97	60%
Canal tour	62	38%
Trolley ride	31	19%
(not as part of canal tour)		
Visitor Center film	29	18%
Working People exhibit	25	15%
Quilt Museum/quilt festival	23	14%
Not sure yet/other possible activities	19	12%
Eating at restaurant	16	10%
Greek	2	
brew pub	1	
Walking around city	16	10%
American Textile History Museum	13	8%
Concert at Boardinghouse Park	10	6%
Mentioned 4 times or fewer:		

Ranger talk/tour, walking by canal, junior ranger program, Canal Day presentations, Kerouac park/grave, Tsongas Center activity, shopping, visiting family, Whistler House, B&M train, Center for Lowell History, St. Anne's Church, Riverwalk, picnic, Irish Festival, Lowell Folk Festival, Suffolk Mill exhibit, driving around city, Brush Gallery, Revolving Museum

ETHNICITY OF VISITORS

Again, this question was designed to give me a *general* sense of what major ethnic groups visitors belonged to. I phrased my question as follows:

> *I'm interested in the ethnic backgrounds of the people who come to the national park in Lowell, to see whether or how those overlap with the ethnic and immigrant history that is shown here. What ethnic groups are in your own family background?*

Most visitors mentioned a blend of ethnicities: "English/German/Irish" and "French Canadian/Irish" were very common. I counted each mention of each ethnicity once in the list below (for example, "English/German/Irish" counted once each toward English, German, and Irish). I have also included answers that problematized or reshaped the category "ethnicity" itself (for example, "American southerner").

Irish	mentioned 67 times
English	64
Yankee/New Englander/"swamp Yankee"	7
White/WASP/Anglo-Saxon/American/Caucasian	9
German	50
French Canadian/French American	21
Other Canadian	4
(included English Canadian, Scottish Canadian, Irish Canadian)	
Other northern European	21
specific groups mentioned	
Dutch	8
Swiss	7
British Isles	2
Belgian	1
Flemish	1
Austrian	1
general northern Europe	1
Other eastern/central European	20
specific groups mentioned	
Russian	4
Armenian	3
Lithuanian	2
Czech	2
Croatian	1
Hungarian	1

Albanian	1
Ukrainian	1
general eastern Europe	5
Italian	19
French	
(may include some French Canadian)	18
Scottish	18
Scandinavian	15
specific groups mentioned	
Swedish	6
Norwegian	4
Danish	3
Finnish	1
general Scandinavian	1
Mixed	13
specific terms used	
"mongrels"	3
"Heinz 57"	3
other	10
Polish	11
Jewish	10
Other southern Europe	6
specific groups mentioned	
Greek	3
Portuguese	3
Asian	4
specific groups mentioned	
Chinese	2
Thai	1
Korean	1
Native American	3
Latino/South American	3
specific groups mentioned	
Brazilian	1
Colombian	1
Latino	1
Africa/Middle East	3
specific groups mentioned	
Israeli	1
Afrikaans	1
Lebanese	1
Black	1
Southerner (U.S.)	1
India	1
Mormon	1
No answer/not sure how to answer question	4

With this question I asked whether visitors felt that their personal or family history was connected in any way with the history being presented at Lowell NHP. Because some groups of visitors gave more than one answer (for example, a woman might answer "yes," her husband, "no"), total responses add up to more than the total 162 surveys conducted.

No connection with Industrial Revolution	96	52%
direct "no"	76	
"not sure"/"not aware of any"	20	
Some connection with Industrial Revolution	86	47%
No answer	1	1%

Many people mentioned some specific connection with the Industrial Revolution/industrial history.

Self or siblings work/worked in factory	6
Parents work/worked in factory	14
Grandparents worked in factory	25
Great-grandparents worked in factory	3
Someone in family (not specified) worked in factory	25

Industries/jobs mentioned specifically

Textiles	31
Garment trade	8
Mining	7
Shoes	5
Family-owned mills	4
Iron/steel	2
Labor organizers	2
Airplanes, paper, railroads, pianos, canal worker	1 each

Places mentioned specifically

Industries in Massachusetts	24
Lowell	9
Lawrence	4
Worcester	3
Billerica	2
Boston, Bridgewater, Brockton, Beverly, Salem, Haverhill, general Massachusetts	1
Industries in New England (other than Massachusetts)	9
Rhode Island	5
New Hampshire	2
Maine	1
general New England	1
Other U.S. industry	11
New York City	3
New York state	3

Pennsylvania	3
the South	1
Wisconsin	1
Non-U.S. industry	7
Germany	3
England	3
France	1

Four people said that although they were not aware of any specific family connections with industrial history, their history "must overlap in *some* way" with the history of the Industrial Revolution, given its breadth.

An interesting subgroup responded with variations on this answer: "No, there's no connection in my family with the Industrial Revolution, although my grandfather did work in a shoe factory." These visitors evidently were not connecting their family histories with the larger history presented at Lowell NHP.

When I analyzed the places of origin for people who said that they did have some personal/family connection to the history of the Industrial Revolution, I found that they very closely matched general visitor patterns for the park. That is, visitors from nearby were no more or less likely to have a personal connection with the Industrial Revolution than visitors from far away.

VISITOR OCCUPATIONS[7]	Park visitors	Lowell residents[8]
Occupation		
Management, professional, and related occupations	66%	28.4%
Service	2%	16.0%
Sales and office	10%	24.4%
Farming, fishing, and forestry	3%	0.1%
Construction, extraction, and maintenance	3%	8.6%
Production, transportation, and material moving	3%	22.6%
Other (unemployed/homemaker/student/etc.)	13%	n/a

7. Categories match the U.S. Census categories for occupation and industry. "Occupation" refers to the specific job a person holds, no matter what the industry (for example, a secretary in an industrial plant would be counted under "Sales and Office," not "Production, Transportation, and Material Moving"). "Industry" refers to the specific sector of society in which a person works. These numbers are somewhat less exact in my survey; if a person answered "secretary" when I asked his/her occupation, I did not always obtain follow-up information about which specific field he/she worked in. However, the preponderance of educational, professional, and administrative workers among park visitors is still clear even if the precise proportions are not entirely accurate. These figures are based on a total number of 288 occupations mentioned by visitors.

8. For purposes of comparing park visitors with the city they are visiting, I am using figures about Lowell's employment patterns from the 2000 U.S. Census.

Industry

Agriculture, forestry, fishing, mining	2%	0.2%
Construction	1%	5.2%
Manufacturing	4%	24.5%
Wholesale trade	0%	3.1%
Retail trade	4%	10.1%
Transportation, warehousing, utilities	2%	4.0%
Information	11%	3.5%
Finance, insurance, real estate	5%	4.5%
Professional, scientific, management, administrative	20%	9.7%
Educational, health, social services	29%	19.9%
Arts, entertainment, recreation, accommodation, food services	5%	7.2%
Other services (except public administration)	2%	4.3%
Public administration	3%	4.1%
Other (unemployed/homemaker/student/etc.)	12%	n/a

Of the 288 park visitors who responded to this question forty one (14%) were retired.

Follow up Surveys

I asked each group of visitors surveyed if they would be willing to fill out and mail back a short follow-up survey about their trip to Lowell. All of my informants took the survey with them; 87 people (54% of the groups surveyed) returned the survey by mail. Two of the surveys were returned blank.

1. (a) *Was there anything you particularly enjoyed or remembered about your visit to Lowell?*

Canal tour	25
Weave-room	16
Boott Mills	13
Worker videos/quotes/histories	11
Learning about history	9
Preservation efforts in city	8
American Textile History Museum	6
Clean/attractive/walkable city	6
Dam, locks, Francis Gate	6
Quality of rangers/guides	6
Quilt Museum, festival	6
Trolley	7
Canal walk	5
Mill buildings	5
Children's activities (including Boardinghouse Park concert, mentioned once)	4

Working People exhibit, boardinghouse	4
"Lowell: The Industrial Revelation" slide show	3
Museums	3
Suffolk Mill exhibit	3
"Wheels of Change" slide show	3
Whistler House	3
Friendly people	2
Kerouac Park	2
Riverwalk	2
Visitor Center	2

Mentioned once: being able to see changes/decline in city, costumed interpreters, bookstore, overall interpretation, seeing similarities with own work, "explanatory kiosks" (waysides?), parking at Visitor Center, quietness of city, low entrance fees, cultural heritage of Lowell, unusual urban park, Folk Festival, 1912 strike video, good signs and literature, visiting family in Lowell, restaurants, Boardinghouse Park concert, learning about immigrant history

1. (b) *Was there anything you did not enjoy or found disappointing?*

Nothing	31
Lack of open places to eat/shop	10
People on streets unsavory, unfriendly	4
Poor signage, got lost	4
City feels unsafe	3
Few people around	3
Not enough interpretation on some subjects	3
Trash in canals	3
Trolley out of order	3
City dirty in places	2
City feels empty, like a ghost town	2
Ran out of time	2
Trolley rides too short	2

Mentioned once: Sports Museum closed, unable to get on canal tour, some historic buildings not open (gatehouses), boardinghouse not developed enough, few maps, no restaurant guide, not enough comparisons with present in exhibits, could connect more with educational institutions, would have liked audio tours, no reasonably priced hotels near downtown, some rangers not knowledgeable, weave room, Quilt Museum expensive, not enough about immigrant opportunities, fewer park tours than previously, exhibitry too static, turbines not operating, exhibits outdated, Park Café, Boardinghouse Park concert offensive, lack of air conditioning on hot day, lack of pedestrian crossings, Visitor Center could do more to orient visitors, not enough technical/engineering information, introduction to ranger talk was dull, not enough children's activities.

2. (a) *Do you think there is value in preserving the history of the Industrial Revolution?*

100% of follow-up respondents answered "yes."

2. (b) *Why did you choose this answer?*

For detailed responses, see Comments A. Recurring themes were:

Industrial Revolution a major shift in U.S./ regional history	20
Understanding the past helps us understand the present	16
A way to see progress, change, development, growth	16
Helps us learn from past mistakes, make a better future	13
Important to understand the past	11
Important for educating children, new generations	10
History generally important for understanding life, identity	9
Interesting to learn about past	6
Learning about/preserving the past is enjoyable	4
Understanding present-day cultural diversity	4
Authentic sites/preservation efforts important	3
Better appreciation of current standard of living	3
Educational value	3
See development of labor/worker struggles	3
Understand forebears' sacrifices, hard work	3
Understand economic history, capital flight, etc.	3
Involved professionally in history field	2
Gain sensory/visual/auditory sense of past	2
Understand current digital revolution	2
Understand role of women	2
Understand role of immigrants	2

Mentioned once: provoke thought, understand U.S. decline from manufacturing power, learn from forebears' ingenuity, tell stories of marginal people, see role of technology in our lives

3. (a) *Can you name any of Lowell's major immigrant groups (past or present)?*

Irish	59
French Canadian (includes French, Quebec, Franco-American, Canadian)	34
Greek	34
Cambodian	24
Italian	20
Polish	16
Portuguese	13
Vietnamese	10
Jewish	8
Hispanic/Latino/Spanish/Latin American	8
Asian	6
Russian	6
South Asian/Indian/East Indian	6
English/Anglo	5
Puerto Rican	5

Chinese	4
Laotian	4
Southeast Asian	4
African	3
African American	3
Armenian	3
Eastern European	3
German	3
Colombian	2
Lithuanian	2
"Mill girls"	2
Scottish	2
Cannot name any	4
No answer	5

Mentioned once: Central American, Czech, Dutch, Middle Eastern, Near Eastern, Romanian, Slovenian, South American, Slavic, Thai, Ukrainian, Welsh, Yankee, Yankee/English

3. (b) *Did you see any evidence of those groups while you were in Lowell? (If so, please describe.)*

No answer	5
Restaurants/bars	24
Greek	6 mentions
Asian	5
Irish	4
Latin American	1
Italian	1
No sign	19
People on street or in restaurants/stores	17
In park exhibits/videos/photos	12
Churches/ethnic organizations	11
Greek	2
Irish	2
French	1
Asian	1
Ethnic stores/markets	7
Canals as signs of Irish presence	6
Festival signs, brochures	3
Water Festival	2
Greek school	1
People on tours	3
Street names, buildings, signs	3
(e.g., L'Union St. Joseph Building)	
"Everywhere," "just look around"	2
Knows people in Lowell ethnic groups	2
No answer	6

Mentioned once: "Some," Portuguese weave room employee, schools, Puerto

Rican flag, Tsongas Arena, friendliness of the Irish, ethnic teen threw rock at canal boat, dirt, crowded apartments, teens disobeyed traffic lights, Asian crafts in museum shops

4. *What is your impression of Lowell as a place to live or work today?*

I characterized responses to this question in one of three ways:
Clearly positive (e.g., "Busy and a nice place. Diverse.")
Clearly negative (e.g., "Lowell gives the impression that its best days are behind it [despite the hype of "revitalization"].")
Ambivalent/neutral (e.g., "It appears to be in a rebirth, but not yet vibrant.")

In cases where one informant made two kinds of statements (e.g., one positive, one ambivalent), I counted each response in the appropriate category. I counted 152 total statements, which broke down as follows:

Clearly positive	55
Clearly negative	37
Ambivalent/neutral	60

For detailed responses, see Comments B. The most common response was for visitors to note Lowell's ongoing revitalization.

There is an ongoing/incomplete revitalization	23
Interesting history/culture	10
Positive impression	9
No impression/not sure	9
Visitor prefers larger/smaller city/more rural area	8
Diverse city	7
Attractive city/downtown	6
Clean/cleaner than before	6
Might like to work here	6
Still needs more/better jobs, better housing	5
Still has depressed image in region	4
Nice to visit, wouldn't want to live here	4
Would not want to live here	4
Blue-collar city	3
Busy place	3
Friendly, welcoming	3
Impoverished	3
Lack of vitality	3
No night life	3
Still struggling	3
Downtown needs more shopping	2
Downtown not attractive/inviting	2
Good to see mills being re-used	2
Noted civic pride	2
Quiet, slow pace	2
Wonders about school quality	2

Mentioned once: high-crime area, successful high-tech sector, attractive suburbs, comfortable, might like to live here, downtown thriving, likes living here but working here not profitable, felt unsafe after dark, inexpensive to visit, easily accessible, little opportunity here, good potential, depressing, some nice restaurants and stores, unfriendly, unwelcoming, educational, liked river area

Comments A

Detailed comments in response to the question: *"Do you think there is value in preserving the history of the Industrial Revolution? Why did you choose this answer?"*

Preservation is important to understanding our past and for personal reflection on our present existence. It provokes thought and promotes understanding of culture.

Let people know the past and so they can enjoy present and do better in future.

You can understand more by seeing and "hearing" the factory and I'm not sure that people fully understand the impact of the Industrial Revolution on other politics.

A significant change in people's lifestyles, wealth.

Every history gives us the knowledge about the truth of life.

History is part of the identity.

It's a very important aspect of our society's development.

To help those of us today put our lives and way of life in context—perspective of those who came before us only a century or so (or less) ago.

The history is a link to the present day. Who we were makes us what we are today.

Without the Industrial Revolution where would we be today? These people made a tremendous contribution to our country.

It's a good way for every generation to think of what happen in the past and what is the best way to improve ourselves.

This was such an important time with the shift away from the agrarian economy. The 19th C. was such an exciting time of changes, including the role of women in our history.

An important chapter in American history, that helped to draw millions of immigrants who essentially created America anew socially, culturally and economically.

Important to maintain historic perspective—

Because it is our heritage.

It's very important to know the past, to keep memory of how things were.

It's important to preserve that time in history so that future generations can see and hear how hard our parents and grandparents worked so hard for their children to have a better and easier life than they did.

- Need to have this comparative focus for understanding contemporary work and industry
- Need to understand the importance of ethnic migration into the U.S., to appreciate contemporary sociocultural diversity

It is important to understand how people behaved in another era and the exploitation they endured to insure that our society does not regress from the advances we have made in civil and human rights of our citizens.

That history is often overshadowed here in this region by Revolutionary War history. Also, it is very interesting to consider the parallels between the Ind Rev and the 20th c. electronic one.

Everybody likes to record and preserve history. And by so doing as in Lowell, it gives us another interesting stopover city to visit on the way to our niece's home in Bar Harbor, Maine.

Those who do not understand the past are doomed to repeat it. I feel that many Asian countries have special insight into the planned industrial communities. You would be surprised to know that Low[ell]'s model has been copied in meticulous detail for manufacturing of most of the commodities. Toyota has an industrial community at the base of Mount Fuji complete with planned hydro-electric power to employee housing replete with modern benefits such as schools for children and amenities to keep the worker bees happy. I have visited at least 70 carbon copies of Lowell from the Mini-Dragons of the Asian rim to German, French, and Italian companies copied and expanded on in detail. I would be happy to supply you with additional correspondence if it would be of benefit. I have been to nearly 40 countries and have had the cooks tour of many such facilities.

Gets to our industrial "roots" to show how industrialism developed.

Industry has changed so much that folks miss how much went before and the struggles people went through—the way things were invented led to the current industry development. Important to see models.

I love history and believe in the statement that knowing history helps us to understand ourselves in the present and to construct a better future.

It's interesting—meaningful—Helps one to understand and appreciate ppl [people] and our country.

We should always know the history of our country, and this is a part that shaped what we are now.

I'm [a] history major and give Cultural Arts Program to 4, 5, 6th grade students in elementary schools.

W/o preservation people in time wouldn't have history.

Our children can actually see how things have changed not just from colonial times, but also from the 1800s–1900s.

It was interesting. Very informative. Value to young people.

Because we learned a lot about the Industrial Revolution.

I graduated with honors in (American) history from New York University. This is a terrific opportunity to visualize what an industrial community of the nineteenth century was like. I came away with a far more sophisticated understanding of life in a textile mill. Workers experienced horrible working conditions (by today's standards).

It's important for our youth to know of our history, especially that our nation was once a strong manufacturing center. Afraid our grandchildren will grow up thinking the whole country is employed as consultants—that no one has to do anything—just talk about it. We hope to bring our grandchildren here.

Crucial to understanding our past and growth in the U.S.

I am an historian of early industrialization in Canada—actually I did my M.A. thesis on this topic.

It's important for future generations to be able and look back on past cultural advances and discouragements.

The Industrial Revolution helped define a period of history and changed the face of America—both in personal consumption and in commercial production.

I think it's important to teach kids how things came to be the way they are today through history.

It was the beginning of what we know today.

To educate future generations.

Just the importance of the time and learning about the mill and the workers is fascinating.

Learn from the past, it's interesting, it's fun.

It is important to know the sacrifices and hardships endured by workers. The elements that made the development of the textile industry possible were all available in this area.

Industrial Revolution helps explain our economy today. Plus, role of Lowell in growth of women's movement, is important.

We need to know our history and what has gone before.

History can be taught/remembered/valued more if it is preserved and presented in an interesting and authentic setting.

Because it is cool to see how people lived before you and how lucky you are. Margie (Age 11)

It makes history come alive. It helps explain today and maybe we can learn and not repeat mistakes!

It's good to know about our past.

Besides being interesting, we need to know this history to try and avoid the same problems in the future (as well as get ideas from the ingenuity of our predecessors). The same issues that we deal with today were issues then, and we can learn from them.

The Industrial Revolution brought as much social change as 1776 or the Civil War. Studying it helps understand the present digital revolution. (I teach the subject at the School of Business Administration, College of William and Mary. I stress the networks . . . i.e., canals, railroads, Internet and Global Information Infrastructure. All the same things are happening . . . overbuilding, financial crises, increase in wealth etc.) Most people do not realize that until the Industrial Revolution everyone was in want of adequate clothing, tools, and other essentials. Neither do most people see today's experience as history repeating itself.

1) Regional history is important in NE [New England] and all we get is Rev. War.
2) This is the story of marginal people—women, minorities, immigrants, the poor, etc.
3) We live in a capitalist economy. We need to focus on our *economic* history as much as George Washington.

It showed our children their roots. Especially with the video of people talking of their younger days working in the mills. (Long hard work.)

It's an important part of our country's history.

There is so much to learn about.

Shows how previous generations worked to improve this country, their lives, and those of their descendants. Serves as a warning that while capitalism provides abundant goods and wealth we must guard against abuses.

It's an important part of who this country is today. I believe in preserving many different aspects of our history.

I think it is important to show our heritage.

Think it is very good to preserve history especially for the younger generation.

It is always valuable to preserve and reflect on historical periods that represent major changes in the human condition.

In our world of change/choice at your fingertips, I think that the path that led us to our present technology could be completely forgotten. The *real* people who forged the way could get lost, with only the men with money receiving any recognition.

All history is worth preserving, good or bad, so that we can learn from it. The Industrial Revolution, in particular, is one of the most important influences on how we live our lives today.

It gives a glimpse into our nation's past, from which we can always learn.

1) We can appreciate how well off (standard of living) that the ave. American today enjoys.
2) Technical aspects of the time-production.

3) Exposing children to "pre-computer" ways of life.

Helps us to all to understand/appreciate the hardships our ancestors endured in building our prosperous nation.

It is a very important part of our past.

We can learn from history. It helps explain who we are and how we progressed.

I think it makes up part of the U.S. history and shows the progress that has been made over time, and changes.

So valuable to the understanding of how our industrial society came to be, as well as the importance of immigration and child labor laws.

We take the current state of the world for granted. History helps us understand how things used to be, and the forces that changed things.

It is very critical to maintain the history. To show the phases of the economic and social development. To have demonstrations of the progresses made over the last 150 years.

We learn where we came from. We learn from history.

I teach this history. It is part of our heritage.

I know our history is what helped shape us today.

There are insights here to effects of global economy. Pursuit of cheaper goods and labor. Also flight of capital.

It's important to see first-hand what working conditions were like, how the modern economy of mass manufacturing began and how important it is to protect workers' rights.

Because of all the history there.

It's a major part of U.S. history, and like domestic stories, more appealing than battlefields.

Knowing our past is both interesting and provides guidance to the future.

Enjoy history and hope it will be kept intact for future generations to see and learn from.

Our heritage is important.

Because a full understanding of today's politics, social milieu, and technology requires some understanding of their antecedents.

The past is always important in understanding the present.

It is part of the American Heritage and an interesting/educational attraction.

Comments B

Detailed comments in response to the question: *"What is your impression of Lowell as a place to live or work today?"*

The community appears a bit impoverished. The history described by NPS is quite interesting. I am not fond of the east coast communities around Lowell for living or working. I prefer the Midwest.

I might be interested to work here if there is a good employment opportunity. I don't want to live here.

My impression is that Lowell would not be a great place to live because of crime and also I have a poor impression of the schools. I think it would be fine working there—I like the immigrant influences and preserved history.

Probably reasonably pleasant.

None.

I don't know.

Favorable—attractive city—new high-tech industry.

It's diverse—proud—interesting and certainly on its way back.

The suburban homes are very lovely.

It seems like a thriving, pleasant community. We really didn't spend time anywhere but the National Hist. Pk.

It is a friendly place.

A nice place to visit. I don't like cities for living.

Did not see enough of city and its people to judge.

Nice to visit—wouldn't live in a city setting.

Too much of a city for me—I like more space.

I prefer bigger city and like really hot weather. . . . If not Lowell is a very pretty small city.

I was born and brought up in Lowell—moved to N.H. in 1970. Lowell has come a long way—for the better—but would not consider moving back to Lowell.

Positive. Working to improve sustainability of city and make the area a better place to live for its residents.

Very comfortable and *clean.*

We were surprised by its density and that it hasn't managed to capitalize on its amazing building stock and proximity to Boston—We assume that it is largely retarded by its long association as a depressed blue collar city (town).

Seemed okay to us, a fairly normal place.

Given the appropriate opportunity, I would move there in a heartbeat. There seems to be a revival underpinned by a sense of renaissance.

It was rewarding to see some of the mills had been converted to housing. It seems that downtown would be a good mix of businesses and people to support them. The center seems neat and clean and a source of pride to the residents.

Like any city, Lowell has pros and cons as a place to live or work.

?

Much more attractive place to work and live—cultural—shopping—sports etc. Festivals—Bread and Roses—We visit but prefer our small town to live in.

The only comparison I have are things that I've heard—high crime rate for years—and what I saw—on my first visit to just a small part of Lowell—definite upgrade—I didn't see nor do I know enough about the city now to know if it would be a good place to live or work today.

Slow—clean—peaceful—quiet—

Since the refurbishment taking place in Lowell, I think of that as very positive.

No opinion from visitor from Chicago Ill.

I like living here but feel that working here isn't profitable.

It appears to be in a rebirth, but not yet vibrant.

Very historical—well preserved. Keep up the good work.

If I lived in Lowell I might be interested in working at the Historical Park.

Lowell seems to be blue collar. Merrimack Street is not particularly inviting. There seems to be no night life. Lowell gives the impression that its best days are behind it (despite the hype of "revitalization").

We were there for a day and a half as tourists—certainly not enough time or information to judge a place's desirability as a place to work or live. We learned little, if anything, about employment, education, cultural activities and opportunities, or residential areas beyond the immediate area of tourist (NPS) attractions. Our immediate impression when driving into downtown (never having been there before) was pleasure at seeing such a vibrant area. However, after packing in as much tourism as possible, we walked up and down the main street and surrounding area in search of a place to eat. The "quick" spots that sounded interesting had closed (we were planning on taking time to eat after tourist sites closed). It was difficult to find a dining spot that appealed. Finally, we settled on one and were disappointed. As we were searching, we observed the atmosphere and mix of people changing (approx. 6 p.m.). We got the uneasy feeling that this might not be a place one might want to be after dark—nothing specific (unless one counts two teenage boys hoisting a third up into a second floor window)—just basing our impression on local tourist areas we are aware of.

Very positive.

Since I was attending a two-day conference and had little time to visit or explore the city, I cannot answer this.

An up and coming city, w/ many future opportunities.

It appears to be a location in a period of improvement and revitalization, with an interesting past—and hopefully, a good future.

I think Lowell is a very welcoming city and has alot to offer—is inexpensive to visit—easily accessible—I think it has overcome its image as an unsafe place to visit.

I wish they would improve the downtown/shopping etc.

Little opportunity.

No interest in city life.

I don't live here now but I think it would be great to work here if my circumstances changed.

Busy and a nice place. Diverse.

Much effort is apparent to improve conditions and create a more prosperous community. There seems to be a need for more employment opportunities and better living conditions.

City appears to suffer from a post-Industrial Revolution hangover. Those big, empty textile mills are depressing. Canals and architecture are superb—NHP is a great site to build around. Retail businesses near NHP indicate town is struggling.

Very interesting with much potential!

It looks much improved over the past couple of decades, but still seems a bit run-down or depressed. I wonder how good the school system is. . . .

An interesting mix—lots of good ethnic restaurants—maybe a tough and large "mill worker blue collar group." Sad to see the mills abandoned and falling down. Depressing.

It's a place that is trying to become economically viable and a good place to live. It's trying to become a destination for tourists and increase the local economy.

It's getting better as a place to work, but I still wouldn't want to live there. It still needs to be cleaned up more and get enough jobs to reduce the poverty.

Not observed from this perspective. Stuck to the historic mills.

It was cleaner than it used to be, and reminds me of Williamsburg, Brooklyn. But it (a) seems like we would need a car to live (b) there is nothing to do if I lived there—movies etc. It seems a place for old people. If there were outlet malls in the old mills it might bring people in over and over. (See the history, do some shopping.) What kind of jobs are there than blue collar? The town does not seem *fun*. It seems like it is no longer dying, and the Lowell Spinners are great, but it is in holding until something compliments [*sic*] the park.

Clean, friendly, historical.

Very nice. Well restored city with many cultural events.

Once thriving city is working hard to come back to its glory. It's undergoing a revitalization.

Seems to have improved since the lows of the 1920s–40s with some new companies moving in but still seems to struggle some.

We are impressed with the job Lowell is doing at preserving its history, and how it is handling different immigration waves. We are only scratching the surface in our short visit.

I didn't see a whole lot of Lowell so cannot really answer.

Quiet. Needed to be better advertised as we got a lot of "WHY STAY IN LOWELL"!! People in Boston were amazed.

Downtown center is pretty good but no interesting shopping. Quilt Museum and Textile Museum and Brush Art were wonderful, but probably of more interest to tourists.

We love Lowell!!

It still has "a way" to go, with an unairconditioned mill still in operation. My mother worked in a spinning room when I was growing up. It saddens me to know that people still do that in such conditions. (And yet, a worker waved to us on the canal boat!) How could I enjoy/appreciate Lowell if my family was mill workers in this year of 2002?

Quite pleasant.

Okay—seems to be revitalizing itself.

• A struggling city.
• There are signs of progress with some nicer restaurants and stores.
• The Quilt exhibits were nicely organized—A catalog would have been nice.

Nicely "reborn" community with quite a bit of diversity.

Probably a good place to work.

Seemed like a nice community.

I wouldn't live in Lowell or work in Lowell. Not a town I would call home—people didn't seem too friendly on the street, and the graffiti isn't an attraction. The local teens were rude if you asked for directions or wouldn't get out of their way if on a sidewalk. Just not pleasant area.

Interesting place—diverse.

It's still in the process of reinventing itself yet again. Good to be on the UP side.

The downtown is well rebuilt. But it remains a low income town. I would not live there.

Better than it used to be a few years ago. Cleaner. Vibrant cultural scene.

It seems clean and very culturally-diverse.

Busy but educational.

Better. Particularly liked Merrimac River area. Very little about modern Lowell on tour.

A very interesting place to work during the day but deserted by night, although as visitors, we enjoyed dining out and exploring the streets.

Too busy to live but we are from a very rural part of the U.S.

Looks like fun. Should be booming in 10 yrs. I remember it in the 50s— forlorn and dead. Has anyone thought to commemorate John Coolidge of Harvard for his role in urging this restoration project?

Good—Glad to see mills rehabilitated as apartments and shops revitalizing and maintaining the downtown area as a habitable area where it would be interesting to live.

There have been interesting changes which I hope reflects a bright future.

Not good, poor.

Favorable, but I may not have conventional tastes.

Difficult to tell from a day visit—but it seemed pleasant enough.

Not the most attractive (downtown). Have not visited the suburbs.

NOTES

1. The term "Lowell experiment" was applied to postindustrial Lowell by Bronwyn King in an article in a National Park Service bulletin shortly after the founding of Lowell NHP. See King 1979. "Visitability" is a term coined by Bella Dicks to describe the goal of culture-based revitalization projects like Lowell's. See Dicks 2003.

2. A New England Council report (2000) articulates many of the key ideas and strategies now being pursued in many places. See http://www.creativeeconomy. org/pubs/documents/CEI_2000_report.pdf.

3. Barbara Kirshenblatt-Gimblett's "World Heritage and Cultural Economics" insightfully explores the concept of "world heritage" in *Museum Frictions: Public Cultures/Global Transformations*, ed. by Ivan Karp and Corinne Kratz, a project of the Center for the Study of Public Scholarship at Emory University (Durham, N.C.: University Press, in press 2006). Available at http://www.nyu. edu/classes/bkg/web/heritage.pdf. For surveys of heritage area development in the United States and internationally, see the U.S. National Park Service's compilation of research on heritage areas at http://www.cr.nps.gov/heritageareas/ REP/research.htm and the website of the Alliance of National Heritage Areas at http://www.ohioeriecanal.org/nationalheritage.html. In particular, Dennis Frenchman's "International Examples of the United States Heritage Area Concept" (http:// www.cr.nps.gov/heritageareas/REP/intlexamples.pdf) addresses how this model has been applied around the world.

4. See, for example, Richard Florida (2005) on the creative class, Charles Landry (2000) on the creative city, B. Joseph Pine and James Gilmore (1999) on the experience economy, the Project for Public Spaces (2000) on placemaking, and Al Ries and Laura Ries (2004) on branding.

5. The AHA-sponsored Conference of State and Local Historical Societies was founded in 1904, the American Association of Museums in 1906, the Mississippi Valley Historical Association (later the Organization of American Historians) in 1907, and the Society for the Preservation of New England Antiquities (SPNEA) in 1910 by a grandson of Nathan Appleton, one of the prime movers behind the creation of Lowell. See Glassberg 1990, Lindgren 1995:26–49, and Wallace 1996:178–221, for useful discussions of the motivations and strategies of some public history-makers in this period.

6. The National Park Service hired its first historian in 1931. In 1933, the federal government transferred its historic battlefield properties and monuments from the War Department to the National Park Service, which had previously been the custodian of sites notable more for archeological or natural rather than historical interest. This transfer, as well as such other New Deal activities as the Historic American Buildings Survey (HABS) and the 1935 Historic Sites Act, stimulated public interest in historic preservation and gave a boost to the nascent craft of public historical interpretation. See Conard 2002:151–58, Mackintosh 1985 and 1986, Townsend 1999:5–10.

An intriguing parallel to the creation of Lowell NHP can be found in the history of Hopewell Furnace National Historic Site in southeastern Pennsylvania. The remnants of this small eighteenth- and nineteenth-century iron-making site were contained within one of many Depression-era parks that used Civilian Conservation Corps labor to reclaim "submarginal" agricultural land in depressed rural areas. As with Lowell, young and iconoclastic historians within the Park Service advocated a new, more holistic kind of national historical park that would focus on labor and social history as well as technological accomplishment. In part, Hopewell Furnace was the Park Service's response to the growing interest in "living history" sites like Colonial Williamsburg; it is an important, although little known, precursor of later industrial history sites and heritage areas. See Glaser 2005.

7. According to a recent survey by the Organization of American Historians, social history was still selected most often by OAH members in completing the "scholarly areas of interest" section of their annual membership forms. Social history was selected 1,396 times, followed by cultural history, 1,148, and political history, 1,033. Organization of American Historians 2003:18.

8. For a useful overview of public history as an international movement, see Liddington 2002. Earlier views of the public history movement outside the United States are found in English 1983, Johnson 1984, and Sutcliffe 1984. On public history in Australia, see Ashton and Hamilton 2000 and Curthoys and Hamilton 1992.

9. Many scholars have written on the performative nature of various aspects of culture. See, for example, Judith Butler 1999 and 1997 on the performativity of gender. For two seminal discussions of language as performance, see J. L. Austin 1955 and Richard Baumann 1977.

10. See Jenkins 1997 for a useful compendium of these discussions within the historical profession in the 1970s and 1980s; Clifford 1988 and Clifford and

Marcus 1986 were among the most influential early works in anthropology's concurrent debate over similar questions.

11. Although a constructivist approach recognizes the incomplete and participatory nature of historical knowledge, constructivism itself can just as easily be used for conservative purposes or by those who seek to limit as well as to extend debate about the past. See Gable and Handler 1996, as well as Handler and Gable 1997:78–101 for a discussion of this strategy.

12. For thorough discussions of heritage as a mode of production, see Kirshenblatt-Gimblett 1998:131–200, and Dicks 2003:119–43. For two largely dismissive views of heritage, see Hewison 1987 and Lowenthal 1998.

CHAPTER 2

1. Detailed survey results are reproduced in the appendix. Visitor survey data are discussed and analyzed in Chapter 6.

2. I chose to focus on the Cambodians for three reasons. First, they form the largest and most visible single block of recent migrants. The fact that Cambodian Americans currently make up a one-third of all students in Lowell schools, and that the city has had a Cambodian-born city councilor since 1999, give Cambodians a particularly high profile among the city's many immigrant groups. Second, many Cambodians in Lowell and elsewhere have self-consciously mobilized cultural performance forms—festivals, dance, music—in an effort to mend some of the social damage caused by the trauma and upheavals of the 1970s and 1980s and to try to knit together a sense of transnational Cambodian identity that includes a far-flung and fragmented community. There are intriguing parallels between these efforts and Lowell's heritage project, in that both are acts of repair in the wake of loss and change. And finally, Cambodians began arriving in Lowell in the early 1980s, just as the national park was beginning to become a visible presence in the city. The park and the Lowell Cambodian community have both passed through their hectic early growth and settlement phases. As they enter a second chapter of their tenure in Lowell, both are consolidating, assessing, and adjusting, and these processes provided opportunities for me to hear many different people articulating their versions of the past and visions for the future and to observe negotiations around these subjects.

3. For many years, anthropologists have debated the pros and cons of doing "indigenous anthropology" or "anthropology at home." Some have argued that the insider's ability to understand the nuances of language and behavior can produce more sophisticated ethnographies, while others insist that an insider familiarity with a culture blinds a researcher to things that would seem strange or obvious to an outsider, as was the case with my failure to look holistically at the professional historians at Deerfield. Others have questioned how we define "home" or "otherness," pointing out that there are many types of alterity—differences of gender, ethnicity, class, and locality—even within supposedly homogeneous and familiar societies (Jones 1970). Anthropologists' habit of looking elsewhere for "otherness," some have suggested, reveals "an inherent affinity between

anthropology and exoticism" that has kept this still largely Western discipline from the kind of intensive study of dominant or Western cultures that we have lavished on other parts of the world (Peirano 1998:106). A flip side of this preoccupation with the exotic, some have charged, is that anthropologists are often lazy about studying our own cultures, assuming we already understand them and thus not doing the same kind of broad study of historical and economic context that we would otherwise undertake as a matter of course (di Leonardo 1998). In general, this debate makes clear that we face the same kinds of relational and representational choices no matter where we conduct our fieldwork, and that the key—at home, as elsewhere—is to be as aware of and transparent about these choices as possible.

For more discussion of "at home" anthropology, see Cerroni-Long 1995, Fox 1991, A. Jackson 1987, Messerschmidt 1981.

4. Such was the case with Handler and Gable's study of Colonial Williamsburg. Some of the responses to the book were written by practicing public historians (Bunch 1999, Norkunas 1999, Zoidis 1999), including those at Colonial Williamsburg itself (Carson 1994). An early and well-known call for anthropologists to "study up" was issued by Laura Nader (1972).

CHAPTER 3

1. The Historic Preservation District, established in 1978 in the legislation that created the national park and its sister agency, the Lowell Historic Preservation Commission (see Chapter 5), establishes strict design controls for buildings within its boundaries. In order to establish and maintain a cohesive landscape resonant of Lowell's industrial past, and to provide for the creation of new waterfront recreational areas, the district includes not only the entire core downtown area but also a good deal of property abutting the canal system and the Concord and Merrimack Rivers. Design standards for the district were established in the Lowell Historic Preservation Commission's 1980 Preservation Plan.

2. Parks throughout the NPS system hire "seasonals" during the busier summer months, and these jobs are very often gateways to highly sought-after permanent jobs in the Park Service. Nearly all of the Park Service employees I interviewed, including high-level administrators, had started as seasonals. Many told me how enjoyable they had found the experience, which appeared to offer greater autonomy and opportunities for discovery and innovation than the more bureaucratically constrained permanent positions. It is noteworthy—particularly in light of my discussion in Chapter 6 of teaching as a "gateway" job into the professional world—that many NPS seasonal rangers throughout the national park system, and perhaps particularly at historical parks, have often been teachers.

3. By 1845, the end of the major development phase in Lowell, the group now known as the Boston Associates comprised about eighty men. Early on embracing the concept of vertical integration, these investors—many of whom had family ties—held overlapping interests in thirty-one textile companies as well as in the corporations that controlled the city's waterpower, railroad, and marketing agencies. At that point, this relatively small group controlled about one-fifth of the

entire industrial capacity of the United States (Dalzell 1987:79).

4. The official title of the Brown Book is "Lowell, Massachusetts: Report of the Lowell Historic Canal District Commission to the Ninety-Fifth Congress of the United States of America." Lowell Historic Canal District Commission, Lowell Team, and United States Congress. Washington: GPO, 1977.

5. When I asked visitors completing my follow-up survey to list anything they had particularly enjoyed or remembered from their visit to Lowell, 29 percent mentioned the mill and canal tours; the next most popular item mentioned was the working weave room, at 18 percent. Although there is a fee for the canal tours, ticket revenue does not cover the entire cost of this expensive operation. Especially now, as they face shrinking budgets, park managers are caught in a balancing act between the costs and benefits of the park's most popular program.

6. The Suffolk Mill waterpower exhibit has recently been redesigned, and reopened in 2006.

7. The possibility of treating such potentially sensitive or controversial subjects more directly in museums—and the likelihood that visitors will react thoughtfully rather than indignantly—is illustrated by the response to a 1997 exhibit on sweatshops at the Smithsonian Institution's National Museum of American History. For discussions of the creation of the exhibit and its generally very positive reception by audiences, see Alexander 2000 and Liebhold 2000.

8. The Federal Election Commission prosecuted McCallum for making $250,000 in excess campaign contributions to Tsongas's presidential campaign (Federal Election Commission Record, vol. 23, no. 2, February 1997. Electronic document, http:// www.fec.gov/pdf/record/1997/feb97.pdf, accessed November 19, 2005).

CHAPTER 4

1. These tour groups were much smaller than the mill-and-canal tour audiences; attendance was likely to be seven to ten people, rather than the twenty-plus for the trolley and boat tours.

2. This session was part of the American Memory Project, created by New York City photographer Bill Hayward. Hayward and an assistant traveled to Lowell as one stop on a national trek on which they photographed people posing with self-created signs and props expressing their sense of their relationship to local places and histories. For on-line selections from this project, see http:// www.theamericanmemoryproject.com/.

3. According to the U.S. Census of 1980, Lowellians who had two parents from the same ethnic group were as follows:

French Canadian	13,928
Irish	12,556
Portuguese	4,769
English	3,833
Greek	3,472
Polish	2,437

(United States Bureau of the Census, 1980 Census of Population and Housing, Census Tracts. Lowell, Mass.–N.H., Standard Metropolitan Statistics Area [Washington, 1983])

4. Population figures cited are from U.S. decennial census records unless otherwise noted.

5. Many community activists and social service workers in Lowell dispute the census counts, arguing that the large numbers of undocumented immigrants—including many visitors who have intentionally overstayed their visas—are not reflected in the official figures. Local people frequently cite the figure of 25,000 to 30,000 Cambodians in Lowell. I am indebted to Professor Jeffrey Gerson at the University of Massachusetts at Lowell, Samkhann Khoeun, former director of the Cambodian Mutual Assistance Association, and Danielle Vacarr at ONE Lowell for information on Cambodian population figures and settlement patterns in Lowell.

6. The statue, a 1985 work by Ivan and Elliot Schwartz, is one of eleven pieces of public art commissioned by the Lowell Historic Preservation Commission and installed during the 1980s. For an in-depth discussion of the politics of public art in Lowell, see Norkunas 2002.

7. For a cogent analysis of Latinos in Lowell, see Gerson 2002.

8. The phrase "No Irish Need Apply" is originally traceable to a few handwritten signs in early-nineteenth-century London but more generally to a hugely popular song written in 1862. This song established an "urban legend" that was widely mobilized by Irish Americans in the nineteenth century as they sought to consolidate their social identity and political power by fostering a sense of collective grievance against the dominant Anglo-American culture. Although there was certainly nativist and anti-Catholic sentiment in this period in the United States, Irish workers were generally sought out by employers rather than being discriminated against, as their experience in Lowell's textile mills amply illustrates. They offered precisely what the growing industrial nation needed—a labor force desperate enough to work for low wages. For discussions of strategic uses of race, ethnicity, and victimization among nineteenth-century Irish Americans, see Ignatief 1996, Jensen 2002, Roediger 1991.

9. An Wang, himself an immigrant from China, combined the prototypical roles of engineering entrepreneur and energetic immigrant, both of which resonated deeply with Lowellians.

10. This backlash included many of the scholarly works that have become touchstones for urban planners and historians, including Jacobs 1961 and Lynch 1960. Another key work was sociologist Herbert Gans's study of the Italian community displaced by urban renewal in Boston's West End (Gans 1965). Remarking on the phenomenon that a sense of ethnic identity and community often follows displacement rather than preceding it, Gans noted that, "The West End as a neighborhood was not important to West Enders until the advent of redevelopment" (104).

11. Like many of Lowell's cultural and educational institutions, the International Institute has been carefully documented as part of the city's self-conscious

collection and preservation of its own history. The Center for Lowell History, a project of the University of Massachusetts Lowell, has archived exhibit material relating to the International Institute at http://library.uml.edu/clh/Inter/In.Html.

12. The Lowell Folk Festival per se began in 1990; its first three years (1987–1989) were actually productions of the National Folk Festival, which moves from one city to another (usually in deindustrialized places like Lowell) on a three-year rotation. The National Council for the Traditional Arts (NCTA), which produces the National Folk Festival, hopes that host cities will be able to sustain annual festivals after the initial three-year run; Lowell has been by far the most successful venue in this regard. The Lowell Folk Festival is now produced cooperatively by the Lowell National Historical Park, the NCTA, the city of Lowell, and the Lowell Festival Foundation, a nonprofit organization created to raise funds for and administrate the festival and some other performing arts events in the city.

13. Other Heritage State Parks in the former industrial communities of Fall River, Gardner, Holyoke, Lawrence, Lynn, North Adams, and Uxbridge are still operating.

14. For an on-line retrospective on the Human Services Corporation, see http://library.uml.edu/clh/ Roots/R1.Html. Besides the Human Services Corporation, Mogan's key allies at this time included members of the Lowell Historical Society, which had helped to create a local history museum, the Lowell Museum, that existed within the Wannalancit Mill from 1976 to 1982.

Legislation to create a national park in Lowell was first introduced by U.S. Representative Bradford Morse in 1972. It was resubmitted annually by Morse and his successor, Paul Cronin, until Congress established the Lowell Historic Canal District Commission (LHCDC) in 1974. By defining a historically significant district and creating a multilevel government commission to plan its preservation and development as a resource, this legislation took an important step toward the creation of a national park and also created a model for the Lowell Historic Preservation Commission that would be set up in 1978. The LHCDC, on which Mogan served as a commissioner, in many ways took over the work of the Human Services Corporation. It was responsible for commissioning the "Brown Book," a consultant-prepared plan published in 1977 that supported the proposal made by Paul Tsongas to the House of Representatives that year. Tsongas's political know-how and connections helped to facilitate its successful passage through Congress in the spring of 1978. For details of these transactions, see Ryan 1987.

15. "Capital" was originally to have its own interpretive area, in a building that once housed the agent for the Boott Cotton Mills. Agents belonged to upper management, charged with overseeing the operations of the mill, so this space would have been a very appropriate location for such an exhibit. The building, however, was also slated to be used for the offices of the park's own managers, who, according to some of my informants, were reluctant to share their work space with the general public. As a result, labor remains more heavily interpreted

than capital in Lowell NHP's exhibits, and the agent's house—sometimes referred to as "the castle" by park workers—remains the exclusive domain of management, just as it was in the days of the cotton mill.

16. There was a pilot project in which twelve U.S. cities (including Boston, but not Lowell) were chosen for the resettlement of clusters of Khmer refugees, but only 8,000 of the 150,000 Cambodian refugees in the United States were resettled in this way. See Hein 1993:72–76 for a discussion of state policies on resettlement.

17. Paraphrased in Coombes 1997; also, on rumor as a means of subaltern resistance, see Spivak 1988a and 1998b.

CHAPTER 5

1. The 17,000 square-foot Visitor Center was constructed at a cost of $14 million and opened in the spring of 1982. The entire two-building complex contains 285,000 square feet of space; one building dates from 1882 and the other from 1902, considerably later than the "golden age" period on which the park's main interpretation focuses (O'Har 1999:72–73).

2. In addition to these properties, the federal government owns (or is still in the process of trying to acquire) many of the gatehouse structures along the canal system, as well as a property that it uses as a maintenance facility next to the Northern Canal.

3. The Tsongas Center is given short shrift in this study, although it is a very important part of what the park does and could easily be the basis for a full-length ethnographic study of its own. It was created in the late 1980s (although not formally inaugurated until the official opening of the Boott Cotton Mills site in 1992) to be a model for collaborative educational activities between the National Park Service and other educational institutions in communities where national parks were located. The founding of the Tsongas Center was not without controversy. One of my interviewees, a highly respected local historian and university professor who had been integrally involved in the evolution of the culture-led redevelopment plans, told me about being part of a group that had argued strongly for a more Mogan-esque vision of what the Tsongas Center could be. They had hoped that the planned center would encompass lifelong learning for all sectors of the community, drawing on university faculty as a resource and seeing "education as a community phenomenon." Instead, for a variety of reasons, which many people saw as politically or financially motivated, the center focuses exclusively on "K through 12" education (elementary and high school), and it has designed its workshop offerings to dovetail closely with state-mandated curriculum requirements.

The Tsongas Center is extremely popular among teachers, who bring 60,000 students a year to its programs. Most of these school groups are from outside Lowell, but the center also has very close ties with the city's own school department. Students in the Lowell system attend at least three workshops over the course of their elementary and high school years. Workshops typically last for a full day and cover such topics as immigration, industrial labor, and waterpower. Half of each workshop takes place in the Tsongas Center's own classroom areas, where students engage in role-playing and hands-on activities; the other half takes them to the park exhibit areas.

The Tsongas Center is responsible for a very large percentage of the total visitorship at the Boott Cotton Mills Museum and the adjacent Working People exhibit, which gives the center considerable clout within the park. In many ways, the Tsongas Center's educational products—workshops, curricula, trainings, and simple familiarity with Lowell via the hundreds of thousands of students who have now been there on field trips—are among the most important and marketable export items in postindustrial Lowell. Its role in familiarizing children from the city's new immigrant groups with the national park may also serve, in time, to create a more culturally diverse park audience than currently exists.

4. In 2002, tenants in the privately owned parts of the Boott complex included a law firm, a computer software system designer, and consultant firms specializing in energy, telecommunications, marketing, and environmental issues. The Boott buildings surround a recently relandscaped courtyard, a remnant of the planned green spaces that Lowell's founders laid out to impart a wholesome pastoral atmosphere to their industrial experiment. The courtyard is now part of an extensive system of river- and canal-side walkways being built with federal funds.

5. This is one of the two buildings in which I lived while I was resident in Lowell.

6. Although the Historic Preservation Commission spearheaded the public art projects, the majority of funding for the works—approximately $100,000 per work—came from businesses and wealthy individuals. The developer of the downtown hotel was the major sponsor for a piece next to the hotel, while the Tsongas family sponsored another piece next to the downtown Wang training center, just across the canal from the hotel. The site-specific works include the statue of the Irish canal-builder in Mack Plaza, mentioned in the first tour; a series of stone pieces with quotes from women workers in the canalside Lucy Larcom Park, which is named for a Lowell writer and former mill girl; and a striking granite construction jutting out into the Pawtucket Canal that appears to be—and is taken by many observers as—the foundation of a vanished mill building. I am indebted to Paul Marion for sharing his knowledge of the public art collection with me.

7. Immediately after World War II, industrial production accounted for 38% of the nation's nonagricultural employment, with services making up only 10% of American jobs. By 1982, services had pulled ahead of manufacturing, and by 1996, accounted for 29% of nonagricultural employment, while manufacturing had fallen to just 15%, smaller than the retail trade sector (Newman 1999:31–32). In Massachusetts, service-sector employment rose by 54% between 1981 and 1999, while manufacturing employment continued to dwindle, decreasing by 35% in the same period (Forrant et al. 2001:2).

8. The main institute of higher education in Lowell is the University of Massachusetts at Lowell. It has roots in both the educational and industrial sectors, having been created by a merger of Lowell Technological Institute (a school for textile studies founded in 1895) and Lowell State College (a teachers' college

founded in 1897). The resulting University of Lowell became one of five campuses of the state public university system in 1991. See http://library.uml.edu/clh/Pv/Pv.Html for a history of the institution. Lowell is also home to one of the two campuses of Middlesex Community College.

9. One day a woman whose car had broken down outside the boardinghouse block where I was living came inside to use the telephone. In the course of giving directions to a friend, it became clear that, although she was a native Lowellian, she was not familiar with specific street names or even with the name of the neighborhood (the Acre) where she had broken down. But she had no hesitation in stating that she was parked in front of "one of those boardinghouse buildings—you know, the ones where the mill girls lived."

10. Wallace was referring to a comment quoted in the *New York Times* about the attitude of merchants in Seneca Falls, New York, to the creation of Women's Rights National Historical Park in their town. Although seemingly uninterested in feminism or women's history, the merchants were very much in favor of anything that would bring people and revenue into the declining downtown. See Wallace 1996:201 and note 178.

11. In 2003, the LDFC had to a pool of approximately $24 million in loan funds.

12. The Lowell Plan hired a consultant firm, American Cities Associates, to generate a planning document that continues to guide much of the city's planning and development. The Lowell Plan also financed and oversaw a cultural plan that has continued to influence cultural policy and implementation in the city.

13. Lowell municipal government consists of a nine-member city council, elected every two years, who choose one of their members for the largely ceremonial role of mayor. The city council also appoints the city's chief administrative officer, the City Manager. This unelected official functions in many ways as a mayor would in a "strong-mayor" system of city government.

14. The fact that Tsongas's right-hand man in Lowell, City Manager Joe Tully, was eventually indicted and convicted of soliciting kickbacks from a developer does not keep many Lowellians from praising his ability to get things done. As one cultural leader said to me, "Joe Tully may have gone to jail, but Joe Tully was an important man in his time, and I'll take Joe Tully any day over a lot of other people." After Tully's conviction, Paul Tsongas asserted, "He was the best city administrator I ever ran into, and had it not been for him, there would not have been a Lowell renaissance," while Peter Aucella stated, "The legacy is there and the verdict doesn't change that" (Lavoie 1988).

15. An Wang himself died in 1990. Wang's buildings, totaling 1.5 million square feet of space, were sold at auction for approximately 1% of their cost. After emerging from bankruptcy in 1993, the company moved away from durable manufacturing and toward a new emphasis on the new-economy staples of development, consulting, and marketing. Lowell's unemployment rate zoomed back up to 10.7%, making the recession of the early 1990s more severe in Lowell than elsewhere in the state or the nation (Gittell and Flynn 1995).

16. Former Secretary of Labor Robert Reich has recently noted the tendency of American politicians to become "born-again manufacturers" when seeking votes, in defiance of the evidence that the loss of American manufacturing jobs is irreversible within the logic of the present system. See http://www.tompaine.com/feature2.cfm/ID/9322.

17. Boston National Historical Park, created in 1974, is a slightly earlier example of this approach not far from Lowell. Boston NHP owns a small amount of property in the former Charlestown Navy Yard and provides interpretive tours and support for several area historic sites, including Boston's Faneuil Hall and other locations on the city's well-known Freedom Trail. The presence of the national park in Boston has helped to channel federal funds to the overall Freedom Trail and other Boston sites. As already noted in Part I, many of the recently created national heritage areas are governed by similar federal commissions in partnership with a range of public and private entities.

18. The ten local members included six people appointed by city government (three by the mayor, three by the City Manager), one appointed by the university, and three seats appointed by the state governor. Four federal agencies—the Departments of Commerce, Transportation, Housing and Urban Development, and Interior—appointed one commissioner each, and there was one National Park Service seat. Commissioners were appointed for two year terms, and the chair was chosen by commission members. For information on the Historic Preservation Commission, I have drawn primarily on my interviews and on George O'Har's draft administrative history of Lowell NHP.

19. Massachusetts Congressional representatives at this time included not only Paul Tsongas in the Senate (until 1984), but Speaker of the House Tip O'Neill; Edward Boland, ranking minority member on the House Appropriations Committee; and Chester Atkins, also a member of the House Appropriations Committee.

20. The rate of $15 to $20 per square foot for office space in the Boott is slightly higher than that in the former Wang complex, now renamed CrossPoint Towers (Tutalo 2003a). The park retains its small waterpower exhibit space in the Suffolk/Wannalancit Mill complex, but its center of gravity is now at the Boott.

21. In the spring of 2002 the Wang towers, now renamed Cross Point, were for sale again for $167 million (Hughes 2002a).

22. Defense procurement contracts in Massachusetts totaled $10 billion annually by 1986, slumped with the end of the Cold War, and have recently picked up again as area defense contractors like Raytheon have been awarded new federal contracts as part of the war on terror. In the general nonprofit and health and human services fields, Massachusetts receives two to three times more federal research and development funding per capita than do any of the next most heavily funded states, California, Colorado, or New York (Forrant et al. 2001:45–46).

23. The federal government defines affordable housing as that which requires no more than 30% of a person's income. Boston's average fair-market rental cost for a two-bedroom apartment in 2002 was $1,419. The minimum wage in Massachusetts is $6.75 per hour. Overall, Massachusetts fair-market rental prices

required an hourly wage of $22.40 to make an average two-bedroom apartment affordable, while the required "housing wage" in Boston was $27.29. Lowell's housing wage in 2002 was $20.48—an increase of 16.1% from the previous year, which saw Boston prices rise by 5.7% and the state average by 5.9%. (National Low Income Housing Coalition 2003).

CHAPTER 6

1. The wearing of the Park Service uniform itself is to some extent an indicator of a specific employee's level of identification with the agency. Frontline and lower-grade employees (including seasonal employees) must wear the uniform at all times. Managers, administrative staff, and those in the interpretive division who work behind the scenes in offices have more personal choice about whether to wear the uniform. Some invariably wear it whether they are appearing in public or not; others do so less often, or never. In general, I found that those who identified themselves explicitly as public historians were less likely to wear the uniform.

2. Major national park exhibits are generally funded by National Park Service money for which parks compete through an annual grant process. The Boott redesign funds were part of a three-part funding package that also covered the redesign of Lowell NHP's Visitor Center and its Suffolk Mill waterpower exhibit. During 2002, I observed nine regular planning Boott-team meetings, attended a community forum on the exhibit and a three-day design charette with park staff and the outside design company they had contracted, and interviewed six of the seven team members and its two historian consultants. I also attended several meetings, community forums, and other activities related to the Visitor Center exhibit redesign. Ironically, the new display has already fallen victim to the inherent instability of Lowell's postindustrial economy: an upscale day spa, featured prominently in a photograph in the "Re-making Lowell" section of the exhibit, recently closed its doors.

3. The exhibit-planning team was directed by the curator, a public historian with a Ph.D. in the history of technology who was relatively new to the park and to the National Park Service. The other seven members of the team included the park's historian, librarian, and collections manager, a part-time staff member assigned as an administrative assistant for the Boott project, two upper-level managers at the Tsongas Industrial History Center (including the director), and a frontline park ranger who also sometimes conducted the Tsongas Center's "Workers on the Line" program. The Tsongas Center, whose school groups account for much of the visitation to the Boott facility, thus had a significant presence on the exhibit team, as did those with a specific public history orientation. As consultants, the team contracted two Ph.D. historians with extensive experience in both academic and public projects. The majority of the people working on the exhibit had graduate-level training in history; in their interviews with me, these people identified themselves specifically with the public history field and its progressive aims.

4. James Green, a historian at the University of Massachusetts Boston who has acted as consultant for some of Lowell NHP's productions, has written of the

somewhat ambivalent socioeconomic mobility and class status in his own recent family history:

> Though my father's job as a teacher made us middle class, his salary was working class, and so were his house, his neighborhood, and his church. He had worked in a candy plant and a paint factory while he earned his master's degree on the G.I. Bill, and then, in the summers, he earned extra money as a milkman and a bricklayer. . . . My dad loved those summer jobs far more than teaching because he had inherited an avocation for building and fixing things from my grandfather who owned and operated his own machine shop in Oshkosh, Wisconsin. (2000:5)

Similarly, the family history of Peter Aucella, whose tour of Lowell is the focus of Chapter 5, reveals this three-generation progression from manual labor to professional work to the "cultural intermediary" role. Aucella's maternal grandfather, an Italian immigrant, was a mason who helped to build the Boston Garden, completed in 1928; Aucella's father became a pharmacist; and Aucella himself has taken an exceptionally active role in the construction of postindustrial Lowell, including— ironically—overseeing the construction of the city's new baseball stadium and hockey arena.

5. Lowell NHP serves various audiences, and counts different types of visitors in its annual visitation figure of approximately three quarters of a million people. Of this number 60% comes from special events such as festivals that the park cosponsors; attendance at the three-day Lowell Folk Festival alone accounts for as more than a third of the park's annual visitation. The approximately 60,000 students attending Tsongas Industrial History Center programs also make up a considerable percentage of the total.

My interest was primarily in traditional national park visitors—that is, adults and families who come to the park out of some combination of recreational and educational motivations. Because the park is dispersed among several sites, many visitors are counted more than once, making it difficult to state precisely how many of these visitors come to the park each year. The 2002 park visitation figures show 90,200 visits to the park Visitor Center, a typical first stop for the kinds of tourists I was studying. Of the people I surveyed, 68% mentioned that they had gone to the Visitor Center. Assuming another 32% who did *not* go to the Visitor Center while visiting the park, one might estimate approximately 132,000 total traditional visitors in 2002. It is this population from whom my visitor survey data were drawn.

6. These data are drawn from 162 short surveys that I conducted orally with a total of 357 park visitors in the summers of 2001 and 2002. I spoke with informants for between 5 and 20 minutes per survey. I also asked each group of visitors if they would be willing to return a follow-up written survey; 54% of my informants did so. For detailed visitor survey data, see the appendix. My Lowell Folk Festival data were collected in the summers of 2001 and 2002 via 2- to 5-minute-long taped mini-interviews with audience members who were standing in the long line at one of the busiest of the festival's food booths.

7. I did not make a comprehensive study of written visitor comments at Lowell NHP. Comments quoted in this chapter are drawn from a compilation made in 1994. I am grateful to Marty Blatt for sharing this data with me.

8. Bella Dicks's research at a coal heritage park in Wales reveals a similar pattern. "Virtually all of the visitors I approached," she notes, "had some close or distant family connection, either to the place or to coal-mining in general" (2003:128).

9. This comment is drawn from the park's visitor comment books of the early 1990s, not from my own survey.

10. See the appendix for specific methodology used to gather these data, and for the complete listing of ethnic backgrounds mentioned by park visitors.

11. This standardization and professionalization have been taking place within the Park Service through two linked programs: "Ranger Careers," a rationalized career progression through measurable skill stages and wage-grade levels, and the Interpretive Development Program (IDP), a series of voluntary training modules focusing on front-line interpretation. For more information on the IDP, see http://www.nps.gov/idp/interp/ and Chen 2003. The latter explicates some of the same ideas I discuss in this chapter.

CHAPTER 7

1. The United States government prohibits naming federal buildings after people who are still living, as Pat Mogan is. However, no one involved in the renovation of the Boott Mills boardinghouse, apparently, was aware of that rule until after the Mogan Center had already been christened.

2. The Center for Lowell History has digitized the brochures for almost all of these exhibits; see http://library.uml.edu/clh/Exhibit.html.

3. This is a rather different view from the "safety-valve" perspective on cultural performance, which sees periodic carnivalesque eruptions as a way of maintaining structure and order in the long run; see, for example, Brandes 1988.

4. My sources for this etymology are primarily anecdotal. One dictionary of unconventional English does include the term "blow-in" ("a newcomer, especially one still unaccepted"), but ascribes an Australian origin to it, perhaps not a surprising connection given that Australia, like the United States, received very large numbers of Irish immigrants (Beale 1989:43).

5. Jeremy Hein (1993) has noted that in the field of refugee administration, too, many Americans have assumed that the European immigrant experience is the natural and universal one. This model—"new arrivals entering an existing ethnic community and successfully adapting with the aid of established residents" (82)—is not applicable to the sudden influxes of refugee groups, yet its popularity among policymakers has led them to support particular resettlement plans, notably the creation of mutual assistance associations, to the exclusion of others that may be more culturally adapted to particular refugee groups.

6. There was contention about the acquisition of the property, even after the owners, H&H Paper Company, had agreed to a selling price of $200,000. The federal government cannot take over real estate until the tenant or owner agrees

to disclaim ownership rights, but H&H refused to do this. Eventually, H&H was evicted from the property (Lowell *Sun* 1983).

7. In fact, the Preservation Plan proposal called for the Human Services Corporation, the organization founded and guided by Mogan, to take a central role in overseeing the planned center. Although there was never an institutionalized partnership between the two entities, Mogan and many of his staunchest allies did sit on the advisory board of the Mogan Cultural Center during its first years, while also serving as commissioners on the Historic Preservation Commission.

8. The commission, the city, and the private corporation developing the Boott Mill complex acquired the property next to the boardinghouse block for $500,000 in 1986 (Lowell *Sun* 1986). After demolition of a "nonhistoric" building on the site, the lot was landscaped and an outdoor performing arts stage constructed by 1990. The interior of the boardinghouse block was gutted and completely rebuilt with an addition on one side, while the original exterior was returned to its nineteenth-century appearance, a task that included replacing the fourth story which had been lopped off earlier in the building's history. The total cost of the renovations to the building was approximately $5,500,000. I am indebted to former Preservation Commission director Peter Aucella for details about these projects.

9. The exhibit designer for the Working People exhibit, as well as for the Boott Cotton Mills Museum exhibit, was the Center for History Now, based in Williamsburg, Virginia. This group, headed by project director Shomer Zwelling and interpretive design manager Avi Decter, had previously worked at Colonial Williamsburg, the H. F. du Pont Winterthur Museum, and other high-profile public history sites. The Center for History Now contracted historians Patrick Malone of Brown University and Gary Kulik, then chair of the Department of Social and Cultural History at the National Museum of American History, as consultants on the Lowell exhibits (O'Har 1999:158).

10. Paul Marion, e-mail correspondence with the author, 10/22/2003.

11. In its 1997 Strategic Plan, the Park Service called this "an important social and cultural issue" (U.S. Department of the Interior 1997:55). For discussion of the issue and its implications for the National Park Service, see Floyd 1999 and 2001, Goldsmith 1994, Wilkinson 2000. Some scholars (for example, Gramann 1996, Woodard 1993) have argued that the problem is not so much "underparticipation" by minorities at national parks, but rather "overparticipation" by whites, an approach that echoes my interpretation of the ritual use of Lowell NHP in Chapter 6.

12. Marion was working as a writer in the university's public relations department, and continued to play a very active avocational role within the heritage establishment. The other two university seats were held by the director of the Center for Lowell History (located in the Mogan Center) and a political science professor whose field of study was urban ethnic politics. As it had during the planning of the Working People exhibit, localness was able to command considerable deference from outsiders. Although there was no executive board or ostensible hierarchy within the committee, it was clear that Marion held a de facto leadership

role. "People are being polite, kind of a seniority thing," he told me. "I have a lot of institutional memory that they're being very respectful of."

13. For example, during the planning for the 2002 Southeast Asian Water Festival, city officials stepped in to fill some of the organizational gaps left by the then-ongoing collapse of the festival's primary sponsor, the Cambodian Mutual Assistance Association. The city wanted to implement a very different parking plan from the one that had been used in previous years. Cambodians on the planning committee clearly knew—but did not want to say—that the tens of thousands of Cambodian attendees from outside Lowell would continue to park in their accustomed places, no matter how much publicity to the contrary was sent out. The issue was never aired; festival-goers parked where they had always parked; and the city's carefully planned system of shuttle buses and parking attendants went unused. The Cambodians clearly preferred to face some low-level resentment after the fact rather than to argue directly against the proposal of the city officials whose help they needed just to mount the festival.

EPILOGUE

1. Roy Rosenzweig and David Thelen (1998) have documented this atomization and individualism among Americans, particularly white Americans, in their search for knowledge about the past.

2. Handler and Gable (1997) note this same phenomenon at Colonial Williamsburg. The work of Pierre Bourdieu (1984), among others, addresses this issue of how elite cultural and educational institutions manage to reproduce hierarchy and hegemonic power despite the frequent intentions of people inside them to overcome entrenched inequalities.

WORKS CITED

Abrams, James F. 1994. "Lost Frames of Reference: Sightings of History and Memory in Pennsylvania's Documentary Landscape." In *Conserving Culture: A New Discourse on Heritage*, ed. Mary Hufford, 24–38. Urbana and Chicago: University of Illinois Press.

Alba, Richard D. 1985. *Italian Americans: Into the Twilight of Ethnicity*. Englewood Cliffs, N.J.: Prentice Hall.

Alexander, Mary. 2000. "Do Visitors Get It? A Sweatshop Exhibit and Visitors' Comments." *The Public Historian* 22(3):85–94.

Ashton, Paul, and Paula Hamilton. 2000. "Blood Money: Race and Nation in Australian Public History." *Radical History Review* 76:188–207.

———. 1996. "Streetwise: Public History in New South Wales." *Public History Review* 5/6.

Austin, J. L. 1955. How to Do Things with Words. Cambridge: Harvard University Press.

Bakhtin, Mikhail. 1965. *Rabelais and His World*. Bloomington: Indiana University Press.

Batteau, Allen W. 1990. *The Invention of Appalachia*. Tucson: University of Arizona Press.

Baumann, Richard. 1977. *Verbal Art as Performance*. Rowley, Mass.: Newbury House Publishers.

Beale, Paul, ed. 1989. *Partridge's Concise Dictionary of Slang and Unconventional English*. New York: Macmillan.

Benjamin, Walter. 1969. "Theses on the Philosophy of History." In *Illuminations*. New York: Schocken.

Bennett, Tony. 1990. *Outside Literature*. London: Routledge.

———. 1995. *The Birth of the Museum: History, Theory, Politics*. London: Routledge.

Benson, Susan Porter, with Stephen Brier and Roy Rosenzweig. 1986. *Presenting the Past: Essays on History and the Public*. Philadelphia: Temple University Press.

Bixel, Patricia Bellis. 1998. Review of *The New History in an Old Museum: Creating the Past at Colonial Williamsburg*. Journal of Southern History 64(3): 584–85.

Blackman, Ann. 1993. "Lowell's Little Acre." *Time*, June 23: 34.

Blatti, Jo, ed. 1987, *Past Meets Present: Essays about Historic Interpretation and Public Audiences*. Washington: Smithsonian Institution Press.

Blewett, Mary. 1976. "The Mills and the Multitudes: A Political History." In Eno Jr., 1976, 161–179. Lowell: Lowell Historical Society.

———. 1989a. "Machines, Workers, and Capitalists: The Interpretation of Textile Industrialization in New England Museums." In Leon and Rosenzweig, 1989, 262–303. Urbana: University of Illinois Press.

———. 1989b. "Revisions Waiting in the Wings: The New Social History at New England Textile Museums." In *The Popular Perception of Industrial History*, ed. Robert Weible and Francis R. Walsh, 11–20. Lanham, Md.: American Association for State and Local History.

Blewett, Peter. 1976. "The New People: An Introduction to the Ethnic History of Lowell." In Eno Jr. 1976, 190–217.

Bluestone, Barry, and Bennett Harrison. 1982. *The Deindustrialization of America: Plant Closings, Community Abandonment, and the Dismantling of Basic Industry*. New York: Basic Books.

Bluestone, Barry, and Mary Huff Stevenson. 2000. *The Boston Renaissance: Race, Space, and Economic Change in an American Metropolis*. New York: Russell Sage Foundation.

Bodnar, John. 1992. *Remaking America: Public Memory, Commemoration, and Patriotism in the Twentieth Century*. Princeton, NJ: Princeton University Press.

Bourdieu, Pierre. 1984. *Distinction: A Social Critique of the Judgement of Taste*. Cambridge: Harvard University Press.

Boyer, M. Christine. 1992. "Cities for Sale: Merchandising History at South Street Seaport." In *Variations on a Theme Park: The New American City and the End of Public Space*, ed. Michael Sorkin. New York: Hill and Wang.

———. 2001. "Twice–Told Stories: The Double Erasure of Times Square." In *The Unknown City: Contesting Architecture and Social Space*, ed. Iain Borden, Joe Kerr, Jane Rendell, and Alice Pivaro. Cambridge: MIT Press.

Boyer, Peter J. 2002. "Rescue at Quecreek." *The New Yorker*, November 18:56–73.

Brandes, Stanley. 1988. *Power and Persuasion: Fiestas and Social Control in Rural Mexico*. Philadelphia: University of Pennsylvania Press.

Brault, Gerard J. 1986. *The French Canadian Heritage in New England*. Hanover, N.H. and London: University Press of New England.

Briggs, Charles. 1996. "The Politics of Discursive Authority in Research on the 'Invention of Tradition.'" *Cultural Anthropology* 11(0): 435–69.

Bruner, Edward, and Barbar Kirshenblatt-Gimblett. 1994. "Maasai on the Lawn: Tourist Realism in East Africa." *Cultural Antropology* 9(2): 435–70.

Bunch, Lonnie. 1999. Review of *The New History in an Old Museum: Creating the Past at Colonial Williamsburg*. *Journal of American History* 86(2):872.

Butler, Judith. 1999(1990). *Gender Trouble: Feminism and the Subversion of Identity*. London and New York: Routledge.

————. 1997. *Excitable Speech: A Politics of the Performative*. New York: Routledge.

Butterfield, Fox. 1982. "In technology, Lowell, Mass. finds new life." *New York Times*, August 10:Section A1.

Campanini, Jim. 2002. "Corporate responsibility and the Spinners." Lowell *Sun*, September 9, 2002.

Carson, Cary. 1994. "Lost in the Fun House: A Commentary on Anthropologists' First Contact with History Museums." *Journal of American History* 81(1):137–50.

Center for History Now. 1984. "Mill Girls Boardinghouse Exhibits: A Conceptual Statement." Archived document, Lowell National Historical Park Library.

Cerroni–Long, E. L. 1995. *Insider Anthropology*. Washington, D.C.: American Anthropological Association.

Certeau, Michel de. 1988. *The Writing of History*. New York: Columbia University Press.

Chambers, Erve. 2000. *Native Tours: The Anthropology of Travel and Tourism*. Prospect Heights, Ill.: Waveland Press.

Chen, Wei-Li Jasmine. 2003. "The Craft and Concepts of Interpretation: A Look at How National Park Service Interpreters Reveal and Facilitate Opportunities for Connections." Dissertation, West Virginia University. Electronic document, http://etd.wvu.edu/templates/showETD.cfm?recnum=2963, accessed April 10, 2003.

Clairmonte, Frederick, and John Cavanagh. 1981. *The World in Their Web: Oligopolistic Capitalism in the Textile Multinationals Today*. London: Zed Books.

Clifford, James. 1988. *The Predicament of Culture: Twentieth Century Ethnography, Literature, and Art*. Cambridge: Harvard University Press.

Clifford, James, and George Marcus, eds. 1986. *Writing Culture*. Berkeley: University of California Press.

Conard, Rebecca. 2002. *Benjamin Shambaugh and the Intellectual Foundations of Public History*. Iowa City: University of Iowa Press.

Coombes, Rosemary J. 1997. "The Demonic Place of the 'Not There': Trademark Rumors in the Postindustrial Imaginary." In *Culture Power Place: Explorations in Critical Anthropology*, ed. Akhil Gupta and James Ferguson, 249–74. Durham, N.C.: Duke University Press.

Curthoys, Ann, and Paula Hamilton. 1992. "What Makes History Public?" *Public History Review* 1:8–13.

Dalzell, Robert F., Jr. 1987. *Enterprising Elite: The Boston Associates and the World They Made*. Cambridge: Harvard University Press.

———. 1991. "The Boston Associates and the Rise of the Waltham-Lowell System: A Study in Entrepreneurial Motivation." In Weible, 1991, 40–75. Lowell: Lowell Historical Society.

Deely, Katherine. 2003. "There's a new haus in Lowell's arts district." Lowell *Sun*, March 5. Electronic document, http://www.lowellcentercity.org/articles/haus.html, accessed July 2, 2003.

Desmond, Jane. 1999. *Staging Tourism: Bodies on Display from Waikiki to Sea World*. Chicago: University of Chicago Press.

Deutsche, Rosalyn. 1996. *Evictions: Art and Spatial Politics*. Cambridge: MIT Press.

Dickerson, Kitty G. 1998. *Textiles and Apparel in the Global Economy*. New York: Prentice Hall.

Dicks, Bella. 2003. *Culture on Display: The Production of Contemporary Visitability*. Maidenhead, U.K.: Open University Press.

di Leonardo, Micaela. 1998. *Exotics at Home: Anthropologies, Others, American Modernity*. Chicago: University of Chicago Press.

Dorst, John. 1989. *The Written Suburb: An American Site, an Ethnographic Dilemma*. Philadelphia: University of Pennsylvania Press.

Drake-Wilson, Diane. 2000. "Realizing Memory, Transforming History: Euro/Americans/Indians." In *Museums and Memory*, ed. Susan Crane, 115–236. Stanford: Stanford University Press.

Dublin, Thomas. 1993[1979]. *Women at Work: The Transformation of Work and Community in Lowell, Massachusetts, 1826–1860*. New York: Columbia University Press.

Edensor, Tim. 1998. *Touring the Taj: Performance and Meaning at a Symbolic Site*. New York: Routledge.

Ehrenreich, Barbara. 1989. *Fear of Falling: The Inner Life of the Middle Class*. New York: Pantheon.

Ehrlich, Bruce, and Peter Dreier. 1999. "The New Boston Discovers the Old: Tourism and the Struggle for a Livable City." In *The Tourist City*, ed. Dennis R. Judd and Susan Fainstein, 155–78. New Haven: Yale University Press.

English, John R. 1983. "The Tradition of Public History in Canada." *The Public Historian* 5:1(Winter 1983):47–59.

Eno, Arthur L., Jr., ed. 1976. *Cotton Was King: A History of Lowell, Massachusetts*. Lowell: Lowell Historical Society.

Evans, Graeme, and Jo Foord. 2003. "Shaping the Cultural Landscape: Local Regeneration Effects." In *Urban Futures: Critical Commentaries on Shaping the City*, ed. Malcom Miles and Tim Hall, 167–81. London: Routledge.

Evans-Pritchard, Dierdre. 1987. "The Portal Case: Authenticity, Tourism, Traditions, and the Law." *Journal of American Folklore* 100:287–96.

Fabian, Johannes. 1983. *Time and the Other: How Anthropology Makes Its Object*. New York: Columbia University Press.

Featherstone, Mike. 1991. *Consumer Culture and Postmodernism*. London: Sage.

Fleming, Tom. 2004. "Supporting the Cutlral Quarter? The Role of the Creative Intermediary." In *City of Quarters: Urban Villages in the Contemporary City*, ed. David Bell and Mark Jayne. Long: Ashgate.

Florida, Richard. 2005. *Cities and the Creative Class*. London: Routledge.

Floyd, Myron F. 1999. "Race, Ethnicity, and the Use of the National Park System." *Social Science Research Review* 1.2:1–24.

———. 2001. "Managing National Parks in a Multicultural Society: Searching for Common Ground." *The George Wright Forum* 18.3:41–51.

Flynn, Patricia M. 1984. "Lowell: A High Technology Success Story." *New England Economic Review*. September/October:39–49.

Forrant, Robert, with Philip Moss and Chris Tilly. 2001. "Knowledge Sector Powerhouse: Reshaping Massachusetts Employment during the 1980s and 1990s." Lowell: Department of Regional Economic and Social Development, University of Massachusetts at Lowell. Electronic document, www.uml.edu/centers/CIC/pdf/knowledge_sector.pdf, accessed May 24, 2003.

Fox, Richard G. 1991. *Recapturing Anthropology*. Santa Fe, N.M.: School of American Research Press.

Freeman, Allen. 1990. "Lessons from Lowell." *Historic Preservation*. November/December:32–39.

Frenchman, Dennis. 2001. "Narrative Places and the New Practice of Urban Design." In *Imaging the City: Continuing Struggles and New Directions*, eds. Lawrence Vale and Sam Bass Warner, 257–82. New Brunswick, N.J.: Center for Urban Policy Research.

Frisch, Michael. 1990. *A Shared Authority: Essays on the Craft and Meaning of Oral and Public History*. Albany: State University of New York Press.

Fuentes, Annette, and Barbara Ehrenreich. 1983. *Women in the Global Factory*. Boston: South End Press.

Fuoss, Kirk. 1998. "Performance as Contestation: An Agonistic Perspective on the Insurgent Assembly." In Pollock 1998, 98–117.

Gable, Eric, and Richard Handler. 1993. "Colonialist Anthropology at Colonial Williamsburg." *Museum Anthropology* 17:26–31.

———. 1996. "After Authenticity at an American Heritage Site." *American Ethnologist* 98:568–78.

Gall, Lawrence D. 1991. "The Heritage Factor in Lowell's Revitalization." In Weible, 1991, 397–405.

Gans, Herbert. 1965. *The Urban Villagers: Group and Class in the Life of Italian-Americans*. New York: The Free Press, 1965.

———. 1979. "Symbolic Ethnicity: The Future of Ethnic Groups and Cultures in America." *Ethnic and Racial Studies* 2:1.

Gennep, Arnold van. 1960[1909]. *The Rites of Passage*. Chicago: University of Chicago Press.

Gerson, Jeffrey. 2002. "Latino Migration, the Catholic Church, and Political Division: Lowell." In *Latino Political Representation in Massachusetts: Struggles, Strategies, and Prospects*, eds. Carol Hardy-Fanta and Jeffrey Gerson. New York: Routledge.

Gittell, Ross J., and Patricia M. Flynn. 1995. "The Lowell High-Tech Story: What Went Wrong?" *New England Economic Review*. March/April: 57–69.

Glaessel-Brown, Eleanor E. 1991. "A Time of Transition: Colombian Textile Workers in Lowell in the 1970s." In Weible, 1996. 341–75. Lowell: Lowell Historical Society.

Glaser, Leah. 2005. *Hopewell Furnace National Historic Site Administrative History*. (Prepared for the Organization of American Historians under cooperative agreement with the National Park Service.) Boston: National Park Service.

Glassberg, David. 1990. *American Historical Pageantry: The Uses of Tradition in the Early Twentieth Century*. Chapel Hill: University of North Carolina Press.

———. 1996. "Public History and the Study of Memory." *The Public Historian* 18:7–23.

———. 2001. *Sense of History: The Place of the Past in American Life*. Amherst: University of Massachusetts Press.

Goffman, Erving. 1959. *The Presentation of Self in Everyday Life*. New York: Anchor Books.

Goldsmith, J. 1994. "Designing for Diversity." *National Parks* 68:20–21.

Goldstein, Dan. 1997. "Dancing on the Margins: Transforming Urban Marginality through Popular Performance." *City and Society* 9(1): 201–15.

Graburn, Nelson H. H. 1976. "Tourism: The Sacred Journey." In *Hosts and Guests: The Anthropology of Tourism*, ed. Valene Smith, 21–36. Philadelphia: University of Pennsylvania Press.

Gramann, J. H. 1996. "Ethnicity, Race, and Outdoor Recreation: A Review of Trends, Policy, and Research". Miscellaneous Paper R-96-1, Vicksburg, Miss.: U.S. Army Engineering Waterways Experiment Station.

Green, James. 2000. *Taking History to Heart: The Power of the Past in Building Social Movements*. Amherst: University of Massachusetts Press.

Grele, Ronald J. 1981. "Whose Public? Whose History? What Is the Goal of a Public Historian?" *The Public Historian* 3(1):40–49.

Grimes, Ronald L. 1982. *Celebration: Studies in Festivity and Ritual*. Washington: Smithsonian Institution Press.

Gross, Laurence F. 1991. "The Game Is Played Out: The Closing Decades of the Boott Mills." In Weible 1991, 281–99. Lowell: Lowell Historical Society.

——— 1993. *The Course of Industrial Decline: The Boott Cotton Mills of Lowell, Massachusetts, 1835–1955*. Baltimore: Johns Hopkins University Press.

Guss, David. 2000. *The Festive State: Race, Ethnicity, and Nationalism as Cultural Performance*. Berkeley: University of California Press.

Halter, Marilyn. 2000. *Shopping for Identity: The Marketing of Ethnicity*. New York: Schocken Books.

Handler, Richard, and Eric Gable. 1997. *The New History in an Old Museum: Creating the Past at Colonial Williamsburg*. Durham, N. C.: Duke University Press.

Harvey, David. 2005. *A Brief History of Neoliberalism*. New York: Oxford University Press

Heartland Industrial Partners. 2001. "Collins and Aikman Completes Acquisition of Automotive Fabrics Operations of Joan Fabrics." Press Release, Sept. 24, 2001. Electronic document, http://www.heartlandpartners.com/news/092401.shtml, accessed May 2, 2003.

Hein, Jeremy. 1993. *States and International Migrants: The Incorporation of Indochinese Refugees in the United States and France*. Boulder, Colo.: Westview Press.

Herzfeld, Michael. 1991. *A Place in History: Social and Monumental Time in a Cretan Town*. Princeton: Princeton University Press.

Hesmondhalgh, David. 2006. "Bourdieu, the Media, and Cultural Production." *Media, Culture and Society* 28(2) : 211–31.

Hewison, Robert. 1987. *The Heritage Industry: Britain in a Climate of Decline.* London: Methuen.

Hopkins, MaryCarol. 1996. *Braving a New World: Cambodian (Khmer) Refugees in an American City.* Westport, Conn.: Bergin & Garvey.

Howe, Barbara, and Emory Kemp. 1988. *Public History: An Introduction.* Malabar, Fla.: Robert E. Krieger Publishing.

Howell, Raymond. 1997. "Tsongas had the heart of a reformer, but the brains of a Lowell ward boss." Lowell *Sun*, January (n.d.). Electronic document, http://www.howellcomm.com/content/articles.asp, accessed January 16, 2003.

Hughes, Vanessa. 2002a. "Cross Point up for sale." Lowell *Sun*, May 22:1,7.

———. 2002b. "Family–owned drug store gives way to Acre renewal." Lowell *Sun*, July 1:1, 4.

———. 2002c. "Lowell antique shop being evicted." Lowell *Sun*, August 3:1, 2.

Ignatief, Noel. 1996. *How the Irish Became White.* New York: Routledge.

Ingrassia, Lawrence. 1990. "Recession haunts city that believed it was saved by high–tech." *Wall Street Journal*, January 25:A1.

Jackson, Anthony. 1987. "Anthropology at Home." Association for Social Anthropology Monographs 25. London: Tavistock.

Jackson, John Brinckerhoff. 1980. *The Necessity for Ruins and Other Topics.* Amherst: University of Massachusetts Press.

Jackson, Shannon. 1998. "Performance at Hull-House: Museum, Microfiche, and Historiography." In Pollock 1998, 261–93.

Jacobs, Jane. 1961. *The Death and Life of Great American Cities.* New York: Random House.

Jameson, Frederic. 1984. "The Cultural Logic of Late Capitalism." *New Left Review* 144:53–92.

Jenkins, Keith, ed. 1997. *The Postmodern History Reader.* London: Routledge.

Jensen, Richard. 2002. "'No Irish Need Apply': A Myth of Victimization." *Journal of Social History* 36.2:405–29.

Johnson, G. Wesley. 1984. "An American Impression of Public History in Europe." *The Public Historian* 6:4(Fall 1984): 87–97.

Jones, Delmos J. 1970. "Towards a Native Anthropology." *Human Organization* 29(4):251–59.

Karp, Ivan, and Steven D. Lavine, eds. 1991. *Exhibiting Cultures: The Politics and Poetics of Museum Display.* Washington: Smithsonian Institution Press.

Karp, Ivan, with Christine Mullen Kreamer and Steven D. Lavine, eds. 1992. *Museums and Communities: The Politics of Public Culture.* Washington, D.C.: Smithsonian Institution Press.

King, Bronwyn. 1979. "The Lowell Experiment." *CRM* [Cultural Resources Management] *Bulletin* 2.4:4.

Kirshenblatt-Gimblett, Barbara. 1998. *Destination Culture: Tourism, Museums, and Heritage*. Berkeley: University of California Press.

Kopkind, Andrew. 1992. "No Miracle in Lowell." *The Nation*, 254(12), March 30:404–8.

Kryston, Cynthia. 1996. "The Interpretive Journey." Electronic document, http://www.nps.gov/idp/interp/101/journey.pdf, accessed April 12, 2002.

Kujawa, Richard. 1998. "The Urban Development Action Grant Program." In *Encyclopedia of Urban America*, ed. N. L. Shumsky. New York: Garland.

Lafleur, Michael. 2003. "Council: New lease a lock." Lowell *Sun*. February 5.

Landry, Charles. 2000. *The Creative City: A Toolkit for Urban Innovators*. London: Earthscan Publications.

Laurie, Bruce. 1989. "The Working People." Review in *Journal of American History* 76(3):874–79.

———. 1990. Response to Robert Weible. *Journal of American History* 77(1):384–5.

Lavenda, Robert H. 1992. "Festivals and the Creation of Public Culture: Whose Voice(s)?" In Karp, Kreamer, and Lavine, 1992, 76–104.

Lavoie, Denise. 1988. "Tully verdict emotions: Surprise to outrage." Lowell *Sun*, December 22:17.

Lefferts, Jason. 2002. "Study: Asian voter registration low in city." Lowell *Sun*, August 5:1,14.

Leffler, Phyllis K., and Joseph Brent. 1990. *Public History Readings*. Malabar, Fla.: Krieger Publishing.

Leon, Warren, and Roy Rosenzweig, eds. 1989. *History Museums in the United States: A Critical Assessment*. Urbana: University of Illinois Press.

Liddington, Jill. 2002. "What Is Public History? Publics and Their Pasts, Meanings and Practices." *Oral History* 30 (1): 83–93.

Liebhold, Peter. 2000. "Experiences from the Front Line: Presenting a Controversial Exhibit during the Culture Wars." *The Public Historian* 22(3):67–84.

Lindgren, James M. 1995. *Preserving Historic New England: Preservation, Progressivism, and the Remaking of Memory*. New York: Oxford University Press.

Lipchitz, Joseph. 1976. "The Golden Age." In Eno Jr. 1976, 80–103.

"Lock Monsters." 2002. Press release, November 6. Electronic document, http://www.lockmonsters.com/gameday_htmlpages/press_releases/press_mccallum.html, accessed October 25, 2002.

Lowell Historic Canal District Commission. 1977. Report of the Lowell Historic District Commission to the Ninety-Fifth Congress of the United

States of America. Sundocs 022–001–00070-1, GPO 1977 0–225–785. Washington: Government Printing Office.

Lowell Historic Preservation Commission. 1980. *Preservation Plan*. Lowell: U.S. Department of the Interior.

Lowell *Sun*. 1979. "Park commissioners sworn in." January 12:9.

———. 1983. "Park service takes over Boott boarding house." September 22:12.

———. 1986. "Final work begins on Mogan Center, museum highlights working people." July 21:9,12.

———. 2002a. "Slow recovery." Editorial. March 12:15.

———. 2002b. "Making a miracle." Editorial. July 29:15.

———. 2002c. "Lost energy." Editorial. August 5:13.

———. 2003. "Home sales, prices remain strong in Bay State." January 28:21.

———. 2005. "Renaissance city." Editorial. June 14:7.

Lowenthal, David. 1998. *The Heritage Crusade and the Spoils of History*. Cambridge: Cambridge University Press.

Lynch, Kevin. 1960. *The Image of the City*. Cambridge: MIT Press.

MacCannell, Dean. 1999 [1976]. *The Tourist: A New Theory of the Leisure Class*. Berkeley: University of California Press.

———. 1992. *Empty Meeting Grounds: The Tourist Papers*. London and New York: Routledge.

Mackintosh, Barry. 1985. *The National Parks: Shaping the System*. Washington, D.C.: U.S. Department of the Interior. Electronic document, http://www.cr.nps.gov/history/online_books/mackintosh1/index.htm, accessed May 15, 2002.

———. 1986. *Interpretation in the National Park Service: A Historical Perspective*. Washington, D.C. : History Division, National Park Service, Department of the Interior.

Maddox, Richard. 1997. "Bombs, Bikinis, and the Popes of Rock'n'Roll: Reflections on Resistance, the Play of Subordinations, and Liberalism in Andalusia and Academia, 1983–1995." In *Culture/Power/Place: Explorations in Critical Anthropology*, eds. Akhil Gupta and James Ferguson, 275–90. Durham, N.C.: Duke University Press.

Madhavan, Narayanan. 2005. "Global service giants step up hiring in India." http://go.reuters.com/newsArticle.jhtml;jsessionid=WYFFOLZL0SU 0QCRBAE0CFEY?type=topNews&storyID=8647691. Accessed June 13, 2005.

Malone, Patrick M. 1991. "Canals and Industry: Engineering in Lowell, 1821–1880." Weible 1991, 139–55.

Malone, Patrick M., and Charles A. Parrott. 1998. "Greenways in the Industrial City: Parks and Promenades along the Lowell Canals." *Industrial Archeology* 24:1:9–18.

Manning, Frank. 1983. *The Celebration of Society: Perspectives on Contemporary Cultural Performance*. Bowling Green, Ohio: Bowling Green University Popular Press.

Marion, Paul. 1989. *Middle Distance*. Lowell: Loom Press.

Marston, Sally. 1991. "Contested Territory: An Ethnic Parade as Symbolic Resistance." In Weible 1991, 213–33.

Marx, Leo. 1964. *The Machine in the Garden: Technology and the Pastoral Idea in America*. New York: Oxford University Press.

McKibben, Bill. 1999. "The End of Growth." *Mother Jones*, November/December:68.

Messerschmidt, Donald A. 1981. *Anthropologists at Home in North America*. Cambridge: Cambridge University Press.

Miles, Steven, and Ronan Paddison. 2005. "The Rise and Rise of Culture-Led Urban Regeneration." *Urban Studies* 42:5–6(May 2005):833–39.

Miller, Marc S. 1988. *The Irony of Victory: World War II and Lowell, Massachusetts*. Urbana: University of Illinois Press.

Mishel, Lawrence, with Jared Bernstein and John Schmitt. 2001. *The State of Working America, 2000–2001*. Ithaca: Cornell University Press/Economic Policy Institute.

Mitchell, Brian. 1991. "Good Citizens at the Least Cost Per Pound: The History of the Development of Public Education in Antebellum Lowell, 1825–1855." In Weible 1991, 115–35.

Moskos, Charles. 1999. "The Greeks in the United States." In *The Greek Diaspora in the Twentieth Century*, ed. Richard Clogg, 103–17. New York: St. Martin's Press.

Murdock, S. H. 1995. *An America Challenged: Population Change and the Future of the United States*. Boulder, Colo.: Westview Press.

Murray, Andy. 2002. "Unraveling the textile heritage." Lawrence *Eagle-Tribune*. February 24. Electronic document, http://www.eagletribune.com/news/stories/20020224/BU_001.htm, accessed November 9, 2002.

Nader, Laura. 1972. "Up the Anthropologist: Perspectives Gained from Studying Up." In *Reinventing Anthropology*, ed. Dell H. Hymes, 284–311. New York: Pantheon Books.

National Historic Preservation Act of 1966. Amended 1992. Washington, D.C.: Advisory Council on Historic Preservation, National Conference of State Historic Preservation Officers, and National Park Service.

National Low Income Housing Coalition. 2003. "Out of Reach 2003: America's Housing Wage Climbs," Washington D.C.: National Low Income Housing Coalition. Electronic document, http://www.nlihc.org/oor2003/, accessed December 2, 2003.

Negus, Keith. 2002. "The work of Cultural Intermediaries and the Endur-
    ing Distance Between Production and Consumption." *Cultural Studies*
    16(4): 501–15.

New England Council. 2000. *The Creative Economy Initiative: The Role of the Arts
    and Culture in New England's Economic Competitiveness*. Boston: New
    England Council. Available online at http://www.creativeeconomy.
    org/pubs/documents/CEI_2000_report.pdf.

Newman, Katherine S. 1999 [1988]. *Falling from Grace: Downward Mobility in
    the Age of Affluence*. Berkeley: University of California Press.

Newsweek. 1981. "Lowell: A Town Is Reborn." September 28:38.

New York Times. 1987. "Killing and school plan stir tensions in Lowell," Octo-
    ber 25:43.

———. 1988. "Broad bilingual plan settles segregation suit," December 14:
    B16.

———. 1989a. "Immigrants' town is divided over measure on language,"
    November 7:B8.

———. 1989b. "Town votes for English as official language," November 10:
    A22.

Noble, David. 1977. *America by Design: Science, Technology, and the Rise of Corpo-
    rate Capitalism*. New York: Knopf.

Norkunas, Martha K. 1999. Review of *The New History in an Old Museum: Cre-
    ating the Past at Colonial Williamsburg*. *Journal of American Folklore*
    112:215–17.

———. 2002. *Monuments and Memory: History and Representation in Lowell,
    Massachusetts*. Washington, D.C.: Smithsonian Institution Press.

Novick, Peter. 1988. *That Noble Dream: The "Objectivity Question" and the
    American Historical Profession*. Cambridge: Cambridge University
    Press.

O'Har, George. 1999. "The Park and the City: Lowell National Historical Park
    and the Rebirth of Lowell." Draft administrative history of Lowell
    National Historical Park.

Olwig, Karen Fog. 1999. "The Burden of Heritage: Claiming a Place for West
    Indian Culture." *American Ethnologist* 26(2):370–88.

Organization of American Historians. 2003. *OAH Newsletter* 31(4).

Osterhammel, Jurgen, and Neils P. Petersson. 2005. *Globalization: A Short His-
    tory*. Princeton: Princeton University Press.

Peirano, Mariza G. S. 1998. "When Anthropology Is at Home: The Differ-
    ent Contexts of a Single Discipline." *Annual Reviews of Anthropology*
    27:105–28.

Pine, B. Joseph, and James Gilmore. 1999. *The Experience Economy*. Cambridge:
    Harvard Business School Press.

Pollock, Della, ed. 1998. *Exceptional Spaces: Essays in Performance and History.* Chapel Hill: University of North Carolina Press.

Poole, Deborah. 1990. "Accommodation and Resistance in Andean Ritual Dance." *The Drama Review* 34:98–126.

Project for Public Spaces. 2000. *How to Turn a Place Around: A Handbook for Creating Successful Public Spaces.* New York: Project for Public Spaces.

Reich, Robert. 2003. "Welcome to the Machines." Electronic document, http://www.tompaine.com/feature2.cfm/ID/9322, accessed November 12, 2003.

Richards, Peter. 1991. "A Study in Community Power. Lowell 1912." In Weible 1991, 265–79.

Ries, Al, and Laura Ries. 2004. *The Origin of Brands: Discover the Natural Laws of Product Innovation and Business Survival.* New York: HarperBusiness.

Robinson, W. Courtland. 1998. *Terms of Refuge: The Indochinese Exodus and the International Response.* London: Zed Books.

Rodriguez, Richard. 1989. "An American Writer." In Sollors 1989, 3–13.

Roediger, David R. 1991. *The Wages of Whiteness: Race and the Making of the American Working Class.* New York: Verso.

Rosenzweig, Roy, and David Thelen. 1998. *The Presence of the Past: Popular Uses of History in American Life.* New York: Columbia University Press.

Ryan, Loretta Anne. 1987. "Lowell in Transition: The Uses of History in Urban Change." Ph.D. dissertation, Columbia University.

Schechner, Richard. 1985. *Between Theatre and Anthropology.* Philadelphia: University of Pennsylvania Press.

———. 1993. *The Future of Ritual: Writings on Culture and Performance.* London: Routledge.

———. 2002. "Performance Studies in/for the 21st Century." *Anthropology and Humanism* 26(2):158–66.

Schouten, Frans F. J. 1995. "Heritage as Historical Reality." In *Heritage, Tourism and Society*, ed. David T. Herbert, 21–31. London: Pinter.

Scott, Christopher. 2002. "Council berates Weber over Manchester deal." Lowell *Sun*, August 14:1, 2.

Shaffer, Marguerite S. 1998. Review of *The New History in an Old Museum: Creating the Past at Colonial Williamsburg. American Quarterly* 50(4):875–84.

Singer, Milton. 1972. *When a Great Tradition Modernizes: An Anthropological Approach to Indian Civilization.* New York: Praeger.

Sloan, Carole. 2002. "Joan Fabrics Acquires Mexico Mill." *Furniture Today.* October 9. Electronic document: http://www.furnituretoday.com/news10-09-02b.shtml, accessed November 20, 2002.

Smith-Hefner, Nancy. 1995. "The Culture of Entrepreneurship among Khmer Refugees." In *New Migrants in the Marketplace: Boston's Ethnic Entrepreneurs*, ed. Marilyn Halter, Amherst: University of Massachusetts Press.

Snow, Stephen Eddy. 1993. *Performing the Pilgrims: A Study in Ethnohistorical Role-Playing at Plimoth Plantation.* Jackson: University Press of Mississippi.

Sollors, Werner. 1989. *The Invention of Ethnicity.* New York: Oxford University Press.

Spivak, Gayatri Chakravorty. 1988a. "Can the Subaltern Speak?" In *Marxism and the Interpretation of Culture*, eds. Cary Nelson and Lawrence Grossberg. Chicago: University of Illinois Press.

———. 1988b. "Subaltern Studies: Deconstructing Historiography." In *Selected Subaltern Studies*, ed. Ranajit Guha and Gayatri Chakravorty Spivak. New York: Oxford University Press.

Stearns, Peter N. 1993. *The Industrial Revolution in World History.* Boulder, Colo.: Westview Press.

Steinberg, Theodore. 1991. *Nature Incorporated: Industrialization and the Waters of New England.* Amherst: University of Massachusetts Press.

Sutcliffe, Anthony R. 1984. "Gleams and Echoes of Public History in Western Europe: Before and After the Rotterdam Conference." *The Public Historian* 6:4 (Fall): 7–16.

Tilden, Freeman. 1977[1957]. *Interpreting Our Heritage.* Chapel Hill: University of North Carolina Press.

Townsend, Jan. 1999. "The Department of Everything Else, Including Historic Preservation." *CRM* [Cultural Resource Management] *Bulletin* 22:4.

Tsongas, Paul E. 1991. *A Call to Economic Arms: Forging a New American Mandate.* Self-published. Electronic document: http://www.bralyn.net/etext/misc/paul.tsongas/calltoecon.txt, accessed May 15, 2002.

Turner, Victor. 1969. *The Ritual Process: Structure and Anti-Structure.* New York: Aldine de Gruyter.

———. 1974. *Dramas, Fields, and Metaphors: Symbolic Action in Human Society.* Ithaca: Cornell University Press.

———. 1982. *From Ritual to Theatre: The Human Seriousness of Play.* New York: Performing Arts Journal Publications.

———. 1986. *The Anthropology of Performance.* New York: Performing Arts Journal Publications.

Tutalo, Frank. 2002. "With jobs going south, 2 Lowell plants to be left vacant." Lowell *Sun*, August 13:1, 6.

———. 2003a. "A boost from the Boott." Lowell *Sun*, February 23:15, 18.

———. 2003b. "Report: Economy walloped region." Lowell *Sun*, March 28:1,2.

United States Congress. 1978. Public Law 95–290 [H.R. 11662]. An act to provide for the establishment of the Lowell National Historical Park.

United States Department of the Interior. 1997. *National Park Service 1997 Strategic Plan.* Washington, D.C..

Urry, John. 1990. *The Tourist Gaze: Leisure and Travel in Contemporary Society.* London: Sage Publications.

———. 1995. *Consuming Places.* London and New York: Routledge.

Wallace, Mike. 1996. *Mickey Mouse History and Other Essays on American Memory.* Philadelphia: Temple University Press.

Ward, Stephen V. 1998. *Selling Places: The Marketing and Promotion of Towns and Cities, 1850–2000.* New York: Routledge.

Watanabe, Paul, and Michael Liu. 2002. "Asian American Voter Registration in Massachusetts: A Preliminary Report on Ten Cities and Towns," Institute for Asian American Studies, University of Massachusetts Boston, July 2002. Electronic document, www.iaas.umb.edu/publications/AA_Vot_Reg_Report.pdf, accessed November 16, 2002.

Weible, Robert. 1984. "Lowell: Building a New Appreciation for Historical Place." *The Public Historian* 6(3):27–38.

———. 1990. Letter to the Editor. *Journal of American History* 77(1):382–84.

———. ed. 1991. *The Continuing Revolution: A History of Lowell, Massachusetts.* Lowell: Lowell Historical Society.

Weil, Francois. 1998. "Capitalism and Industrialization in New England, 1815–1845." *Journal of American History* 84(4):1334-54.

Whisnant, David. 1983. *All That Is Native and Fine: The Politics of Culture in an American Region.* Chapel Hill: University of North Carolina Press.

Wieffering, Eric. 1991. "Lowell Rides from Bust to Boom and Back." *American Demographics* 13:11(12–13).

Wilkinson, T. 2000. "The Cultural Challenge." *National Parks.* January-February: 20–23.

Wolf, Eric. 1983. *Europe and the People without History.* Berkeley: University of California Press.

Woodard, M. D. 1993. "Leisure among African-Americans: Towards an Indigenous Frame of Reference." In *Managing Urban and High-use Recreation Settings,* ed. P. H. Gobster, 122–26. St. Paul, Minn: U.S. Department of Agriculture, Forest Service, North Central Forest Experiment Station.

Wright, Helena E. 1989. "Selling an Image: Views of Lowell 1825–1876." In *The Popular Perception of Industrial History,* ed. Robert Weible and Francis R. Walsh, 141–63. Lanham, Md.: American Association for State and Local History.

Zaroulis, Nancy. 1976. "Daughters of Freemen: The Female Operatives and the Beginning of the Labor Movement." In Eno Jr. 1976, 105–26.

Zizek, Slavoj. 2000. "Why Do We All Love to Hate Haider?" *Eurozine,* April 13, 2000. Electronic document, http://www.eurozine.com/article/2000-04-13-zizek-en.html, accessed July 5, 2005.

Zoidis, Marilyn. 1999. Review of *The New History in an Old Museum: Creating the Past at Colonial Williamsburg. Journal of Social History* 33(1):196–97.

Zukin, Sharon. 1982. *Loft Living: Culture and Capital in Urban Change*. Baltimore: Johns Hopkins University Press.

———. 1995. *The Cultures of Cities*. Oxford: Blackwell.

INDEX

CATHY STANTON was born and raised in Canada and has lived in the United States since 1983. She earned her B.A. and M.A. as an adult student at Vermont College, and her Ph.D. in the Interdisciplinary Doctorate Program at Tufts University, where she concentrated on cultural anthropology and heritage studies. She currently works as a teacher, writer, and consultant. Her interests include cultural performance, public history and memory, museums, myth and ritual, heritage, and tourism. *The Lowell Experiment: Public History in a Postindustrial City* is her first nonfiction book. Ms. Stanton lives in Athol, Massachusetts, with her husband and cats.